ALSO BY CYI

MUSHROOM: *A Global History*

A HASTINESS OF COOKS:
A Practical Handbook for Use in Deciphering the Mysteries of
Historic Recipes and Cookbooks

IN THE SHADOW OF RAVENS: A Novel

WISDOM SOAKED IN PALM OIL:
Journeying Through the Food and Flavors of Africa

MEATBALLS & LEFSE:
Memories and Recipes from a
Scandinavian-American Farming Life

STOVES & SUITCASES:
Searching for Home in the World's Kitchens

Take A Goose or A Duck

Eclectic Essays on English Cookery through the Ages

Cynthia D. Bertelsen

TURQUOISE
MOON PRESS

Take a Goose or a Duck

Eclectic Essays on English Cookery Through the Ages

©2022 Cynthia D. Bertelsen

Most of the essays in this collection first appeared on the "Cynthia D. Bertelsen's G & T" blog.

Cover photo: Sonsedskaya
Frontispiece illustration: John Parkinson's Paradisi in Sole. Paradisus Terrestris
Cover and book design: Cathy Gibbons Reedy
1. Cookbooks—England—History 2. Cooking—Great Britain—History
3. Cooking, English 4. Domestic Space—England—History 5. Gastronomy

ISBN; 978-1-7345579-3-0

Turquoise Moon Press
Gainesville, FL

TURQUOISEMOONPRESS.COM

For my beloved grandmother,
Winnie Estelle Gibson Purdy
(1890-1969)

You always listened and shared the best stories, too.
I still dream of your carrot cake.

England does not know her wealth.

~ Florence White, *Good Things in the Kitchen*

CONTENTS

The Roaft Beef of Old England.

A Favourite CANTATA.

Taken from a celebrated PRINT of the ingenious Mr. HOGARTH.

RECITATIVE.

'TWAS at the gate of Calais, Hogarth tells,
　Where fad defpair & famine always dwells,
A meagre Frenchman, Madame Grandfire's cook,
As home he fteer'd his carcafe, that way took;
Bending beneath the weight of fam'd SIR-LOIN,
On whom, in vain, he often wifh'd to dine;
Good Father Dominic by chance came by,
With rofy gills, round paunch, and greedy eye;
Who, when he firft beheld the greafy load,
His benediction on it he beftow'd;
And, as the folid fat his fingers prefs'd,
He lick'd his chaps, and thus the Knight addrefs'd:

Air—A lovely Lafs to a Friar came.

O rare Roaft Beef, lov'd by all mankind,
　If I was doom'd to have thee,
When drefs'd and garnifh'd to my mind,
　And fwimming in thy gravy,
Not all thy country's force combin'd,
　Should from my fury fave thee.
Renown'd SIR-LOIN, oft-times decreed
　The theme of Englifh ballad;
On thee ev'n kings have deign'd to feed,
　Unknown to Frenchman's palate;
Then how much doth thy tafte exceed
　Soup-meagre frogs and fallad!

RECITATIVE.

A half-ftarv'd foldier, fhirtlefs, pale, and lean,
Who fuch a fight before had never feen,
Like Garrick's frighted Hamlet, gaping ftood,
And gaz'd with wonder on the Britifh food.
His morning's mefs forfook the friendly bowl,
And in fmall ftreams along the pavement ftole.
He heav'd a figh, which gave his heart relief,
And then in plaintive tones declar'd his grief.

Air——Foote's Minuet.

Ah! fatre Dieu! vat do I fee yonder,
　Dat look fo tempting red and vite?
Begar it is Roaft Beef from Londre;
　Oh! grant me van letel bite.

But to my guts if you give no heeding,
　And cruel fate dis boon denies,
In kind compaffion unto my pleading,
　Return, and let me feaft mine eyes.

RECITATIVE.

His fellow guard, of right Hibernian clay,
Whofe brazen front his country did betray,
From Tyburn's fatal tree had hither fled,
By honeft means to gain his daily bread.
Soon as the well-known profpect he defcry'd,
In blubb'ring accents dolefully he cry'd,

Air——Ellen a Roon.

Sweet beef, that now caufes my ftomach to rife,
Sweet beef, that now caufes my ftomach to rife,
　So taking thy fight is,
　My joy that fo light is,
To view thee, by pailfuls runs out at my eyes.

While here I remain my life's not worth a farthing,
While here I remain my life's not worth a farthing,
　Ah, hard-hearted Loui!
　Why did I come to you;
The gallows, more kind, would have fav'd me from
　ftarving.

RECITATIVE.

Upon the ground, hard by, poor Sawney fate,
Who fed his nofe, and fcratch'd his ruddy pate;
But when old England's bulwark he efpy'd,
His dear lov'd mull, alas! was thrown afide:
With lifted hand he blefs'd his native place,
Then fcrubb'd himfelf, and thus bewail'd his cafe.

Air——The Broom of Cowdenknows.

How hard, oh! Sawney, is thy lot,
　Who was fo blithe of late,
To fee fuch meat as can't be got,
　When hunger is fo great!
O the beef! the bonny bonny beef,
　When roafted nice and brown;
I wifh I had a flice of thee,
　How fweet it would gang down.

Ah! Charley, hadft thou not been feen,
　This ne'er had happ'd to me;
I wad the de'il had pick'd mine e'en,
　E'er I had gang'd wi' thee.
　O the beef, &c.

RECITATIVE.

But, fee! my Mufe to England takes her flight,
Where health and plenty focially unite;
Where fmiling Freedom guards great GEORGE's
　throne,
And whips, and chains, and tortures are not known.
Tho' Britain's fame in loftieft ftrains fhould ring,
In ruftic fable give me leave to fing.

Air——The Roaft Beef of Old England.

As once on a time a young Frog, pert and vain,
Beheld a large Ox grazing o'er the wide plain,
He boafted his fize he could quickly attain.
　O the Roaft Beef of Old England,
　And O the Old Englifh Roaft Beef.
Then eagerly ftretching his weak little frame,
Mamma, who ftood by, like a knowing old dame,
Cry'd, Son, to attempt it, you're furely to blame.
　O the Roaft Beef, &c.

But, deaf to advice, he for glory did thirft;
An effort he ventur'd, more ftrong than the firft,
'Til fwelling and ftraining too hard made him burft.
　O the Roaft Beef, &c.

Then, Britons, be valiant—the moral is clear;
The Ox is Old England, the Frog is Monfieur,
Whofe puffs and bravadoes we never need fear.
　O the Roaft Beef, &c.

For while by our commerce and arts we are able
To fee the Sir-loin fmoking hot on our table,
The French may e'en burft, like the Frog in the fable
　O the Roaft Beef, &c.

Figure 1. The Roast Beef of Old England, A Cantata

INTRODUCTION

IT'S TIME TO SHAKE OFF THE DUST from old beliefs about English cuisine. And American, too, for that matter.

I passionately believe that it's time to go back to the roots of American cuisine—don't laugh, there is such a thing—and give credit to the English. Of course, in this story, you will find elements of oppression, appropriation, and just plain classism.

Studying the past is never easy. The many culinary transformations and exchanges from one culture to another through time and space resulted in what you see today in kitchens around the world.

Yet, if you believe contemporary chefs, food writers, and even diners, the flowering of England never happened in the kitchen. With the modern mad rush to discover the newest, shiniest repasts possible, culinary gatekeepers and influencers ignore the wealth of English cooking and have done so for decades. Some call this culinary appropriation. But this way of thinking is "presentism," the tendency to judge the past through the lens of present-day sensibilities.

Might it be said that a great deal of what people today consider peculiar to the American kitchen is actually appropriated from English cooking?

This is not a popular opinion.

Many scholars and famous food writers believe that rampant culinary appropriation denies credit due to enslaved cooks and others.

By delving deeper into the subject of English cooking, I realized that English cooking was anything but bland and uninteresting. Not at all in need of spicing before, during, and after the colonial period in America. English cooking, greatly influenced by French cuisine—at the upper levels of society at least—gave us the jellies, pickles, pies, roasted fowl and meats, cakes, quick and yeast breads, pastries, all associated with so-called traditional American cuisine.

When I read Mary Randolph's *The Virginia Housewife* on a cold, snowy afternoon many years ago, it—published in 1824—revolutionized my thinking about English food. Despite the current insistence that Mrs. Randolph included recipes using African techniques or appropriated them from enslaved cooks, those particular recipes are few, a fact that's quite evident with a thorough examination of the book. To wit: "You may take America out of England, but you can't take England out of America." Social scientists commonly regard the kitchen as one of the last places where human cultures change, where assimilation comes up against a solid, almost impenetrable wall.

And Mrs. Randolph's cookbook serves as a reliable witness to that. Filled with recipes hailing back to England, cooked in planation kitchens in Virginia, *The Virginia Housewife* spoke cuisine with a very English accent.

English cooking remains the Mother Cuisine for historical American cooking despite the current hunger for the faddish, the exotic, and the extreme in the kitchen. And for much contemporary cooking as well.

However, in support of this contrary opinion, consider Harvey Levenstein's comment in *Revolution at the Table*: "Even before independence, waves of immigrants from Europe and Africa washed onto America's shores, but left few traces of their cuisines on the American table."

I also take solace and sustenance from a brilliant article by Stephen Schmidt, "Southern Cooking: When Did Southern Begin?"

Schmidt suggests that the defeated people of the post-Civil War South turned to the sumptuous food of their defunct plantations, thereby grabbing onto an illusionary and glorious culinary past. He takes his cue from Eugene Walter, author of Time-Life's *American Cooking: Southern Style*. Walter, a native of Mobile, Alabama, and as Southern as one soul can be, states in stark and stinging prose that:

> During the years after the Civil War the region took its tone,
> set its style, cocked its snoot, decided to become set in its ways
> and pleasurably conscious of doing so. Traditions became
> doubly important; the South set about glamorizing its past and
> transforming anecdote into legend. And among the rites and
> observances, none were more important than those of the table.

Enslaved cooks prepared most of the food, at least among the wealthier antebellum strata, true. Still, that culinary repertoire rested firmly on English cooking traditions. And plantation cuisine differed significantly from today's Southern, now a stereotype of barbecue, fried chicken, and myriad unchanging side dishes.

Many soul food dishes considered Africa-influenced derive from English or French cooking methods: pies, cakes, pickles and preserves, breaded fried meats such as chicken or pork or beef, soups thickened with nuts—an old medieval way of using nuts. Black-eyed peas, watermelon, rice, okra, sesame seeds, peanuts (native to the Americas), and collard greens do not play a huge role in American cooking overall, contrary to popular lore. You'll find these ingredients in only a few dishes, such as Hoppin' John, gumbo, benne wafers, and peanut chicken, among others. Today, much of what authors consider "soul food" appeared only *after* the American Civil War.

As for smoked meats, one glance at the history of English smoked hams and bacon makes it clear that smoked meat was nothing new to the English in the New World.

Nor to the Romans. Take a look at Cato's recipe for smoked ham in *De Agricultura*:

> After buying legs of pork, cut off the feet. One-half peck ground Roman salt per ham. Spread the salt in the base of a vat or jar, then place a ham with the skin facing downwards. Cover completely with salt. After standing in salt for five days, take all hams out with the salt. Put those that were above below, and so rearrange and replace. After a total of 12 days take out the hams, clean off the salt and hang in the fresh air for two days. On the third day take down, rub all over with oil, hang in smoke for two days...take down, rub all over with a mixture of oil and vinegar and hang in the meat store. Neither moths nor worms will attack it.

Culinary practices don't suddenly appear out of thin air but rather testify to a long and complicated heritage.

Yet, certain mythologies still exist.

In *Iron Pots and Wooden Spoons*, prolific food writer Jessica Harris implies that enslaved cooks were responsible for introducing greens—such as collard greens— into the diets of their masters, stating as follows:

> Foods were being grilled and vegetables were being added to what in Europe had been mainly a protein and carbohydrate diet. One historian goes as far as to credit the slaves [*sic*] with adding greens and green vegetables to the slaveholder's diet and thereby saving countless numbers from nutritional deficiencies.

But a glance at John Evelyn's *Acetaria: A Discourse of Sallets* dispels the notion that the English eschewed greens. In *Classical Southern Cooking*, Damon Lee Fowler says, "Anyone who thinks early Englishmen and ergo, early Americans, were indifferent to vegetables should be tied to a chair and made to read this book."

In fact, English people ate smoked pork and greens for centuries before migrating to the New World. So too the concept of pottages made with various greens, some precooked and stirred into simmering soups and other liquids. Consider *Eli-*

nor *Fettiplace's Receipt Book*, dating to 1604, a few years before the first Jamestown colonists set sail for Virginia from Blackwall, near London. Her recipe for "Chicken with Spinach Sauce" testifies to the cooking of meat with greens. Editor Hilary Spurling reminds us that Gervase Markham recommends "thick sippets with the juyce of sorrel and sugar" for roast chicken.

And Stephen Schmidt writes:

> I did spot some native southern inventions—a few of which are
> still known today, like beaten biscuits and hominy griddle cakes—
> but, for the most part, the book [*The Virginia Housewife*] outlined
> the same cuisine that was in vogue among the privileged classes of
> the North in Randolph's day: genteel English cooking interspersed
> with a few American dishes such as pumpkin pudding, soda-
> leavened gingerbread, and doughnuts. *Hess, in fact, acknowledges
> Randolph's pervasive Englishness; her notes are largely given over to
> tracing it.* [Emphasis mine.]

To claim that the spicing of American food only came through the provenance of certain groups of cooks, such as immigrants or enslaved African cooks, is to miss a very vital point. By the time the Jamestown settlers arrived in 1607, the world had been enjoying a revolution in taste that began with thriving global trade. With their seafaring skills, the English joined the Portuguese and the Spanish in seeking wealth and spices and power. They did not arrive on the shores of Cape Henry with palates limited to blancmange or boiled salted beef.

Exactly.

Ironically, the popularity of "The Great British Baking Show" showcases the wealth of English culinary history, even as it limits the topic to baking.

So why *Take a Goose or a Duck?*

This book explores and celebrates English cooking before the twentieth century. However, bits and pieces refer to England during the war years of the self-same century and slightly beyond.

Fourteen years of strict rationing clipped the wings of nearly an entire generation of English cooks. That sad turn of events, in turn, led food historians as renowned as Karen Hess and others to soundly—and unfairly—trash English cooking as bland, boring, and blah. Hess herself writes in *Martha Washington's Booke of Cookery*: "Still [in spite of other influences such as African and Native American, etc.], the way of our [United States] cooking is English, much as common remains the basis of our law."

And what of the title of this book? What does it mean to "Take a Goose or a Duck?"

It alludes to a bizarre and frankly sadistic recipe in William Kitchiner's *The Cook's Oracle* of 1822, a sordid reminder that culinary trends occur throughout history. As Diane Ackerman notes in *A Natural History of the Senses*:

> This [culinary sadism] was all sponsored by the peculiar notion that the taste of animal flesh could be improved if the poor thing were put through hell first. Dr. William Kitchiner, in *The Cook's Oracle*, cites a grotesque recipe, by a cook named Mizald, for preparing and eating a goose while it is still alive.

Kitchiner's, or rather Mizald's, recipe begins with the words, "Take a Goose or a Duck ...."

What follows is a standard historical English cookbook textual quirk.

"Take" appears as the first word in many recipes, a usage stemming from the Latin word *recipere*. A practice that began in bygone days, it flourished in early English cookery texts, appearing at times as "Nym water" and "Nym swete mylk." "Nym" reflected the connection of English to German, in this case *nehmen* "to take."

But the recipe in *The Cook's Oracle* is anything but standard:

> Take a GOOSE or a DUCK, or some such *lively creature*, (but a goose is best of all for this purpose,) pull off all her feathers, only the head and neck must be spared: then make a fire round about her, not too close to her, that the smoke do not choke her, and that the fire may not burn her too soon; nor too far off, that she may not escape free: within the circle of the fire let there be set small cups and pots full of water, wherein salt and honey are mingled: and let there be set also chargers full of sodden apples, cut into small pieces in the dish. [...]

Shiver. I could scarcely believe what I saw when I first read this recipe. *Take a Goose or a Duck* serves as a tribute to all the animals thus tortured.

An informal history of English cooks, cookbooks, and cuisine, *Take a Goose or a Duck* brings together my somewhat unorthodox and often quirky reflections on English cooks, cookery books, and cooking. And culinary appropriation. I offer them here, updated and aired out like dust sheets in an English manor house, ready for the enjoyment of guests.

Cheers!

[Note: Most of the cookbooks discussed in *Take a Goose or a Duck* can be read online through such resources at Gutenberg.org, archive.org, and others.]

Figure 2. Frontispiece, Hannah Woolley's *The Queene-Like-Closet*

Cookbooks *Do* Tell Tales

THE SOUND OF FLESH SMACKING the table jerked me out of my reverie. My skin prickled as I stared at the red-faced man at the head of the table.

"I won't stand for it," the new head of Special Collections yelled, his high-pitched voice that of a petulant child.

"I don't want to see any more dirty recipe books added to the collection. We have enough of those useless things as it is. They're like hash, a big mess!"

Absolute silence hung in the air like an ill-placed burp. Or worse ....

Eleven other angry women besides me scrunched down around the table, all staring at their hands, mouths twisting with unspoken words

Then Carol stood up.

"Sir, these books testify to a lot more than mere hash."

Carol whispered a "bless your heart" under her breath.

Hash, with its unpleasant companion word "rehash," conjures up visions of an unholy mess, a quivering glop of leftovers slipping around on a plate, a dish best unseen and stuffed into a "coffin" (also known as "cofyn," archaic terms for pie crust). Quite unappetizing.

But Carol was having none of that kind of talk. One of the so-called elders of a group assisting the library in acquiring antique cookbooks and manuscripts, she kept the floor. In her posh Charlestonian accent, honed to a fine sharpness by her distinguished family background, Carol explained why those community cookbooks represented vital pieces of culinary history.

To give the man credit, he quieted.

In a nutshell, those "dirty" cookbooks tell how the transfer of knowledge changed from the privileged wealthy few to ordinary men and women, empowering them through one of the greatest intellectual inventions ever: printing.

Printing revolutionized everything.

I learned this firsthand.

Under my mother's watchful eye, I first ventured into my childhood kitchen, where she taught me how to cook the five or six dishes in her repertoire. She told me what needed to be done, the steps involved in making oven-fried chicken or creamed hamburger on white rice. Nothing written on a slip of paper, not even a napkin. Nevertheless, despite those basic recipes firmly entrenched in my mind, I wanted to know and understand more about cooking. No, I *needed* to know. Thus, I slowly accumulated cookbooks and, hence, a cooking knowledge far beyond what I could glean from my mother or grandmother.

After years of collecting, I owned several hundred cookbooks, carting them along with me as I moved to several developing countries to live and work. Servants and upper-class locals expressed amazement at my reliance on all those cookbooks.

"Didn't your mother teach you to cook?" one line of questioning went. At the same time, another—unspoken—thought focused on what could only be my incompetence with a saucepan. Why else would I need a cookbook?!

Through these experiences, I realized just how powerful literacy and access to books have been. Cookbooks from all over the world allowed me freedom at the stove, thanks to the revolutionary invention of printing.

Printing, oh, how we take it for granted! Aside from writing, until computers appeared, printing probably counts as the most critical intellectual invention in the history of humankind. To phrase it another way, the words and ideas of thinkers could move from place to place through cheaper published materials. Thought would no longer be halted or silenced by neither geographical location nor the chains and prison cells holding dissidents and heretics. No longer would the clustering of knowledge rest solely in the hands of a privileged few—priests, political leaders, and an educated elite.

Some authorities suggest literacy began in order to keep track of grains and other foodstuffs, an example of the timeless imperative of economics. Money is the root of all things?

That said, over seventy-five percent of the earliest printed books continued to deal with religious subjects, not secular topics. And certainly not cookery. Henry Notaker discovered that only 100 "different [cookbook] titles" appeared between the 1470s and 1700. But those books made a difference. Thanks to early print cookbooks, or *aide-mémoires*, Notaker writes, "the mind gets a greater freedom to more original thought and new speculation."

In other words, the need to memorize everything became less critical.

And as Stephen Mennell mentions in *All Manners of Food*, "In cooking, as in the case of other social phenomena like codes of manners, fashions in clothing, or styles of eating, printing also very much facilitates the process of social emulation—of the habits, styles and interests of one class or stratum by another."

This scenario indeed occurred in England, as English edged out Latin, a trend toward the vernacular inspired by Geoffrey Chaucer's *The Canterbury Tales* and one of the earliest English cookbooks, *The Forme of Cury.*

But before delving into specifics about English cookbooks and their history, a few necessary words about just how cookbooks and recipes evolved.

*The man who can dominate a London dinner table
can dominate the world.*

~ Oscar Wilde

Figure 3. Antique Cutlery

WHAT'S A COOKBOOK? WHAT'S A RECIPE?

BEFORE I GO ANY FURTHER HERE, I must first define a few terms. "Cookbooks" and "recipes." Until the technology of printing emerged, cookbooks appeared in manuscript form, written, copied, passed around, plagiarized, embellished, and molded into the format still used today.

Merriam-Webster defines these unique literary forms as follows:

[1]cook·book

noun \-,bûk\

: a book of recipes : a book of directions explaining how to prepare and cook various kinds of food

Recipe:

1 : PRESCRIPTION 2 : a set of instructions for making something from various ingredients 3 : a formula or procedure for doing or attaining something

As we know them in the West, aside from Babylonian cuneiform tablets, cookbooks first came to life via handwritten manuscripts on vellum. Many early cookbooks recorded medicinal practices, tips, and health advice. Henry Notaker suggests early culinary manuscripts often contained up to fifty percent medicinal receipts, along with culinary information. This practice ensued from beliefs like humoral theory, seeing food as medicine and medicine as food.

Cookbooks later represented cooks' attempts to share and preserve knowledge, the essentials of their trade, for their underlings and successors, in the form of *aide-memoires*. After all, it wasn't until 1448 that the printing press revolutionized the world in ways far beyond the dreams of Johannes Gutenberg, its visionary inventor. At least in Europe. The Chinese and Koreans actually invented this boon to humankind around 800 A.D., approximately 500 years earlier than Gutenberg.

It took European printers a while to apply the new technology to receipt books. The first printed cookbook—Platina's *De Honesta Voluptate et Valetudine*—appeared in 1470. Likely first written in 1464 or 1465, it is based heavily on the work of Martino de Rossi, also known as Martino da Como. And in England, *The Boke of Cokery* became the first published cookbook in English, printed by Richard Pynson around 1500.

Prescriptive, aspirational, and functional—these terms describe the contents of many cookbooks, then and now.

In the early days of writing, a recipe included nothing more than a list of ingredients, maybe, at a minimum. As time passed, cooks added more information. Action words appeared.

Take "Take," for example.

Our verb "to take"—as used in recipes, at least the old ones—implies violence, doesn't it?

Take a deeper look at the use of "take."

According to the *Oxford English Dictionary*:

The earliest known use of this verb in the Germanic languages was app. to express the physical action 'to put the hand on', 'to touch' the only known sense of Gothic *têkan*. … *take* becomes in its essence 'to transfer to oneself by one's' own action or volition (anything material or non-material)'.

And there's at least one specific meaning as well, directly related to this discussion:

> **b.** To catch, capture (a wild beast, bird, fish, etc.); also of an animal, to seize or catch (prey).

Look, too, at Webster's once more. Just to cinch the matter, up turns the following commentary:

> *transitive verb* **1** : to get into one's hands or into one's possession, power, or control: as **a** : to seize or capture physically <*took* them as prisoners> **b** : to get possession of (as fish or game) by killing or capturing

"Take" takes on a wholly different sense as the tie to violence emerges.

The tools of the kitchen—knives, for one—permit other similar acts (burn, boil, strain, wring, pound) beyond "taking."

Thus, the reason why so many vintage receipts start with the phrase "Take … *whatever*."

And all that taking leads to ingredients, the stars of all culinary dramas. Modern or medieval, any recipe essentially instructs cooks like me and you to

"Take" something. Which can only mean the bounty of the garden, the market, or the larder, crocks filled to the top edges with fermenting cabbage. Or perhaps a haunch of fresh beef, chicken pieces, or a whole live goose or squawking duck.

Yet there is a method to the madness.

Whether in books or in manuscripts or on their own, recipes convey vast worlds of knowledge and information. Rules. But not rules. Realizing this requires a different way of seeing and thinking, akin to guidelines, not rigidity. (Though some would beg to differ!)

Although appearing replete with the messiness of hash, medieval recipes were quite clear to their audience. Written recipes served as *aide-mémoires* to cooks and stewards charged with orchestrating enormous feasts and banquets for their wealthy and royal masters. Changes occurred over time. Instead of seemingly random placement of recipes on scattered pages, recipes appeared according to type of dish: soup, meat, or sweets. Later, authors and publishers preferred to list recipes by order of serving at table. Although these practices seem obvious nowadays, the structure and arrangement of recipes in cookbooks were anything but in the beginning.

Recipes turned out to be complex, with individual words conveying tremendous *a priori* knowledge. Tomlinson writes, "A recipe in a cookbook is embedded in a nest of assumptions, prior cultural and technical knowledge, connections between types of instructions, and the ability to bridge all of these so that the recipe can be followed."

According to the *Oxford English Dictionary*, the first use of the word for a food recipe appeared in 1595 in *Widowes Treasure*, in conjunction with directions for making Ipocras.

Well, almost.

Barbara Ketchum Wheaton, a renowned culinary historian, writes in *Savoring the Past: The French Kitchen and Table from 1300 to 1789*, "A recipe artificially isolates the actions and ingredients needed to prepare a single dish. ... A recipe is a cross-section of a portion of the work going forward in a kitchen. From it, one begins to get a sense of how cooking was done."

As the number of possible permutations with ingredients increased, the need for writing down recipes—or guidelines/*aide-mémoires*—evolved into household management manuals and later into cookbooks.

But it behooves me, and you, Dear Reader, to remember something, though. Cookbooks, even the ones described here, represent the works gatekeepers deemed worthy of publication. So, without those ghosts of cookbooks past, the story of English cookery and cookbooks still remains incomplete.

And that's exactly what drew me into the world of cookbooks, especially those published in England, about English cooking.

No hash there!

Let your Food be simple, and Drinks innocent
and learn of Wisdom and Experience how to prepare them aright.

~ Thomas Tryon

XXXV - PERYS EN COMPOSTE

Take Wyne an Canel, and a gret dele of Whyte Sugre, an set it on þe
fyre and hete it hote, but let it nowt boyle, an draw it þorwe a straynoure;
þan take fayre Datys, an pyke owt þe stonys, an leche hem alle þinne, an
caste þer-to; þanne take Wardonys, an pare hem and sethe hem, an leche
hem alle þinne, and caste þer-to in-to þe Syryppe: þanne take a lytil
Sawnderys, and caste þer-to, an sette it on þe fyre; an ȝif þow hast charde
quynce, caste þer-to in þe boyling, an loke þat it stonde wyl with Sugre,
an wyl lyid wyth Canel, an caste Salt þer-to, an let it boyle; an þan caste
yt on a treen vessel, and lat it kele, and serue forth.

— Harleian 4016 (about 1450 A.D.) —

Figure 4. British Lion

In Defense of English Cooking, or, George Orwell Revisited

ERIC ARTHUR BLAIR.

Remember him?

Here's a hint: Born 1903 in Motihari, Bengal, India, to British parents.

No?

Okay. What about George Orwell. Remember him?

Of course, you do.

Blair chose George Orwell as his *nom de plume*.

Yes. Think *Animal Farm, Burmese Days, Shooting an Elephant.* And certainly *1984,* the bane of high school students everywhere, giving rise to the prophetic phrase, "Orwellian world." With good reason, Orwell is enjoying posthumous popularity many years after his death in 1950, thanks in part to Rebecca Solnit's *Orwell's Roses.*

But, if you're a food-obsessed person, as I am, Orwell's work means something other than Big Brother and Winston Smith and a barnyard full of talking animals.

Orwell's memoir of his youthful poverty, *Down and Out in Paris and London,* chronicles days spent in those cities. Working at various low-paying, filthy jobs, including a stint as a hotel *plongeur* or dishwasher near Paris's famous *Place de la Concorde,* he, as you might guess, ruminates about food, not uncommon for a chronically hungry person:

> You discover what it is like to be hungry. With bread and
> margarine in your belly, you go out and look into the shop
> windows. Everywhere there is food insulting you in huge, wasteful
> piles; whole dead pigs, baskets of hot loaves, great yellow blocks
> of butter, strings of sausages, mountains of potatoes, vast Gruyere
> cheeses like grindstones. A snivelling self-pity comes over you at
> the sight of so much food.

Given Orwell's intimate acquaintance with hunger, it then comes as no surprise that food often appears in his writing, often enshrined amid discussions of social class.

Two Orwellian essays on food come to mind.

In "In Defence of English Cooking," an article he wrote in 1945 for *The Evening Standard*, Orwell defends British cooking. He sounds a great deal like the homesick Mark Twain in *A Tramp Abroad*. Twain lists a whole plethora of American dishes—sixty—while sitting in a damp hotel room in Venice, Italy, where he yearns for the foods of his homeland. Many of which were actually English in origin. Of course, Twain meant the following recipe as satire (or did he?):

RECIPE FOR NEW ENGLISH PIE

To make this excellent breakfast dish, proceed as follows: Take
a sufficiency of water and a sufficiency of flour, and construct a
bullet-proof dough. Work this into the form of a disk, with the
edges turned up some three-fourths of an inch. Toughen and
kiln-dry in a couple days in a mild but unvarying temperature.
Construct a cover for this redoubt in the same way and of the
same material. Fill with stewed dried apples; aggravate with cloves,
lemon-peel, and slabs of citron; add two portions of New Orleans
sugars, then solder on the lid and set in a safe place till it petrifies.
Serve cold at breakfast and invite your enemy.

Twain's recipe pointed out a still-prevailing attitude toward English food. Many dishes still prevalent in the United States—at least among home cooks and some chefs—trace their genealogy to English antecedents. Roast beef? Apple dumplings? Apple pie? Roasted potatoes? Mashed potatoes? Trout? Oysters?

Orwell sings the praises of nearly every traditional English dish.

However, his most telling bit of food writing lay hidden for years.

In an unpublished article, "British Cookery," commissioned by the British Council in 1946, Orwell dissects what it is to be British by discussing food and meals commonly eaten in his day. Unfortunately, it reads almost like a caricature of British cuisine. Perusing it, I quite expect a grimacing Mr. Bean to pop out from the woodwork.

Contrary to statements he made in "In Defence of English Cooking," Orwell laments numerous deficiencies in British cooking time and again.

"Fish in Britain is seldom well cooked."

"British pastry is not outstandingly good …."

Yet, he extols the fillings in those pastries. Take lemon curd, not dissimilar to the filling in Lemon Chess Pie, one of the little-known glories of American cooking. A dish with deep roots in the English kitchen. He lavishes praise on the "Sunday joint," apples, and—surprisingly—English bread. I sense deep emotions in his writing about this food.

In the minds of many American cooks and chefs, the reputation of English cooking is so bad that it simply doesn't appear on their culinary radar. This state of affairs is quite ironic, given the influence of English cuisine on the American palate, which is far greater than most other immigrant cuisines.

To highlight this relationship, comb through each cuisine—American and English—dish by dish. Similarities abound if you look. A bigger picture will emerge.

Few researchers do this.

Reading vintage cookbooks and essays, such as those penned by Twain and Orwell, confirms a very portentous point: English cuisine did not just stop being important in the United States once the English lost the Revolutionary War.

In *Good Things in England*, from 1932, Florence White states, "England does not know her wealth" in the kitchen.

And neither does America.

White tries to paint that picture with a foray into British cooking from various periods in English history. She digs pretty deeply into the past at times. The relationships often surprise, just as DNA testing reveals hidden family relationships, skeletons in the closet.

Today, food writers need to recognize the incredible diversity and variety of the foods that fueled England, a land of empire builders, yeomen, tradesmen, adventurers, and seafarers. History, violent and benevolent as it often is, cannot, and never should, be erased just because it doesn't fit present-day sensibilities. Presentism has no place there.

George Orwell provides the last word here, reiterating the positive side of English cookery:

> In addition, no one who has not sampled Devonshire cream, stilton cheese, crumpets, potato cakes, saffron buns, Dublin prawns, apple dumplings, pickled walnuts, steak-and-kidney pudding and, of course, roast sirloin of beef with Yorkshire pudding, roast potatoes and horseradish sauce, can be said to have given British cookery a fair trial.

England's food is indeed history-rich, intriguing, and distinct, as you will see in the following pages.

Reading a recipe, preparing and consuming it are, in the end, the word and the body become one.

~ Janet Theophano

[24.] CRANE

Loke thu have good broth & cler & good blaunched almondys grynd
hem & tempre hem up with thin broth & drawe it hulle it wel & do it on
the fyer charge it wel with amydon or with flour of rys do ther to qwyth
ginger & a perty canel sugre qwybibes & clowes a perty gres & salt.

— John Crophill, *Commonplace Book*, <1485 —

CAELII
APITII, SVM
MI ADVLATRICIS
MEDICINAE ARTIFICIS,
De re Culinaria libri
Decem.

❧

B. PLATINAE CREMONEN-
*sis De Tuenda ualetudine, Natura rerum, & Popinæ
scientia Libri x.*
PAVLI AEGINETAE DE FA-
cultatibus alimentorum Tractatus,
AlbanoTorino Inter-
prete.

*

APVD SEB. GRYPHIVM
LVGVDVNI,
1541.

Figure 5. Apicius, 1541

THOSE ROAMING ROMANS: THE HERITAGE OF APICIUS

FAT DORMICE AND STUFFED PEACOCKS ASIDE, it was Greek to them, literally.

Roman cuisine, that is.

I never gave much thought to Roman cuisine, the vomitoriums putting me off, if you know what I mean. But, given that Rome occupied and ruled England for 367 years, the impact on food habits could be nothing but profound. Right?

The Romans first descended on the unwitting Britons in 43 B.C. under orders from Emperor Claudius. Then Julius Caesar showed up in 55 B.C. and again in 54 B.C. Soon thereafter, he met the tips of several knife blades in the Roman Senate, bestowing his name on a Shakespearean tragedy, as well as the ominous Ides of March. Not until around 83 A.D.—when Julius Agricola smashed the Caledonians at Mons Graupius—did the Romans gain control of Britannia, their name for that green and pleasant land.

In *The Gallic Wars*, Julius Caesar describes the people he encountered, " ... Britons dye themselves with woad ... and as a result, their appearance in battle is all the more daunting." Woad, as you know, is indigo. Sadly, he writes little about their food. Apparently, it wasn't worth writing home about. However, archaeological evidence points to emmer wheat, spelt, and barley among the grains consumed. Cattle supplied a significant source of protein for Iron Age people on the island. Seeds of wild mustard and other greens emerged from the earth as archaeologists dug into ancient sites.

On the other hand, and quite indirectly, the most important written resource for Roman cooking in England comes from *Apicius*, to a certain extent a controversial cookbook also known as *De re coquinaria*.

Dating to the first century A.D. and a famous culinary work attributed to Marcus Gavius Apicius, the Latin text of the eponymous *Apicius* reflects the vulgar variety of that language and likely dates to the fourth century. But, as Sally Grainger states in "The Myth of Apicius," there appears to be no "voice," no sense of a single author, in fact, no Marcus Gavius Apicius. Apicius the man, the author conjures up nothing more than a cognomen, a nickname acquired because of some quirk or other idiosyncrasy that a person becomes known for. And Marcus Gavius became the butt of many derisive comments over the years. Pliny, for example, created a rumor that Apicius ate flamingo tongues.

Rather than a masterpiece mirroring the culinary genius of one man, one cook, *Apicius* represents a compilation of recipes. Likely set down by working cooks schooled in the techniques and lore of Greek cuisine, where technique and practice merged. In Roman culture, however, technique remained the purview of the learned, and practice became the bailiwick of the enslaved. No merging of the two there.

Romans based their system of slavery not on race but rather on geography. Some enslaved people originated in North Africa, but most hailed from Europa and Greece. Cooks generally were enslaved. Grainger believes enslaved people serving as cooks enjoyed a basic, fundamental form of literacy, at least enough to account for *Apicius*, the cookbook. Yet high-class Romans such as Cicero, known for his rhetorical skills, considered "cook" one of the "disgraceful" occupations, along with fishermen, fishmongers, butchers, and poultrymen.

And what is known about cooking in Roman Britain depends in part on words written in the pages of *Apicius*, the first English language version edited by Joseph Dommer Vehling in 1936.

Getting back to dormice, I've never seen one. But apparently, Mr. Vehling believes that I, as an American, wouldn't find that animal too far a stretch in the pot and on the plate. "Dormouse, as an article of diet, should not astonish Americans who relish squirrel, opossum, muskrat, "coon," he states, rather emphatically.

Really, Mr. Vehling?

He follows his translation of the recipe in *Apicius* with a few notes describing what early Romans wrote about dormice, "*Glis*, dormouse, a special favorite of the ancients, has nothing to do with mice. The fat dormouse of the South of Europe is the size of a rat, arboreal rodent, living in trees."

From Book VIII, Chapter IX of *Apicius*, the stuffed dormouse recipe sounds quite sophisticated. Romans considered dormouse a delicacy and created special spaces to raise—and fatten—them, called *gliraria*. Forget about cages or open-air enclosures. Instead, *gliraria* turn out to be terracotta jars with ledges inside, creating space for nuts such as acorns, walnuts, and chestnuts. Dormice could thus scurry about on the ledges, creating a sort of ancient hamster wheel. Aside from all that scrambling, eating and sleeping filled their days as they grew chubbier from inactivity and abundant food.

In Vehling's version of *Apicius*, I find:

Galen, III, de Alim.; Plinius, VIII, 57/82; Varro, III, describing the glirarium, place where the dormouse was raised for the table. Petronius, Cap. 31, describes another way of preparing dormouse. Nonnus, Diæteticon, p. 194/5, says that Fluvius Hirpinus was the first man to raise dormouse in the glirarium.

[396] STUFFED DORMOUSE

: "Laser" refers to laserpitium, an extract of a wild giant fennel (silphium). stuffed with a forcemeat of pork and small pieces of dormouse meat trimmings, all pounded with pepper, nuts, laser, broth. Put the dormouse thus stuffed in an earthen casserole. Roast it in the oven, or boil it in the stockpot.

As for "laser," modern cooks will have to be satisfied with some form of fennel or anise. Why? Ancient Romans gobbled so much silphium that the plant became extinct.

Although silphium is but a whiff of memory now, Roman contributions to the cuisine of Europe, and Britain in particular, are legion.

The famed Roman legions, and their elite generals, yearned for the tastes of home. So much so that the following ingredients came to be standards in British cooking:

Mint. Coriander. Rosemary. Radish. Garlic. Chervil. Dill. Parsley. Oysters. Garum. Asparagus. Turnips. Cabbages. Celery. Onions. Leeks. Cucumbers. Shallots. Globe artichoke. Peas. Figs. Medlars. Sweet chestnut. Cherries Plums. Apples. Mulberries. Walnuts. Grapes. Wine. White mustard. Black pepper. Ginger. Cinnamon.

Along with dormice fattened in *gliraria*, Romans raised rabbits in *leporaria*. They also introduced pheasants, geese, guinea fowl, peacocks, pigeons, brown hare, and white cattle.

Archaeological evidence points to other food items as well. For example, bones serve as a prominent marker for inclusion in diets. Leafy green vegetables require seed evidence because of the obvious decomposition of green leafy vegetables even on a day-to-day basis in the modern kitchen! Dr. H.E.M. Cool's *Eating and Drinking in Roman Britain* offers one of the few specific and in-depth treatments of Roman culinary practices during Roman times.

Cool's references to leafy green vegetables in Roman Britain are of great interest, making it clear that greens formed a vital dietary component on that island very early on. However, some American culinary historians believe greens only arrived in the colonial American diet via the slave trade and the skill of African cooks.

Cool's research says otherwise.

He writes, "Brassica seeds are not uncommon, indicating that leafy vegetables such as cabbage and rape were probably eaten. ... It is also probable that the leaves of vegetables that would normally today be eaten as root vegetables, such as beet and turnip, were eaten. ... The range of the green vegetables exploited may have been wider than it is today."

And a final glance at *Apicius* suggests that green leaves often appeared in the pot and in bowls, many times just the phantom silphium, but in some cases cabbage and others:

From Book III, Chapter IX
[87] Young Cabbage, Sprouts
Boil the sprouts; season with cumin, salt, wine, and oil; if you like add pepper, lovage, mint, rue, coriander; the tender leaves of the stalks, stew in broth: wine and oil be the seasoning.

Yes, indeed. Early Britons knew what to do with greens.

We dined together on beef and greens,
brought from the cook's shop in the neighbourhood ....

~ Tobias Smollett

Figure 6. Geoffrey Chaucer

PILGRYMES, PASSING TO AND FRO: CHAUCER GOT IT RIGHT

SOMEHOW, I MANAGED TO GET THROUGH many years of schooling without ever cracking open a copy of Geoffrey Chaucer's *The Canterbury Tales*. Fleeting references to it sprung from other pages, though, in classes on medieval history. Unfortunately, Middle English quotes requiring a dictionary stopped me from pursuing this remarkable book, the first written not in the scholarly Latin of the time but rather in the words spoken by Everyman on the streets, in shops and in homes, both high and low.

Born around 1343, Chaucer came from a good merchant family and thus made a good marriage. He worked at day jobs, as writing didn't pay big money then either. First, as customs controller for the port of London beginning in 1374 and then as clerk of the king's work starting in 1389, Chaucer rubbed shoulders daily with the rich and powerful.

Despite those somewhat plebian beginnings, Chaucer wrangled a position as a page in the household of the Duchess of Clarence, wife of the third son of John of Gaunt. John proved to be a staunch advocate for Chaucer throughout his life, acting both as patron and protector.

Chaucer cherished books from an early age and loved to read, retaining minute details of what he read in Latin, French, Italian, and Anglo-Norman.

Because he traveled as a diplomat for the Crown, he became familiar with Italian and French literature in the vernacular. His first poetic work—*Book of the Duchesse,* an elegy for John of Gaunt's deceased wife—attests to his closeness to the King. As Chaucer climbed the ladder from page boy in an aristocratic household to luminary at Court, many significant events occurred. Taken prisoner in Reims on a mission to France during the Hundred Years' War, Chaucer's protector, King John himself, paid part of the ransom for Chaucer's release.

In other words, Chaucer wasn't a starving writer moldering in a garret someplace.

The Canterbury Tales is not a food book per se. Nor a cookbook. But it reflects the food culture of the times. There's a definite, if not spoken, tie-in with a late fourteenth-century cookbook, *The Forme of Cury*. Chaucer read his work at King Richard's court, too, so he might well have eaten food found in *The Forme of Cury*.

All these life experiences served Chaucer well when he filled goose quills with ink and wrote *The Canterbury Tales*.

Pilgrimage acted as a great social leveler in Chaucer's day. His cleverness in choosing that aspect of medieval English life proved to be genius.

The Canterbury Tales begins at the Tabard Inn on the south side of the River Thames. Harry Bailly owns the Inn and wagers a sumptuous dinner for thirty pilgrims, a carrot of truly magnanimous proportions in a time when food was not easy to come by. "… a soper at oure aller cost."

Chaucer originally planned on including 120 such tales but only finished twenty-two before he died on October 25, 1399, buried at Westminster Abbey in what became The Poets' Corner. Plague may have taken him.

He used a literary device—framing—putting his characters together via the pilgrimage motif. Each of the thirty pilgrims is tasked with telling two tales on the way to Canterbury and two on the way back. But not all tell a story due to Chaucer's death.

Comprised of a pretty motley mix, the pilgrims hope to arrive at the tomb/shrine of Thomas Becket. As archbishop of Canterbury, he met with a bloody demise on the altar of his cathedral. Vicious thugs hired by King Henry II murdered him. Why? Becket refused to allow Henry a role in setting ecclesiastical policies.

Chaucer's poem, for it is that, exemplifies the roots of the heroic couplet, where the poet creates lines composed of ten syllables with "alternating accents and regular end rhymes."

What really interests me is not poetic forms but rather the cooks.

Yes, there are two, despite just "The Cook's Tale." Both serve bourgeois figures, especially the cook for The Franklin. The Guildsmen also enjoyed the services of their own cook, the very one telling the tale, unfinished as it is.

The Canterbury Tales testifies to Chaucer's erudition. Mentions of gods and legends and the Crusades then bring the first mention of food: The Squire is an apt carver at The Knight's table, though that gentleman be his father and not his true master. Food appears again with the Nun, the Prioress, who possesses exquisite manners at table, not splattering food or drink all over her vestments nor dipping her fingers too deeply into the sauce. As for The Monk, Chaucer mentions his girth and his love for a fat swan, roasted whole.

Chaucer describes other pilgrims with eagle-eyed observations of their dress and manner. He offers no food references until he arrives at The Franklin, a landowner free by birth but not noble. This particular man was "Epicurus' very son," loving his "morning sop of cake in wine." Generous to a fault, The Franklin set a mighty fine table with all manner of victuals: bread, ale, wine, "bake-meat pies," fish, meat, plump partridges, a list that made my mouth water. But then came phrases hinting that perhaps his cook ran around the steaming hot kitchen, fearing his master's tongue if the sauce weren't "hot and sharp."

Allusions to humoral theory pop up from time to time, too. For example, The Summoner likes garlic, onions, and wine, which were deemed unhealthy at the time, so these likes reflect poorly on him.

And that brings to mind The Cook, a poor fellow with a nasty, suppurating ulcer on his left leg.

Chaucer's characters all either represent real people he's known or heard of. The stuff of stereotypes.

Bailly says of The Cook, seemingly repeating accusations common about cookshops and cooks in London at the time,

> You've stolen gravy out of many a stew,
> Many's the Jack of Dover you have sold
> That's been twice warmed up and twice left cold;

The critical point here is the proliferation of cookshops, testifying to the popularity of takeaway food, no surprise since many people had no kitchens or couldn't afford the fuel to cook with. Most people, if they could, grew vegetables, primarily worts and potherbs, a practice so common as to not be mentioned in the culinary literature of the day.

As an introduction to medieval English life, Chaucer's *The Canterbury Tales* offers an often-humorous dissection of society, food, and religious life, all central to his world.

By God, if women had written stories,
As clerks had within here oratories,
They would have written of men more wickedness
Than all the mark of Adam may redress.

~ Geoffrey Chaucer

LYFTE THAT SWANNE.

Take and dyghte hym as a goose but let hym have a largyour brawne & loke ye have chawdron.

— Wynkyn de Worde, *The Boke of Kervynge*, 1508 —

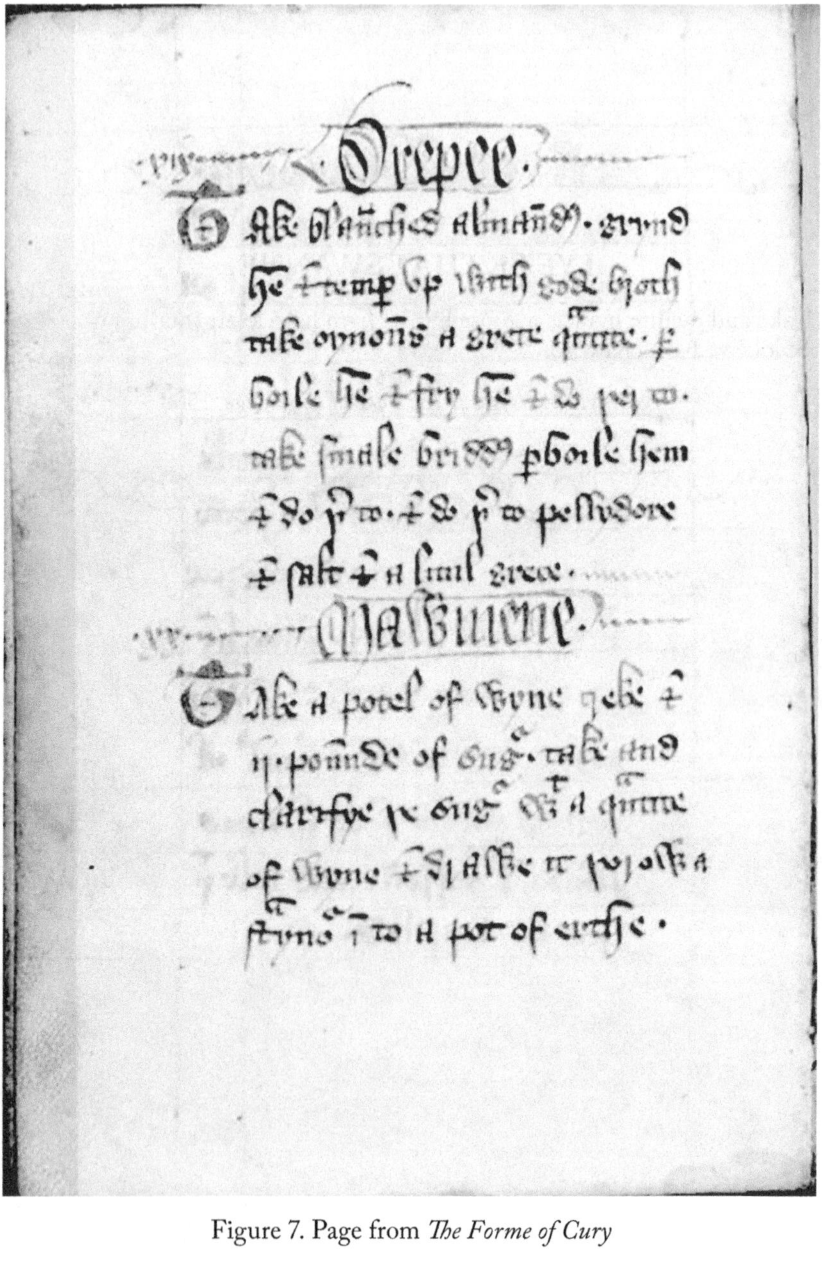
vii. Drepee.
Take blaunched almaundes. grynd
hem & temper up with gode broth
take oynouns a grete quantite. &
boile hem & fry hem & do þerto.
take smale briddes parboile hem
& do þerto. & do þerto pellydore
& salt & a litel grece.
viii. Mawmenee.
Take a potel of wyne greke &
ii. pounde of sugur. take and
clarifye þe sugur with a quantite
of wyne & drawe it thurgh a
straynour in to a pot of erthe.

Figure 7. Page from *The Forme of Cury*

KING RICHARD'S COOKS: THE FORME OF CURY

*Thys fourme of cury ys compyled of þe mayster cokes of kyng Richard þe secund...
by assent of Maysters of physik and of phylosophye.*

NO DOUBT EDWARD, Lord Stafford, bowed and knelt and wobbled on his knee as he lifted the heavy scroll to the queen that day. And not just any queen, but Elizabeth I herself.

The exact date for this transfer may have been around 1587. Samuel Pegge suggests that year in his version of *The Forme of Cury*, printed in 1780 by Nichols, and then in the possession of Gustavus Brandu, curator of the British Museum at the time.

Pegge believes that Lord Stafford may have been only fifteen years old when he handed this earliest English cookbook to the queen. That document, with 196 recipes, dates to the 1420s. Then a scribe copied it from yet another copy, making it like a nested series similar to Russian matryoshka dolls. To me, anyway!

Most authorities believe *The Forme of Cury*—the first English cookbook — appeared in scroll form around 1390 and led the long parade of English cookbooks.

During the Crusades, King Richard II's cooks compiled 200 recipes, several with names influenced by the Saracens, or Arabs. Its listings of ingredients boggle the mind, giving the boot to the idea that cooks of the times produced pottages and nothing else. For example, in the sauces included in the scroll, you see the invisible hand of the Doctoure of Physique, who advised the cooks on how best to balance the humors.

Don't be misled by the word "cury." "Cury" stems from a Middle English word for "food." It has nothing to do with English infatuation with the superb cuisine of India. You won't find the wonderful dishes you might associate with modern India or a curry house in London. The Royal court doled out spices to the kitchen via a section of the household called the "spicery," where the Lord Steward watched over the fragrant and highly valuable seasonings crucial for the dishes of the day's menus.

A word of caution appears necessary here. In its earliest permutation, *The Forme of Cury* is not a book as we think of it, but a scroll of vellum strips. A household manual, or *aide-memoire* in the style of those days, *The Forme of Cury* provided cooks and their staff guidelines for food preparation, banquets, and daily meals. While not cooks per se, pursers and stewards used the "book" while ordering food-stuffs for the household.

Perhaps *Forme* evolved in competition with French chef Taillevent's *Le Viandier*, which appeared simultaneously. No one knows for sure. But one thing is for certain: *The Forme of Cury*'s recipes reflect a sophistication not generally understood by filmmakers and modern-day writers who focus on medieval life.

Filled with 1,096 recipes, the scroll now rests in the British Library. The Library sums up *The Forme of Cury* quite concisely as being the first to "mention olive oil, cloves, mace, and gourds in relation to British food." Recipes included "what were then luxurious and valuable spices, including caraway, nutmeg, cardamom, ginger and pepper." The scroll also includes instructions "for cooking strange and exotic animals, such as whales, cranes, curlews, herons, seals, and porpoises."

This description fails to mention saffron. Sugar, ditto. Analyses of the recipes in *The Forme of Cury* compared to *Le Viandier* suggest that recipes contain thirty-nine percent saffron and twenty-three percent ginger. In contrast, recipes in *Le Viandier* tally up to seventeen percent saffron and twenty-six percent ginger. Compared to *Le Viandier*, twenty-seven percent of *The Forme of Cury*'s recipes required sugar instead of thirteen percent in the French work.

Other percentages were as follows:

Ingredient Comparisons Between *The Forme of Cury* and *Le Viandier*

Ingredient	*Forme of Cury*	*Le Viandier*
Almonds	28%	13%
Beef	3%	14%
Cinnamon	11%	15%
Cloves	9%	14%
Fish/Seafood	22%	29%
Game Bords	9%	9%
Goose	1%	1%
Mace	4%	1%
Parsley	5%	9%
Pepper	14%	10%
Pork	13%	10%

Poultry	15%	13%
Rabbit	4%	2%
Sheep/Mutton	1%	3%
Venison	2%	3%

A mere glance at this list emphasizes the incredible diversity of the ingredients available to cooks of the day, at least the talented souls working for English nobles and royalty. It also illustrates the relatively close connection between the two culinary cultures.

I often wonder who those people were and what they would say if they could speak. And so, I dreamed up a fictional rendition of Richard's master cook, imagining the man, for it was a man, no doubt:

My lord, King Richard II, took me to his service as Master Cook. He is a grand vivandier, possibly the best of all of the Christian kings. His table always boasts the latest delicacies, even when he journeys from one estate to another, far and wide across this green land of England. He especially loves the magnificent sotelties that I, and my cooks, create for him, solid castles constructed with coffin dough. In the year 1390, my lord beseeched me to lay down on vellum with my pen the many dishes that warm his heart on those cold evenings of ceaseless rain.

So I did, with the help of my men. To the benefit of the young lads new to the travail of the kitchen, I wrote the receipts with plentiful attention to the ingredients, the method of cooking, and added a word or two about the way King Richard prefers his food to be served at table.

When word seeped out that we'd recorded our kitchen's secrets, all and sundry came, slyly begging for a glimpse of the 196 recipes we scratched on the vellum, made from the finest of calfskin.

Oh, the luxury and joy of serving the lords and their ladies such dishes as porpoises, cranes, herons, and seals! Gold leaf, the finest of the fine, we use all that to flourish the messes of the King. The health of the King we forebear, with advice from the learned doctors of physick. Safroun finds its way into our pots, and yellows what it touches at will.

Capouns In Councys. XXII. Take Capons and rost hem right hoot þat þey be not half y nouhz and hewe hem to gobettes and cast hem in a pot, do þerto clene broth, seeþ hem þat þey be tendre. Take brede and þe self broth and drawe it up yferer, take strong Powdour and **Safroun** and Salt and cast þer to.

Take ayrenn and seeþ hem harde. Take out the zolkes and hewe the whyte þerinne, take the Pot fro þe fyre and cast the whyte þerinne. Messe the dishes þerwith and lay the 3olkes hool and flour it with clowes.

Transliteration of Recipe

Take capons and roast them right hot that they not be half enough or half done and chop them into pieces and cast them into a pot in thereto clean broth, boil them till they be tender. Take bread and the same broth and place it all on the fire, take strong powder and saffron and salt and cast thereto. Take eggs and seethe them hard. Take out the yolks and chop the whites therein, take the pot from the fire and cast the whites therein. Lay out the dishes therewith and lay the whole yolks and flour/sprinkle the dish with cloves.

The names of those anonymous cooks faded along with the ink on the scrolls. Still, one thing is for sure: they seem to have had tremendous respect for their sovereign's taste in food, saying they'd written the book for "the best and royallest vyaundier of alle cristen kynges."

Unquiet meals make ill digestions
~ William Shakespeare, *The Comedy Of Errors, Act 5, Scene 1*

Here after foloweth the order of meates how they must be served at the Table with their sauces for fleshe dayes at dynner.

The fyrste course.

Potage or stewed broath.
Bolde meate or stewed meate.
Chekins and Bacon.
Powdred beyfe.
Pyes.
Goose.
Pygge.

Roosted beyfe.
Roosted veale.
Custarde.

— *A Proper newe Booke of Cokerye* (mid-16th c.) —

Figure 8. Sir Toby Belch Coming to the Assistance of Sir Andrew Aguecheek

"GINGER SHALL BE HOT I' THE MOUTH, TOO"

IF ANYONE EVER FILMS A MOVIE about ginger's long and fascinating history, I pray Leonardo DiCaprio plays the lead. Imagine him sporting a multi-colored pair of hose, leaping from bow to stern on a flimsy wooden caravel ... chewing ginger to avoid the curse of seasickness.

Anyway, Shakespeare described ginger (*Zingiber officinale*) as "hot in the mouth." Confucius dictated rules about cutting it. No poets have praised it, not yet.

Before Shakespeare was a gleam in the eye of God, ginger enjoyed quite a long and noble history.

In ancient Bengal, in a time out of mind, people discovered a hot spicy yellow root—related to turmeric and galangal—and dubbed it *sringavera*, meaning "horned root" in Sanskrit. Ginger, a rhizome plant almost twin to bamboo and easy to grow, quickly spread throughout Asia. Chinese and Japanese cooks soon learned to pair ginger with fish because ginger eliminated fishy odors. As a cure for seasickness, ginger had no equal, and early Chinese sailors swore by it.

The Romans and Greeks incorporated huge quantities of ginger in their cooking by 100 A.D. Homesick Roman legionnaires posted in Britannia and Gaul demanded ginger (and got it) to spice up their less-than-fresh food. Thus, ginger took hold in Europe, where it dominated the art of cooking throughout the Middle Ages.

During the Age of Discovery, sailors on long voyages chewed ginger to combat seasickness. English cooks made these "ginger pills" more palatable for the sailors by baking cookies and cakes flavored with ginger. Ginger became so ingrained in English cooking that cooks laced traditional English Christmas Eve carp heavily with ginger. So important was ginger for the English palate that special containers for it sat on the dining table, alongside salt and pepper shakers. English settlers bound for the New World carried ginger in their luggage, and that is how ginger first came to America.

Tingly yellow ginger imparts a particular pep and prance to gingerbread boys and bestows the snap in gingersnaps.

Ginger turned up in many English recipe books during the Renaissance. *A Book of Cookyre Very Necessary for all such as delight therein*, compiled by the mysterious A.W., includes a number of ginger-studded recipes for poultry, as indicated by the following offering:

To bake Chickins.
Season them with cloves, mace, sinamon ginger, and some pepper, so put them into your coffin, and put therto corance dates Prunes, and sweet Butter, or els Marow, and when they be halfe baked, put in some sirup of vergious, and some sugar, shake them togither and set them into the oven again.

Bake Sparowes, Larkes, or any kinde of small birds, calves feet or sheepes tunges after the same manner.

Here's another example, from the 1691 *A New Booke of Cookerie*:

To smoore an old Coney, Ducke, or Mallard, on the French fashion.
PArboyle any of these, and halfe roast it, launch them downe the breastwith your Knife, and sticke them with two or three Cloues. Then put them into a Pipkin with halfe a pound of sweet Butter, a little white Wine Uergis, a piece of whole Mace, a little beaten Ginger, and Pepper.

Then mince two Onyons very small, with a piece of an Apple, so let them boyle leisurely, close couered, the space of two howers, turning them now and then. Serue them in vpon Sippets.

On the other side of the Atlantic, America's Revolutionary War soldiers received rations of ginger, probably for the same reasons that Roman soldiers clamored for it. As the years went by, American housewives added ginger mostly to cakes, cookies, ice cream, and pumpkin pies. Ginger ale and ginger beer became popular. Christmas sweets hogged most of the ginger. And that's still the case.

Ginger began to take on other cooking roles when massive waves of other immigrants came to America. Ginger teases the palate in Indian curries, Moroccan stews, and West African chicken and peanut sauces. Asian cooks re-introduced the idea of pairing ginger with fish and shellfish. Used gingerly, ginger indeed reduces the fishiness of fish.

For the modern cook, ginger appears widely in markets, available in both fresh and ground form. Fresh ginger keeps well in the fridge and in the freezer when wrapped in foil and bagged in plastic. Just cut off what is needed and refreeze.

Store ground ginger, made from the dried root, in a glass jar in a cool, dry, dark place. Substitute ground ginger for fresh only when fresh cannot be found in any grocery store or Asian market. Use only one-fourth the amount of ground ginger for fresh ginger. Remove large pieces of fresh ginger from the finished dish or finely grate it before cooking. Why? Biting into a large chunk of fresh ginger can be hotly unpleasant, to put it mildly.

For no less an authority than the famous English herbalist, John Gerard, said, "It heateth in the third degree," seconding Shakespeare's adage: ginger indeed sits "hot in the mouth."

Now about that movie, Mr. DiCaprio....

Sir Toby Belch: Dost thou think, because thou art virtuous,
there shall be no more cakes and ale?
Clown: Yes, by Saint Anne, and ginger shall be hot i' the mouth, too.
~ William Shakespeare, *Twelfth Night*. Act II. Scene 3

Figure 9. Portrait of John Evelyn

John Evelyn: Cook, or, the Seventeenth-Century Man Who Would Be a Locavore

SOMEHOW, AND HOW I WISH IT WERE SO, it would be nice to time-travel, to sit at table with the people I'm meeting through their words, written in long-dead hands with quill pens and India ink.

One of my new "acquaintances," if such a word be the correct way of putting things, goes by the name of John Evelyn.

Seventeenth-century English author John Evelyn chronicled upper-class life in his *Diary*, which eventually ran to six volumes when published. Like Samuel Pepys and James Boswell, he's known primarily for prolific diarying. Still, his apparent hypergraphia led him to produce many other works, including a cookery manuscript, published by Prospect Press as *John Evelyn, Cook: The Manuscript Receipt Book of John Evelyn*, a hymn to salads called *Acetaria;* and a tome about trees and forests—*Sylva, or, A Discourse of Forest Trees*.

You might ask, "Why should I care about a guy who died way back in 1706?" After all, he's a writer whose books ooze with a somewhat "hobbledehoy prose," as Helen Simpson of the *London Literary Supplement* once put it. In one of his portraits, he resembles the archetypal noble fop, posed with his hand caressing a disturbing human skull.

The old saying, "Don't judge a book by its cover," applies here. Born in our times, Evelyn, one of the founders of the Royal Society, would be one of today's greatest advocates for the Earth. A staunch supporter of afforestation, Evelyn also worked to curtail air pollution in the London of his day. Cooks who love gardening will find a kindred soul in John Evelyn. Of vegetarians, he says they are "more acute, subtil, and of deeper penetration" than those who relish meat. And he considers a meal with meat sorely lacking if no salad rests near his fork at the same time.

Evelyn's cookery manuscript contains 353 receipts, ranging from Wormwood Ale to French Bread.

For me, a person for whom cheesecake beats out all other desserts (except for chocolate, of course), John Evelyn's recipe for cheesecake cinches it. Cheesecake literally became mother's milk when my son was born, for I gobbled down many a

Sara Lee cheesecake when 3 a.m. hunger pangs woke both of us.

One sleep-deprived night, while staring at the ceiling, it occurred to me that cheesecake and chess pie really share a common ancestry.

So, after perusing Evelyn's recipe and delving into the messiness of rennet-making, I think I see a strong kinship between the cheesecakes and lemon chess pies I love so much.

A cookbook that surfaced from the archives of the City of Westminster offered a few clues about early cheesecakes in England. "The Cookbook of Unknown Ladies" is a manuscript cookbook from around 1761. However, many of the recipes tell tales of a far earlier time, perhaps one hundred years earlier. Among the many fascinating recipes, one speaks to my curiosity about lemon chess pies and lemon meringue pies and lemon curd.

Lemmon Cheese

A qurt of good thick sweet creame. Put to it the juce of four lemons as as mutch peel as well give it an agreeable flavour. Sweeten it to your taste & add a littile peach or orange flower water if you like it. Whip it up as you would for sellabubs but very solid. If you have a tin vat, put a thin cloath in it & pour in your cream. If not, put it in a napkin and tye it pritty close. Hang it up to let the whey run from it. Make it the night be fore you use it. Garnish it with currant jelliy or candied oranges.

Look at Evelyn's recipe for cheesecake now. I wonder who the "wee" is that he refers to? Him? His wife? His cook or cooks? All of them, merrily stirring the pot while the fire belches choking smoke?

154. An Excellent receipt for Cheesecakes, which wee make

Take 3 quarts of New Milk ren it pretty cold and when it is tender come drayn it from the whay in a strainer then hang it up till all the whay be drained from it, then change it into dry cloaths till it wett the Cloth no longer then straine it through a course haire sive, mingle it with 3 q^{rs} of a pound of fresh Butter, with y^r hands, take halfe a pound of Almonds beaten with rose water as fine as Curd, then mingle them with the yolks of tenne Eggs and neere a Pint of creame. A nutmeg grated sugar and a little salt when y^r Coffins [pie crusts] are ready and going to sett into the Oven, then mingle them together, the Oven must be as hot for a pigeon pye lett the scorching be over halfe an houre will be them well, the Coffins must be hardned by setting into oven full of branne, prick them with a bodkin [sharp instrument], which brush out with a wing, then put in the cheesecake stuff, you may leave 2 whites in the eggs if you like it best so.

The word "ren," when combined with "it," probably refers to "rennet." John Nott, the Duke of Bolton's chef and author of the 1726 *Cooks and Confectioners Dictionary*, emphatically mentions this in his recipe for cheesecake. Earlier on, Robert May writes it as "run it pretty cold" in *The Accomplisht Cook*. E. Smith includes specific details for extracting rennet in *The Compleat Housewife*:

"Making a Runnet-Bag"

Let the calf suck as much as he will just before he is kill'd, then take the bag out of the calf, and let it lie twelve hours covered over in stinging nettles till it is very red; then take out your curd, wash your bag clean; salt it within-side and without; let it lie sprinkled with salt twenty-four hours; then wash your curd in warm new milk, pick it, and put away all that is yellow and hollow, keep what is white and close; then wash it well, and sprinkle it with salt; when the bag has lain twenty-four hours, put it into the bag again, and put to it three spoonsful of the stroaking of a cow, beat up with the yolk of an egg or two, twelve cloves, and two blades of mace; put a skewer thro' it, and hang it in a pot; then make the rennet water thus:

Take half a pint of fair water, a little salt, and fix tops of the red buds of black-thorn, as many sprigs of burnet, and two of sweet-marjoram; boil these in the water, and strain it out; when it is cold put one half in the bad, and let the bag lie in the other half, taking it out as you use it, make more runnet, which you may do six or seven times; three spoonsful of this runnet will make a large Cheshire or cheddar-cheese, and half as much to a common cheese.

According to Rachel Feild's *Irons in the Fire*, "... sorrel, bedstraw, nettles, and many other hedgerow herbs were used to make cheese at almost any time of the year, without the sacrifice of calf, lamb, or piglet."

The eggs, the milk, and the tartness of the cheese carried over into some of the earliest recipes for pies that traveled to the New World with English settlers.

John Evelyn speaks frankly, honestly, and rues those who parade their food expertise a tad bit untruthfully. Take Receipt #146: A very good cake. [The original annotation.] Then, this, added later, according to the editor: "Mrs. Black[wood?], if it had bin given right which upon triall does not answer." One senses the sharp tip of the quill pen grinding into paper smudged with a yellow smear (egg yolk?) and the glassy look of a grease stain (butter?).

Sometimes, frankly, there is nothing new under the sun.

Honestly.

Omnia explorate; meliora retinete
(Explore everything; keep the best.)

~ Evelyn family motto

TO MAKE CONSERUE OF STRAWBERIES, WITH THE VERTUE OF THE SAME. CHAPTER. XXX.

TAke Strawberies .i. quart clene picked and washed, set them on the fyre til they be soft, strain them put thereto two times as much suger in powder, as waight of the strawberies, let them seeth tyll the suger be incorporated wt ye straberis put it in a Glasse or earthen Pot well glased. The vertue of the same. The conserue of Strawberies is good again

— John Partridge, *The Treasurie of commodious Conceits*, 1573 —

GERVASE MARKHAM

Engraved by Burnet Reading from an Original by T. Cross

Published by T. Rodd, 2, G. Newport St. Long Acre.

Figure 10. Portrait of Gervase Markham

GERVASE MARKHAM AND THE FIRST (DOCUMENTED) ENGLISH COOKBOOK IN AMERICA?

CLOSE YOUR EYES AND IMAGINE the splintery wooden deck of an English ship, moored at the London docks, on a warm afternoon in 1620. See the man? Thin, wiry, bent almost double from the weight of the tooled leather chest grinding into his blistered back.

Sweat rolls down his gaunt cheeks and blinds him for a minute as he grabs for the dirty white cloth slung around his neck. He wipes his face and curses, the day being hotter than any in living memory, London usually cool and so rainy that black mold bloomed like the flowers of spring, overnight. The last wooden chest lies at his feet, the one that Richard Berkeley ordered delivered to Mr. Thorpe in Jamestown via the ship *Supply*, companion to the *Mayflower*. The letter to George Thorpe said, not that he a mere docker could read it, that the chest contained some precious goods:

> "Markhams and Goouges booke of all kynd of English husbandry
> and huswifry, and others for the orderinge of silk and silkwormes
> are nowe sent, which take into your owne hands from Thomas
> Lemis, otherwise you will bee defrauded of them." (p. 400, Virginia
> Co. Records, volume III, letter to George Thorpe from Richard
> Berkeley and John Smyth, September 10, 1620)

In other words, George Thorpe could expect Gervase Markham's *The English Housewife* once the *Supply* docked at Jamestown, in faraway Virginia.

Who was Gervase Markham, and why have so few writers about early American cuisine mentioned him, except in passing, if at all?

His quirky, pixy eyes belie his prolificity as a writer, who some dub the first so-called hack writer in modern history, and possibly the first to import an Arabian horse into England.

And possibly one of William Shakespeare's rivals? In his tepidly received *Shakespeare's Rival*, Robert Gittings suggests Gervase Markham could well be the man Will skewered here and there in sonnets and plays. Markham may indeed have inspired Shakespeare's character, Don Adriano de Armado, in "Love's Labor Lost."

Don Armado, as you might recall, was given to highfalutin words and spoke in long paragraphs, fancying himself a pal of the King's. In reality, courtiers surrounding him saw nothing but a joke when they looked at him. If they looked at him at all.

If Shakespeare felt the urge to lampoon Markham, the copious output of this expert on husbandry, cookery, dairying, brewing, and other sundry subjects likely piqued Will's jealousy. Prior to Markham, rare indeed were books on yeomanry or skills for successful country life. Markham's *The Book of St. Albans* from 1486 was one of very few precursors of the genre. So too John Partridge's *The Treasurie of Commodious Conceits, & Hidden Secrets and May be Called, the Huswives Closet, of Healthfull Provision*. These works signify a change in thinking about life. As Spiller says, "In the medieval period … the mechanical and technical were guild practices and thus generally part of oral culture." Then their secrets appeared in print.

Influenced by Alexis of Piedmont, writers began to view knowledge in a different light. Antonio Pérez-Ramos suggests this change be described as "the maker's knowledge" (*verum factum*). In other words, knowing *how* to do/make something results in greater knowledge about its nature, a switch from Aristotelian ideas. Thus was born the "secrets" trend, which ended, more or less, around 1650, focused on specific and unique knowledge. This trend, though, opened the "closet" for the culinary recipe book.

Markham wrote about horses, cattle, and cookery, among many other topics. Here we are most concerned about his two-part tome, *Countrey Contentments*, of which *The English Housewife* formed the second part. His cookery followed the English manner, from first to last. As he himself wrote:

> … let it be rather to satisfie nature then our affections, and apter
> to kill hunger then revive new appetites, let it proceed more from
> the provision of her owne yarde, than the furniture of the markets;
> and let it be rather esteemed for the familiar acquaintance she hath
> with it, then for the strangenesse and raritie it bringeth from other
> Countries.

Culinary historian Karen Hess often mentions Markham in *Martha Washington's Booke of Cookery*, based on Jane Ludwell Parke's copy of a seventeenth-century manuscript cookbook. It arrived in Virginia with Jane's stepmother, Frances Culpeper, wife of Governor Sir William Berkeley, governor of Virginia from 1641 to 1652 and again from 1660 to 1677. Two of the recipes—both incomplete—interpreted by Ms. Hess concerned boiled fowl, in this case, chicken:

To Boyle Chicken
Pull & draw them, then put parsley & [in their] bellies; boyle ym
with water, & salt, 7 [ ] butter, vinegar, 7 some of ye [ ] in; beat
ym together, yn cut [ ] If you can get gooseberries [ ] put in a little
sugar, 7 [ ]

Markham, if his book was indeed in the colony by 1620, could very well
have written the standard procedure for what might best be described as stewed
hen. Either that or cooks adapted his recipe/technique and then copied them into
manuscript cookbooks of the day:

An Excellent Way to Boil Chickens
If you will boile Chickens, young Turkies, Pea-hens, or any house-
Fowle daintily, you shall after you have trimmed them, drawne
them, trust them, and washt them, fill their bellies as full of Parsly
as they can hold; then boile them with salt and water onely till they
be enough: then take a dish and put into it veriuice, and butter,
and salt, and when the butter is melted, take the Parsly out of the
Chickens bellies, and mince it very small, and put it to the veriuice
and butter, and stirre it well together; then lay in the Chickens, and
trimme the dish with sippets, and so serve it foorth.

According to Florence White's *Good Things in England*, Markham's treatment of chicken appears as late as the eighteenth century in Worcester in England,
including the sippets, or triangular pieces of toasted bread. Frankly, the recipe
closely resembles fricassees. Markham also devotes some ink to stewed chicken.
A dish very familiar to me from my childhood, based as it was on recipes from my
grandmothers, both with strong ties to the British Isles.

Gervase Markham's opus, so broad, so profuse, earned him the reputation of
a bit of a hack in his day. Nevertheless, his cookery book of 1615 remained in print
until 1683. The lack of scholarly attention given to Markham's work suggests that
Hannah Glasse's *The Art of Cookery, Made Plain and Easy* enjoyed great popularity
in England's American colonies. Glasse's book was for sale in Williamsburg, Virginia, as attested by advertisements in *The Virginia Gazette*. However, aside from
Markham's work, other cookbooks arrived in Virginia according to fashion and the
increasing presence of women's voices in the genre. Recall, though, at the time, few
women could read and write, estimated at only five to ten percent.

Markham soon faded from the culinary scene. Robert May's *The Accomplisht
Cook* appeared in 1660. Nine years later, Sir Kenelm Digby's *The Closet Of Sir Kenelm*

Digby Knight, Opened hit booksellers' stalls, usurping Markham's work. Both merit a deeper look at the formation of cookery in the New World, as does Markham.

Shakespeare need not have worried, for few now remember Gervase Markham. This is a shame because Markham's work deserves more study and comparison with manuscript cookbooks of the time.

Little did that docker know what he held in his hands as he tossed that chest on board the *Supply* that September day in 1620.

The man who can dominate a London dinner table can dominate the world.

~ Oscar Wilde

TO MAKE A TARTE OF RYCE.

Boyle your Rice, and out in the yolkes of two or three Egges into the Rice, and when it is boyled, put it into a dish, and season it with Suger, Sinamon, and Ginger, and butter, and the iuyce of two or three Orenges, and set it on the fire againe.

— Thomas Dawson, *The Good Housewife's Jewell*, 1596 —

COMPLETE SYSTEM

OF

COOKERY.

In which is set forth,

A Variety of genuine RECEIPTS,
collected from several Years Experience
under the celebrated Mr. de ST.CLOUET,
sometime since COOK to his Grace the
Duke of *Newcastle*.

By WILLIAM VERRAL,
Master of the *White-Hart* Inn in *Lewes*, *Sussex*.

Together with an INTRODUCTORY PREFACE,

Shewing how every Dish is brought to Table,
and in what Manner the meanest Capacity shall
never err in doing what his Bill of Fare contains.

To which is added,

A true Character of Monf. de ST. CLOUET.

LONDON,
Printed for the AUTHOR, and sold by him;
As also by EDWARD VERRAL Bookseller, in *Lewes*:
And by JOHN RIVINGTON in *St. Paul's Church-yard*, *London*.

M DCC LIX.

Figure 11. Title page, William Verrall's *Complete System of Cookery*

Recipes from the White Hart Inn: An Eighteenth-Century Cookbook for Today's Cook

THE DIARIST SAMUEL PEPYS, no mean observer of human foibles that relieve the monotony of day-to-day human life, recorded—almost in real-time—the Francophilic transformation of the English nobility after the 1660 Restoration of the Stuart monarchy. Since Pepys devoted a portion of his library to cookery, it's not surprising that his diary records some of the culinary aspects of the Restoration. One of Pepy's most favored books bore the title *L'école parfaite des officiers de bouche*, written by Jean Ribou. Pepys owned the third edition, published in 1676.

From even a quick reading of Pepys, what happened was that the upper-class English soon equated French cuisine with political power. The hoity-toities of the Whig government nearly all eventually employed French male cooks, thus making French cuisine the food of diplomacy. The precursor, as it were, of the cigar-smoke-filled saloon teeming with Tammany Hall types.

How did this transpire? Why did proud Englishmen fail to ask, "Where's the beef?"

Royal English exiles, Charles II and James II in particular, "disappeared" in France while waiting out the political turmoils of the Cromwellian period. After the Restoration in 1660, when the Stuart monarchy marched (or sailed) home, French influence sailed with them and soon permeated English court life.

William Verrall's *Recipes from the White Hart Inn* reveals a splendid example of that truism.

During the heyday of Whig political power in eighteenth-century England, the Duke of Newcastle enjoyed the services of a chef named M. Pierre de St.-Clouet. Unfortunately, that gentleman decided to cut and run to the service of another. That other someone was William Keppel (Earl of Albemarle), the Duke of Newcastle's friend and British ambassador to France. Later Keppel became governor of Virginia, where traces of his name, Albemarle, still dot the landscape here and there.

Clouet's popularity arose partly because of his culinary specialization: he cooked a form of *nouvelle cuisine* popular in the 1730s.

Fortunately, William Verrall, who worked as *sous* chef with Clouet at the Duke of Newcastle's estate, wrote *A Complete System of Cookery*, recording the recipes with which Clouet so enchanted the Duke of Newcastle.

The recipes hide a most delicious, gossipy story. Just the scandal for *People* magazine or *The National Enquirer* of our day.

Human nature being what it is, regardless of era or place, the Duke of Newcastle complained to his friend Albemarle that he needed a new cook, badly. Since Clouet, the object of his despair, worked for Albemarle, for whom the situation could have been anything but comfortable, Albemarle consulted Clouet on the issue. Together they came up with a chef named Hervé (Hervey in Franglish).

But, alas, like Cinderella's ugly older sister mooning over the handsome fairytale prince, Hervé couldn't capture the heart of the Duke. And this is where the story really becomes a classic: Newcastle wrote (in French) to his old cook, Clouet, pouring out his soul:

> It may be that the new cuisine does not please us here, but I cannot believe that he [Hervé] has mastered the art. His soups are usually too strong and his entrées and entremets are so disguised and so mixed-up that nobody can tell what they are made of. He never serves small hors d'oeuvres or light entrées, and he has no idea of the simple, unified dishes that you used to make for me and which are so much in fashion here, such as veal tendons, rabbit fillets, pigs' and calves' ears, and several other little dishes of the same kind. . . . In other words, he has no resemblance to your ways and your cuisine, and to what I require.

Clouet responded firmly in phonetically written French:

> As regards his mixed-up entrées and entremets, French cuisine has never been anything but mixtures. This is what gives it that great variety which places it above all the other cuisines of Europe. Masters who do not like these mixtures should be so good as to inform the cook of this, and to let him know how they wish to be served, so that the cook can show his skill by conforming to their desires.

So it went for the Duke of Newcastle, who wished to both impress his guests and conduct political shenanigans in his dining room.

That's why it's fortunate that Will Verrall put pen to paper.

With *Recipes from the White Hart Inn,* modern readers get a taste of what the

Duke of Newcastle missed as he watched Clouet abscond to the household of his friend Albemarle.

Mr. Verrall begins his book with a haughty sniff at the ragtag equipment that passed for a *batterie de cuisine* in even upper-class English households of the times. Stir in the English and French antagonisms brought about by long enmity, and you end up with a fine kettle of fish indeed.

Here's what our Will says to the cook in one such establishment, he being hired to cater for a large party, he being a publican with his family's White Hart Inn, which still stands. The passage reads like a skit on "Saturday Night Live," with Will Ferrell winking and quipping:

> Pray, Nanny, says I, where do you place your stewpans, and the other things you make use of in the cooking way?
> La, Sir, says she, that is all we have (pointing to one poor solitary stewpan, as one might call it,) but no more fit for use than a wooden hand-dish.
>
> Ump, says I to myself, how's this to be? A surgeon may as well attempt to make an incision with a pair of sheers, or open a vein with an oyster-knife, as for me to pretend to get his dinner without proper tools to do it; here's another stewpan, soup-pot, and any one thing else that is useful; there's what they call a frying pan indeed, but black as my hat, and a handle long enough to obstruct half the passage of the kitchen.

Mr. Verrall, you learn as you turn to the original title page of his *A Complete System of Cookery*, spent time—likely two and a half years—as the sous chef of "the celebrated Mr. de St.-Clouet, sometimes since Cook to his Grace the Duke of Newcastle."

A few days after the dinner he served despite Nanny's "poor solitary saucepan," Mr. Verrall ran into the gentleman at whose house he'd cooked:

> Will, says he, why here you have made a strange racket at our house. My maid talks of nothing but you; what a pretty dinner you sent to table, and so easy, that it seemed no more trouble to you than for her to make a Welch rabbit [*sic*]; but says, that if she had such a set of kitchen goods as yours, and a little of your instructions, she could do it all very well.

Mr. Verrall then continues by describing how the English noble kitchen might attain the heights of gastronomical bliss afforded by following in the footsteps of French chef M. de St.-Clouet. Of course, he's a bit apprehensive about what Clouet might say:

> What my friend Clouet will say when he hears of this rash
> adventure of mine [publishing the cookbook] I cannot guess; but
> this I'm sure of, he'll be my voucher that it is all authentic.

Mr. Verrall's book never enjoyed the popular acclaim handed to Hannah Glasse's *The Art of Cookery, Made Plain and Easy*. However, *Recipes from the White Hart Inn / A Complete System of Cookery* affords a glimpse of the types of dishes that led the Duke of Newcastle to plead like a spurned lover for the return of his chef, the remarkable M. Pierre de St.-Clouet.

Thomas Gray, the English poet, annotated his copy of Verrall's book with several comments linked to fish recipes. Mr. Verrall's *Recipes from the White Hart Inn* includes the following chapters: Soups, Fish, Gros Entrees of Meat, Petit Entrees, Hors d'Oeuvres, Entremets, and Thomas Gray's Recipes. Note the loose and easy treatment—nay, tormenting—of the French language.

One reason for the lack of contemporary popularity of Mr. Verrall's book lies in the English preference for heavier food, but also in acrimonious, anti-French reviews skewering Will's book. Here's a part of one, illustrating the differences of social class inherent in the Whig preference for French cooks versus other servants:

> With respect to this performance, we wish it may not be said or
> thought, that more is meant than meets the ear. It is intitled, *A
> Complete System of Cookery; but, what if it should prove A Complete
> System of Politics, aye, and of damnable politics, considering the present
> critical situation of affairs! If not a system of politics, at least, it may be
> supposed to be a political system trumped up in favour of our inveterate
> enemies the French. Nay, the author forgets himself so far as even to
> own, in the preface, that his chief end is to shew the whole and simple
> art of the most modern and best French cookery. Ah, ha! master William
> Verrall, have we caught you* tripping? We wish there may not be some
> Jesuitical ingredients in this French cookery. If there is any thing
> of that sort in the oven, we hope you have had no finger in the pye.
> (*The Critical Review, or, Annals of Literature, Volume 8, 1759, p. 284.*)

Plus ça change, plus c'est la même chose!

Everything stays the same, that is, when it comes to human nature, jealousy, and pique!

Speaking of fish, what follows is a list of some of the fish recipes Will included in his tome:

Turbot in the Italian Way

Pike with Forcemeat and Caper Sauce

Carps Done in the Court Fashion

Matelotte of Carps

Fricasee of Eels, with Champagne or Rhenish Wine

Soles with Forcemeat, Sauce of Minced Herbs

Salmon in Slices Mr. Clouet's Fashion, with Crawfish Sauce, or Prawns

Fillets of Soles, with Herbs in a Brown Sauce

Fillets of Whitings Marinaded, and Fry'd with Parsley

Fricasee of Tench, with Whitings Livers

Fillets of Mackerel, with Fennel and Gooseberries

Broiled Weavers, with Bay Leaves, with Sauce Pouvrade

Grudgeons en Gratin, with Livers of Whitings

Crawfish, with the Spawn or Eggs of a Lobster

Forcemeat of Lobster in the Shells

Attelets of Oysters, with Clear Gravy, Broiled

Another recipe featuring fish is:

Anchovies, with Parmesan Cheese (Des anchois au parmesan)
Fry some bits of bread about the length of an anchovy in good oil or butter, lay the half of an anchovy, with the bone upon each bit, and strew over them some Parmesan cheese grated fine, and colour them nicely in an oven, or with a salamander, squeeze the juice of an orange or lemon, and pile them up in your dish and send them to the table.

This seems to be but a trifling thing, but I never saw it come whole from the table.

That's our Will for you!

Recipes from Will Verrall's White Hart Inn would not be out of place on modern restaurant menus or served in home kitchens: turkey braised with chestnuts, rabbit with champagne, and ham hocks with peach fritters. Fairly precise instructions and enough decipherable quantities make it possible to actually cook from this latest offering in Penguin's Great Food Series, including classics by M.F.K. Fisher, Elizabeth David, Charles Lamb, and Mrs. Beeton.

He hath eaten me out of house and home;
he hath put all my substance into that fat belly of his.

~ William Shakespeare, *Henry IV*, Part 1: Act 2, Scene 1

36. TO PRESERVE COWCUMBERS ALL THE YEERE

You may take a gallon of faire water, and a pottle of verjuyce, and a pinte of bay salt, and a handfull of greene Fennel or Dill: boile it a little, and when it is cold put it into a barrell, and then put your Cowcumbers into that pickle, and you shall keepe them all the yeere.

— Sir Hugh Plat, *Delightes for Ladies*, 1602 —

Figure 12. Illustration from Martha Bradley's *The British Housewife*

GREENS AND ROOTS IN SEASON, OR, MARTHA'S LOCAL FOODS IN AN EIGHTEENTH-CENTURY COOKBOOK

MARTHA BRADLEY'S EIGHTEENTH-CENTURY TOME, *The British Housewife*, has long fascinated me for all her detail and precise instructions. And, most of all, for her emphasis on local foods, centuries before Alice Waters or Michael Pollan woke to the idea of farm-fresh food.

Another point I want to reiterate here is that the English knew what to do with fresh vegetables, not needing the tutelage of anyone to teach them otherwise.

For those who live above 35 degrees longitude, January offers very little in the way of freshly grown local vegetables. The need for food preservation loomed large. In other words, food processing.

These days cookbooks proliferate at the speed of light, or so it seems. Books similar in spirit to Mrs. Bradley's crop up like mushrooms, seemingly overnight. Many entice their readers by waggling carrots and kale in front of them. Catering to the current fad of locally grown fresh food, this joining of "local" and "fresh" is frankly a bit of a misnomer. Especially when there's a few inches of snow that refuses to melt, not to mention the mercury hovering at -10°F.

After a week of solid clouds, snow, and misery, I decided to brave the icy mountain road down to the local grocery store. First, I checked to see what Mrs. Bradley recommends for a small household and not a grand manor house in January.

Serialized initially in 1756, Martha's cookbook later appeared as a complete two-volume work in 1758, totaling a whopping 725 pages. The book—organized by season, with a month-by-month compendium of ingredients—well represents several trends ongoing in England at the time, namely 1) female authors were becoming mainstream contributors to cuisine, something that did not happen in France until much later; 2) subtle disdain for French culinary ways was increasing, although Martha Bradley included many French dishes, and 3) even women of the lower classes could better themselves through cooking.

Her book never quite reached the pinnacle of commercial success enjoyed by Elizabeth Raffald or Hannah Glasse. Truth be told, Bradley co-opted several of Glasse's recipes, as was common practice in her day. Her work also shows signs of the influence of Patrick Lamb and Vincent La Chapelle. Yet Gilly Lehmann titled her analysis of eighteenth-century British cookbooks as *The British Housewife*. In contrast to, say, Elizabeth Raffald, not much is really known about Martha herself, save what appears on the title page. But Mrs. Bradley's personality comes through loud and clear in her book, serving as an excellent introduction to her attitudes toward many things, and not just cooking!

> Our Cook ... will be able to shew that an English girl, properly instructed at first, can equal the best French Gentleman in everything but Expence. It is only in the being better taught at first, that these Foreigners excel our own people; let them have the same Advantages, and they may defy them. It is this we have endeavoured to give them in the present Book, and we hope we have hitherto succeeded.

And she firmly believed that practice makes perfect:

> Practice is all; for as the Children play at Bilbecket till they can catch the Ball every Time for many Minutes in the same Manner the Cook will be able to toss a hundred Pancakes without missing once, when she is accustomed to the Method of it.

Note that Mrs. Bradley aims her book at readers in the country (or provinces), and London as well. She suggests that the cook, the housekeeper, and the gardener will find something useful in the book by emphasizing those professions in a larger font. The keyword throughout appears to be "Ingredients." Bradley states that she covers fresh provisions, but her greatest emphasis lies with pickling and preserving. Following that comes the signal that the book serves as a guide to getting through the year, seasonality as it were, a "Bill of Fare for each Month."

Beginning, of course, with January, which I eagerly studied.

Of January, Mrs. Bradley says, "January is the dead season." Not much optimism is there!? She goes on to say, "In the Course of this month there is less variety than in any other; the Cook therefore with the utmost Care to make the best of what Nature affords."

Bradley promises a wide range of dishes, but not for January, not costly ones either, foretelling the surge toward economy in the cookbooks of the nineteenth century. Grand households do not greatly concern the author. "Foreign" ingredients appear, too, affirming the increasing commerce and travel of the British as their empire bloomed. She even suggests that illiterate persons will benefit from her book, due to the "curious copper plates" ... "by which even those who cannot read will be able to instruct themselves." Finally, in the end, Mrs. Bradley lets it be known that she comes from Bath, a very fashionable place to be indeed, and she possesses "upwards of Thirty Years Experience." She ends her advertisement, for that is what it is, with a most telling word: "Practice."

Thus, Bradley seals the deal by pointing out her street creds, ensuring that her platform, brand, niche, whatever, rests with the reader knowing of "what is necessary to be done in Providing for, Conducting, and Managing a Family throughout the Year." Mrs. Bradley's contribution to the world of cookery takes many tacks, but very possibly the greatest of them is this: a female author writes for the housewife and not the lady of the manor.

I ask you to answer me fairly: is not additional eating
an ordinary Englishman's ordinary idea of Christmas day?

~ Anthony Trollope

Figure 13. Illustration, Richard Bradley's *The Country Housewife and Lady's Director*

NOW IS THE WINTER OF MY DISCONTENT: MORE WORDS OF WISDOM FROM MARTHA B.

MOST WRITERS LIVE THE SAD TRUTH ABOUT WRITING: it's usually hard, thankless work, it's typically unrewarding financially, and it's always an absolute tyrant. Procrastination and avoidance win hands down when a writer wakes up and dreads the trip from the bed to the desk. Which is just about every day.

But writing, for me, is like eating. Necessary. No, let me rephrase that: writing's more like breathing. Vital. I can't not do it. (Double negative—very naughty of me....)

In the Shakespearean winter of my discontent, at the rise of a snow-shrouded sun, I pondered the grit of writers who wrote long before me, plugging away, with scant payback during their lives.

Especially the women.

Women often could not even dream of publication. Condemned to dresser drawers and leather-bound attic trunks, their writing filled page after futile page. Pages destined never to be read by anyone except the writers themselves. But many of their words still exist. Discovered in those moldering trunks, those moth-infested dressers, all this lost writing comes to the fore with digitization.

Martha Bradley had the good fortune of finding a publisher for her words, but she also found a modern publisher who brought her work into my world, too.

The postperson dumped a huge Royal Mail sack on my front porch. In that strange parcel, wrapped in brown paper and tied with cotton string, I found a six-volume copy of Martha's book, *The British Housewife*. Inside the bright red paperback covers lay a facsimile edition of this remarkable book, reprinted by Prospect Books in 1997. Unlike Mrs. Raffald, Martha did not enclose a picture of herself, nor did she expound much on her qualifications on the title page. Nor is there a long, digressive paean to any patron or patroness, as was so common at the time in many books, not just cookbooks.

She begins to instruct the housewife in the niceties of cooking with the seasons. Of March, she makes no particular comment, but just marches on with instructions on roasting, boiling, frying, and ends with sage advice on the fruits of the March garden, including the growing of flowers, saying, "March is a busy Month for the Person who takes Pleasure in a Flower Garden."

I only know Martha through her words, through the precise directions she gives in the recipes and other material. She apparently has no qualms about borrowing recipes from other published works. Primarily Hannah Glasse's and Vincent La Chappelle's, an act that would get her into serious trouble today, but par for the course in earlier times. She's organized, she understands how a cook's mind works. And she greatly admires French cooking, although there is a weak attempt at that subtle disdain from time to time.

With the usual high hopes and the longings that underlie so much of a writer's soul, Martha sat in her lodgings in Bath, England, the city where she'd cooked for thirty years, and wrote her cookery book. Yet, despite the unique seasonal arrangement and the richness of information found in her enormous book, all that proved insufficient. The book flopped financially. Only one edition ever left the publisher's workshop. Almost immediately, Martha found her book relegated to the modern equivalent of the remainder table. Her desire to be all things to all readers—lady of the manor, servants, gardeners, healers, and animal husbandmen—doomed her work. Another fault lay with her insistence on featuring Frenchiness in her recipes.

Ah, the fickleness of the reader. The obtuseness of the writer?

How so the latter?

It just so happens that Britain and France went to war in the New World in 1756. The French and Indian War, also known as the Seven Years' War. Hardly the time to tout French cuisine.

Poor Martha, she picked the wrong political climate for publishing. Unlike her predecessor, Richard Bradley, no relation, who enjoyed moderate success with his 1728 *The Country Housewife and Lady's Director*. Martha also failed to recognize a trend in British cooking that began around 1750. Gilly Lehmann remarks on this in her introduction to Martha's book, quoting a certain Reverend Stotherd Abdy after the wedding of Susanna Archer, a member of the Houblon family, country gentry thanks to their seventeenth-century trade-made fortune:

> *Monsr ... Cook [French chef hired for the wedding] had taken his leave, and that we should feel too sensibly [...] the want of everything hard named & out of the wayish as to eating; and that we must now be reduced to plain mutton and apple dumplin[sic]. We, instead of being mortified at this account sincerely rejoiced at hearing it, as our eyes had*

not blest with such a sight for above a week. When we came to table we had the pleasure of seeing seven good eatable dishes, and could really tell what they were, and we enjoyed our meal thoroughly.

I imagine that Martha felt the tyranny of writing, too, as she climbed out of her feather bed on a wintery March morning, staring out at leafless trees and drooping rose bushes, little knowing that 260 years later, a cookbook lover in the former British colony of Virginia would be reading her book. And gearing up to cook from it, too.

My definition of man is a cooking animal. The beasts have memory, judgement, and the faculties and passions of our minds in a certain degree; but no beast is a cook.

~ James Boswell

Figure 14. Rhubarb and Spice Seller

Boxing Day / St. Stephen's Day: Some Ancient Truths About Social Class and Food

BOXING DAY. WHAT IS THAT? Hint: It has nothing at all to do with boxing, the sport.

The day after Christmas now passes for a normal day here in the United States. Normal, if you mean more shopping (and gift returns). *Goodness, when will Aunt Tilly ever remember that I hate the color pink? Another pink sweater this year!*

Yet, in other parts of the world, from the earliest days of the Roman Catholic Church and later, December 26 took on significantly special symbolism. One of the original seven deacons in the early Church, Saint Stephen died on December 26. A victim of stoning, or so the legend goes, he became the Church's first martyr (protomartyr) for the faith. Ironically, Saint Paul (Saul of Tarsus) condoned Saint Stephen's death before his, Saul's, own conversion. The Christmas carol, "Good King Wenceslas," refers to Saint Stephen.

After the Norman Conquest in 1066, the devout English built over forty-six churches in Stephen's honor. During the Middle Ages, various customs became associated with this day.

In England, and other countries where England profoundly influenced the local culture, people celebrate December 26 as Boxing Day. Boxing Day began as a day of gift-giving to people in service. It may also have originated with distributing the contents of the local parish church's almsgiving box to the poor.

Boxing Day most likely is the precursor to the "Christmas gift" memories of enslaved Africans on Southern plantations. Planters—many with roots in the British Isles—followed those old practices, with a few changes.

Current practice still encourages people to give to the poor and perform charitable acts in Great Britain on Boxing Day.

It all sounds so nice and pat and convenient. And nice, as in "kind." Yet, as with most current holidays, mostly Christian, the real story delves into a nebulous past much further back.

In Ireland, an ancient ritualistic practice dubbed Wren's Day traditionally took place on December 26. Young boys flitted from door to door, begging money for a "dead wren" they carried on a stick, supposedly stoned to death. Today, the unhappy wren is not real, but the joviality is. This mummer-like tradition really represents a remnant of ancient Druidic wren sacrifices to honor the winter solstice.

As they wen alongt, they sang:

"I have a little box under me arm,
Under me arm, under me arm,
I have a little box under me arm,
And a Penny or Tuppence'd do it no harm."
Or:
"The wren, the wren, the king of all birds,
On St. Stephen's Day was caught in the furze,
Up with the penny and down with the pan,
Give us a penny to bury the wren."

Food plays an interesting role in the various celebrations surrounding Saint Stephen's Day.

In Poland, people throw oats at the priests and walnuts at each other—things supposedly symbolic of the stoning. These practices occurred in very ancient times as fertility rituals. In Sweden there's talk of "wild hunt," called "Staffan's Race." This ancient custom took place on St. Stephen's Day, calling up fertility mythology and lots of alcohol. Many of these customs also exist in the British Isles.

As recently as the early nineteenth century, in Ireland at least, preparations for Christmas still included the slaughter of animals, chiefly pigs and cows, in anticipation of December 25. The gentry received the choicest cuts (and those form the basis of many of the nostalgic recipes we cook, recipes that made their way into period cookbooks). For the peasantry and common people, the division of meat among village dwellers tells another story:

The head, tongue and feet: the blacksmith
The small ribs attached to the hindquarters: the tailor
The kidneys: the doctor
The udder: the harper
The liver: carpenter
The marrowbone: the odd-job man
The heart: the cowherd
A choice piece each: the midwife and the stableman
Black puddings and sausages: the ploughman.

Several recipes attest to the historical importance of food in this saint's festivities, including St. Stephen's Pudding (like plum pudding), Stephen's Beigli (Hungarian bread roll with either walnut or poppyseed filling), and Podkovy (St. Stephen's Horseshoes). Ernst Schuegraf includes recipes for all these dishes in his *Cooking with the Saints: An Illustrated Treasury of Authentic Recipes Old and Modern*.

In her charming little book, Darina Allen, *The Festive Foods of Ireland*, includes a recipe for St. Stephen's Day Stew, rich with salted meats, turkey, and vegetables. Obviously not an ancient recipe with Druidic roots (turkey? No way until after 1492). Nonetheless, the stew stimulates the salivary glands. She suggests using a hay box to keep the stew warm. Hay packed around the outside of the hay box insulates the contents. Yet, turkey sandwiches are now one of the most common dishes served on Boxing Day.

Save that hay bale from your porch after Halloween. It's excellent for keeping run-of-the-mill casseroles warm, too, come to think of it.

The Diet of the Londoners consists chiefly of Bread and Meat,
which they use instead of Herbs. Bread is there as in Paris,
finer and courser, according as they take out the Bran.
This I observ'd, that whereas we have a great deal of Cabbage,
and but a little bit of Meat, they will have Monstrous pieces of Beef;
I think they call 'em Rumps, and Buttocks, with a few Carrets,
that stand at a distance as if they were fright'd; nay I have feen a thing
they call a Sir-Loin, without any Herbs at all, so immense, that a French
Footman could scarce set it upon the Table.

~ M. Sorbiere

Figure 15. Title page, Alexis Soyer's *A Culinary Campaign*

VICTORIAN SENSES
AND SENSIBILITIES

JAMIE OLIVER'S FIGHT to bring nutritional nirvana to West Virginia might remind you of somebody.

That somebody was Alexis Benoît Soyer, a flamboyant French chef born in 1812, the same year as Abraham Lincoln. Soyer died in 1858 because of contracting Crimean fever. Very probably typhoid, though. He'd worked alongside Florence Nightingale, to reduce the pain and suffering of British soldiers sent to the Crimea. As the poet Alfred Lord Tennyson wrote in his poem, "The Charge of the Light Brigade," it was "not to reason why, theirs but to do and die."

Before Soyer so gallantly sailed to the Crimea at his own expense, he took up the cause of the London poor, particularly the Huguenot *émigré* silk weavers in Spitalfields and the starving millions in Ireland.

He set up London soup kitchens with the help of wealthy benefactors, mostly women. When the desperate British government sought him out in 1847 to deal with the starving Irish, he stepped up to the stove and doled out 6000 meals a day in less-than-ideal conditions. Making the most of the media of the day, Soyer wrote copious letters to *The Times*.

Like Nightingale, he attempted to create nutritious food, using some of the nutritional knowledge emerging from the work of scientists like Justus von Leibig, who touted the benefits of beef extract and proposed its use for laborers and people suffering from illnesses.

Thus, was born Soyer's famous "Famine Soup." Soyer claimed that this soup could sustain a healthy working man.

Ingredients for Famine Soup (Large Quantity):
12-1/2 lbs leg of beef
100 gallons of water
6-1/4 lbs drippings
100 onions and other vegetables
25 lbs each of flour (seconds) and pearl barley
1-1/2 lbs brown sugar
9 lbs salt

Ideally, in looking at the ingredients, the drippings, sugar, flour, and barley would supply energy and spare the protein in the beef from being used as energy. Depending on what cooks tossed into the pot, the soup also likely contributed vitamins and minerals in some quantity. Soyer recommended celery leaves, turnips, and the green ends of leeks, which we moderns usually throw away. *You do that, don't you?* He figured out that a quart of this soup cost ¾ d. Unfortunately, many critics pounced on Soyer and upbraided him for misrepresenting the nutritional value of his soup. Twelve pounds of meat to 100 gallons of water *does* make a pretty "skinny" soup.

But Soyer's heart sat firmly in the right place, as he made clear in *Soyer's Charitable Cookery, or the Poor Man's Regenerator*:

Though I have fulfilled my promise by giving publicity to my Receipts for Food, which I have composed for the poor, it has been suggested to me by the benevolent, to publish a small pamphlet with the following receipts, which might prove useful to humanity at large, having the great advantage of being very cheap and easily made. I have also added a few simple receipts for dishes, which may be made at a trifling expense, by copying which, every labouring family may reduce their expense, and live much better than they have hitherto done.

Punch quipped about this "Famine Soup," saying it was "not Soup for the Poor, but rather, Poor Soup!" In creating a stereotypical French chef named "Alcide Mirobolant," William Makepeace Thackeray parodied Soyer in *Pendennis*, a novel published in 1849.

Soyer served as the first chef of the Reform Club in London and hobnobbed with the rich and powerful. Because he never learned to write in English, he turned to F. Volant and J. R. Warren to write a prolific stream of cookbooks, including books, to better the nutrition of soldiers and the poor.

You will find many of his books on Google Books. Titles include *The Gastronomic Regenerator: a Simplified and Entirely New System of Cookery ... Suited to the Incomes of all Classes; Soyer's Charitable Cookery, or the Poor Man's Regenerator; The Modern Housewife or Menagère; The Pantropheon, or History of Food and its Preparation; Alexis Soyer's Shilling Cookery for the People; Soyer's Standard Cookery for the People; Soyer's Culinary Campaign, Being Historical Reminiscences of the Late War ... ;* and *Instructions to Military Hospital Cooks in the Preparation of Diets for Sick Soldiers ... the Receipts,* by G. Warriner and A. Soyer.

The impact of most migrating French chefs might not have reached the same level as Soyer's. As late as the Gulf War in the early 1990s, the British army still relied on his camp stove design. But there is still much to be discovered concerning

French chefs' long-reaching influence on English culture, both before and after the French Revolution of 1789.

It is to be regretted that men of science do not interest themselves more than they do on a subject of such vast magnitude as this; for I feel confident that the food of a country might be increased at least one-third, if the culinary science was properly developed, instead of its being slighted as it is now.

~ Alexis Soyer

Figure 16. Queen Victoria

FRANCATELLI, TOO

CONTINUING ON WITH MY EXAMINATIONS of English cookery books, it's time to turn to a nineteenth-century English chef named Charles Elmé Francatelli.

But before we get to the man of the moment, and the meat of the matter, let's pause for a second and revisit Mr. Manfred Görlach.

Who?

Görlach underwrote one of the few linguistic analyses of the written recipe as it appears in English. Happily, Mr. Görlach recognized the importance of Chef Francatelli and his work, particularly his *A Plain Cookery Book for the Working Classes* of 1852. Görlach contrasted Francatelli with that doyenne of English cookery writing, Mrs. Isabella Beeton, who revealed her own fondness for French cuisine in her door-stop-sized tome, *Book of Household Management* of 1861.

Görlach's conclusions? That Francatelli modified his words to reach a less-literate readership.

Francatelli published various cookery books, such as *The Modern Cook* in 1845. Still, his *Plain Cookery Book for the Working Classes* stands out among the others. There is no indication why Francatelli "stooped," so to speak, to the verbal level of the social classes diametrically opposed to the royal court. Likely he intended to provide practical guidance to those who severely needed it.

And the language Francatelli uses in *Plain Cookery* reads far differently than the style characteristic of his other books. According to Mr. Görlach, eight criteria exist for examining cookery books and their recipes linguistically:

1) Form of heading

2) Full sentences or telegram style

3) Use of imperative or other verbal forms

4) Use of possessive pronouns with ingredients and implements

5) Deletion of objects

6) Temporal sequence, and possible adverbs used

7) Complexity of sentences
8) Marked use of loanwords and of genteel diction

Görlach concludes:

In contrast to his other books, and to Mrs. Beeton, Francatelli's language shows obvious accommodation to the class of expected readers; the most striking feature is probably the extreme variation in form, as if he is intentionally flouting the conventions firmly entrenched in culinary handbooks, by the time. ... . Although Francatelli talks down to his readers, he is not free of inkhornisms.

Inkhornisms? Wonderful word!

Many of Francatelli's dishes definitely do not sound French: *"cow-heel broth, bubble and squeak, sheep's pluck,* and *a pudding made of small birds."* Laura Mason and Catherine Brown allude to these dishes in their 2004 edition of *Traditional Foods of Britain.*

So, who exactly was Charles Elmé Francatelli?

Charles Elmé Francatelli, born 1805, entered the world as an Englishman of Italian ancestry. He studied French cookery in France under famed chef Antonin Carême, thus misleading people into thinking he was French. At one point, Francatelli briefly served as chef to Queen Victoria from 1840 to 1842. But his primary loves were cooking, mostly for private clubs such as The Reform Club, and writing. His myriad cookbooks—the above-mentioned *The Modern Cook* and *A Plain Cookery Book for the Working Classes,* as well as *French Cookery: The Modern Cook, The Cook's Guide and Housekeeper's & Butler's Assistant,* and *The Royal English and Foreign Confectionery Book*—reflected the many changes occurring in the known world after the French Revolution.

Don't forget that French cuisine enjoyed a long history in England.

Francatelli simply fell into a pattern established after the Restoration, when French cooking became associated with Papism and Jacobites. Roman Catholic families of the seventeenth century, like the Carters and the Verrallls, hired French chefs, who cooked quite authentically. Apparently. Chefs like Louis Eustache Ude remained aware of Roman Catholic fast days, as he added various accommodations for those days in his stellar work of 1813, *The French Chef.*

Of course, by the second half of the nineteenth century, nobody remembered those pesky little details.

Victorians like Francatelli oversaw the heyday of French cooking in England. Their influence spread far and wide, across the globe to India, to Kenya, to Ghana, and points even further afield. Under the pseudonym "Lady Maria Clutterbuck," Charles Dickens's wife Catherine even penned *What Shall We Have for Dinner?,* a small book of menus meant to help households plan dinner parties and whatnot.

Colin Spencer, in *British Food*, sums up the whole issue of French cooking in England:

> What the British thought was French cooking was a radical
> adaptation towards their own tastes ... many of these so-called
> French influences were medieval, and had been enjoyed here
> for hundreds of years; after the Reformation we had forgotten
> about them.

Especially sheep's pluck, one would hope ... but not if haggis is your pleasure.

*"He has given us plenty of merriment, I am sure," said Fred, "and it would be
ungrateful not to drink his health. Here is a glass of mulled wine ready to our
hand at the moment; and I say, 'Uncle Scrooge'!"*

"Well! Uncle Scrooge!" they cried.

*"A Merry Christmas and a happy New Year to the old man,
whatever he is!" said Scrooge's nephew.*

~ Charles Dickens

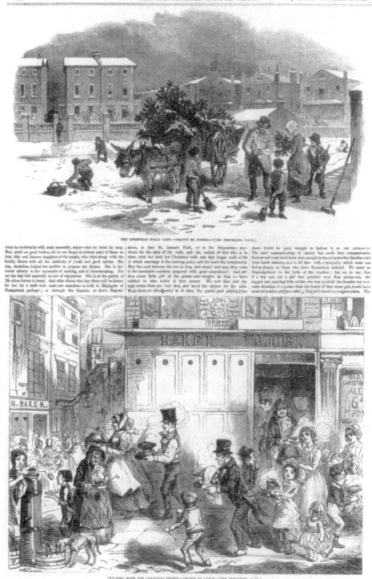

Figure 17. Londoners Fetching Christmas Dinner

Post-Victorian, But Still Victorian

I GLANCE DOWN AT MY FEET. The rectangular box lying on the doormat—about the size of the old New York City Yellow Pages—looks light enough, just like all the other book-filled Amazon boxes streaming into my house. But my back twinges alarmingly as I lean over to pick it up. This monster weighs about twenty pounds!

What book could I have ordered weighing that much? Do publishers even print such elephantine books anymore? Sometimes. The buzz a while back in foodie circles focused on the heft of several recently released cookbooks, as if it were something new to see beefy doorstoppers muscling out ninety-pound weakling paperbacks.

Heaving the box onto my kitchen counter, I grab a paring knife and slide it through the tape holding the box together.

Then the light bulb blazes.

I remember "The Aga with a Saga," a news story in the *Daily Mail* about a hidden Victorian kitchen in Wales, boarded off for sixty years. Estate-owner Archie Graham-Palmer and his wife Philippa discovered a vintage cookbook there, along with period pots and pastry cutters. Unfortunately, none of the news stories revealed the title of this cookbook in the midst of playing up the "Downton Abbey" overtones. Mr. Graham-Palmer remarked in an interview that the family needed an army of cooks to prepare the recipes.

Curious, I contacted Mr. Graham-Palmer about this. He graciously replied: the mystery cookbook they found carried a slightly presumptuous title, *The Ideal Cookery Book*, by Margaret Alice Fairclough, first published in London in 1908 by George Routledge and Sons, Limited. The Graham-Palmers' book dates to 1911.

And that's what nestles under the bubble wrap in that box. Available online, too, *The Ideal Cookery Book* comes complete with almost 300 illustrations, including forty-eight color plates drawn by Alexander Hamilton Sands.

Note that I am not going into a lot of discussion of individual recipes. You, the reader, might find it more exciting to stumble over the choice nugget or two yourself, those that always surface in these delicious old books.

Ms. Fairclough served as principal at the Gloucester Road School of Cookery at 84 Gloucester Road in London. Other than that, she flits through the pages, a phantom lady in white wielding an opinionated pen, giving precise measurements and instructions. I would venture to guess that you and I could actually cook these recipes and see some pretty fabulous results.

She derived many of her recipes from Charles Herman Senn's book, *Senn's Century Cookbook* of 1901 and Auguste Escoffier's *A Guide to Modern Cooking* of 1903, translated into English from French in 1907. *The Ideal Cookery Book* illustrates just how pervasive French cuisine became among the British upper class in the nineteenth and early twentieth centuries.

Most recipe titles appear in French, rarely followed by an English translation. No surprise there, really, given the desire of the British upper classes for French food and the status it conferred. But Ms. Fairclough's training provides another reason for *The Ideal Cookery Book*'s emphasis on all things French: she trained at the National Training School for Cookery, with Mr. Senn, who cooked at the Reform Club with the French chef Alexis Soyer.

Most chapters begin with brief admonishments and rules of cookery necessary to enhance the successful cook's output. As I turn the pages, the firm creamy paper shows no sign of acid rot eating away words after over 100 years. I find a chapter (X) devoted to Indian Dishes (Curries, ETC.). All called for the tinned curry powder becoming more and more popular in England at the time. Ms. Fairclough didn't fuss with French linguistics here: the recipe titles speak the King's English. What could be blunter than Chapter XXV: Invalid Dishes—Invalid Drinks? Another chapter—Chapter XXX. Breads, Cakes, Biscuits, ETC.—focuses on what looks like typical British home baking recipes, an interesting feature of this French-inspired book. The book omits the housekeeping-related features that defined earlier British cookbooks such as Mrs. Beeton's.

Some speculations and what-ifs seem to be in order now.

Might we surmise that the chief cooks/chefs in households like the Graham-Palmers' were always French? Or that the cooks knew enough kitchen French to muddle through? Seeing a tome like this one, found in a British kitchen, brings up a lot of questions. What about literacy in general? The prevailing idea about cooks is that they were slovenly, illiterate, and difficult. However, evidence suggests the contrary. Cooks needed to be literate AND numerate. And many of them were. In *The Expert Cook in Enlightenment France*, Sean Takats digs deeper into this topic.

Could this mean that the cooking of the very earliest English settlers in North America, at Jamestown and Plymouth, represented a "purer" form of English food than we see later? When the Huguenots arrived in Virginia around 1701, their manner of cooking and serving food jibed surprisingly well with what they found already in place?

Cookbooks *do* indeed tell tales, don't they?

One cannot think well, love well, sleep well,
if one has not dined well.

~ Virginia Woolf

Figure 18. Isabella Beeton

ISABELLA BEETON, MANAGING A HOUSEHOLD

IN MANY REGIONS OF TODAY'S WORLD, people try to discover themselves as they approach thirty or forty or fifty, thinking nothing of it, taking their longevity for granted. So, it's sobering to look at the accomplishments of people such as John Keats and Percy Bysshe Shelley and Isabella Beeton. All of them died before the candles on their birthday cakes numbered thirty. Yet they left mature works of near-immortal greatness.

In Britain today, "Mrs. Beeton" is a culinary trademark. Not unlike "Betty Crocker," whom General Mills created in a Frankensteinian moment, looking to boost sales by appealing to Every Housewife in America.

There's a difference between the two ladies. Mrs. Beeton was a real, breathing, living personage who wrote a monster of a book: *The Book of Household Management Comprising information for the Mistress, Housekeeper, Cook, Kitchen-Maid, Butler, Footman, Coachman, Valet, Upper and Under House-Maids, Lady's-Maid, Maid-of-all-Work, Laundry-Maid, Nurse and Nurse-Maid, Monthly Wet and Sick Nurses, etc. etc.—also Sanitary, Medical, & Legal Memoranda: with a History of the Origin, Properties, and Uses of all Things Connected with Home Life and Comfort.*

What a mouthful of a title!

Abbreviated to *BOHM* for short, thank goodness.

The writing of cookbooks often becomes fraught with injured egos and accusations bordering on the libelous. Or with charges of plagiarism, as in the case of Ann Cook and Hannah Glasse, described by Regula Burnet and Madeleine Hope Dodds in separate publications in the 1930s

But "… Mrs. Beeton *was* a plagiarist."

So states biographer Kathryn Hughes in *The Short Life and Long Times of Mrs. Beeton*, nearly 139 years after the death of the twenty-eight-year-old author Isabella Mary Mayson Beeton, also known as Mrs. Sam Beeton.

Kathryn Hughes is not the only twentieth-century writer to fling the dreaded "P" word. Elizabeth David, famed mid-twentieth century English food writer, pointed the tuning fork at Isabella, too. And whispered all but the word "plagiarism," in an article titled "Isabella Beeton and Her Book." David also enumerates what happened to Isabella's book after her death and the many revisions that followed.

Isabella took a leaf, so to speak, from the pages of several other English cookbooks popular at the time. Works by female authors such as Hannah Glasse, Maria Rundell, and the well-known Eliza Acton.

Acton's *Modern Cookery for Private Families* provided Isabella with much material for *BOHM*. She grabbed words from William Kitchiner's *The Cook's Oracle*, too. Portions of Jean Anthelme Brillat-Savarin's *The Physiology of Taste* and Thomas Webster's *Encyclopaedia of Domestic Economy* fell to her pen as well. A Mrs. William Parkes wrote a great deal of the latter book, providing cost information and listing ingredients at the beginning of her recipes. Thus, Isabella really didn't invent something new under the sun.

Born 1836, in Cheapside, London, Isabella was the oldest daughter in a family of 21 children, which she called a "living cargo of children." At age nineteen, she married Samuel Orchard (or Orchart as some researchers write it) Beeton. Sam Beeton made his fortune by publishing Harriet Beecher Stowe's *Uncle Tom's Cabin* in Britain. He adorned the book with the telltale beehive symbol/logo of his company. Isabella served as his editor, copy editor, and compiler from 1859 to 1861 for *The Englishwoman's Domestic Magazine*, which Sam launched in 1852. She also wrote a monthly cooking supplement for the magazine. In October 1861, Beeton published the twenty-four "supplements" as a single volume.

The problem? She didn't know much about cooking—her own sisters called her "an indifferent cook." A damning quote from a letter from Mrs. Henrietta Mary Pourtois English testifies to this situation. Henrietta married Robert English in 1835, formerly a footman to George IV. Well-versed in the ways of the kitchens of noble households, she also worked in the grand ancestral homes of the English aristocracy. Mrs. English wrote to Isabella Beeton, July 21st, 1857. In her letter, Mrs. English questions for whom Isabella was writing the book. Her missive reads in part:

"Cookery is a Science that is only learned by Long Experience and years of Study, which, of course, you have not had …."

Charges of plagiarism against Isabella take on a different perspective with this letter from her contemporary, Mrs. English. For Mrs. English is blatantly telling Isabella to "lift" the recipes from other sources, namely *Simpson's Cookery*! This is, according to Hughes, the way that cookery books had been put together from time immemorial.

At that time, the Beetons sought support for Isabella's *magnum opus*, *BOHM*, its ornate front piece painted by Henry George Hine.

The ensuing tone of *BOHM* resembled the voice of a comfortable, middle-aged lady appalled at the declining standards of competent womanhood. Isabella was primarily concerned with women's financial extravagance, ostensibly driving their families into ruin. Never mind their husbands with their gambling, horseracing, and other sundry vices!

Isabella began her book with a poignant preface:

> I must frankly own, that if I had known, beforehand, that this book
> would have cost me the labour which it has, I should never have
> been courageous enough to commence it. What moved me, in
> the first instance, to attempt a work like this, was the discomfort
> and suffering which I had seen brought upon men and women by
> household mismanagement. I have always thought that there is no
> more fruitful source of family discontent than a housewife's badly-
> cooked [*sic*] dinners and untidy ways.

The book features a number of interesting, somewhat unique characteristics, or at least features not common in many of the cookery books published at the time. Many now-classic phrases and sayings first appeared in *Household Management*:

"Dine we must, and we may as well dine elegantly as well as wholesomely."

"A place for everything and everything in its place."

"In cooking, clear as you go."

In addition to anecdotal stories and history peppered throughout the recipes, Isabella quotes poets Byron, Milton, Keats, and Tennyson in the chapter on "Dinners and Dining." She creates a usable index, numbers and alphabetizes the recipes within the chapters, estimates cost information, measures preparation time, and includes the number of servings for each recipe. She also pays attention to the seasonality of ingredients, in the same vein as Martha Bradley.

A moralizing tone characterizes many cookery books of the past, a trend that came and went like waves at the seashore, sometimes present during certain time periods, and then absent for a while. *BOHM* takes on the fashionable moralizing tone of the nineteenth century. Forty-six intensive, detailed chapters, beginning with "The Mistress of the Household" and ending with "Legal Memoranda" comprise the book. The title page oozes ripely with Victoriana. Over 1,112 pages make it a massive book, with 900 pages devoted to nearly 1400 recipes.

The detailed engravings/illustrations—some in color—are outstanding, a very different feature for a book of its price (7S 6d). The first review appeared a year after publication in *Athenaeum*. Even so, sixty thousand copies were sold during that first year alone.

It is one of the first cookbooks to publish recipes in a format that we find so familiar. Isabella also supposedly tested every recipe with her maid, but Hughes is skeptical about that. She chose recipes for middle-class homes, with few of the fanciful flourishes favored by Charles Elmé Francatelli, chef to Queen Victoria and author of another popular, contemporary book, *The Modern Cook*.

Like a marriage, Beeton's book impacted tremendously on Englishwomen's cookery, for better or worse. She supplies a list of prepared/canned foods available at the time, including prices. One section focuses on the nutritional value of various foods. There, she is quite on the money, quite accurate indeed, despite the advances in nutritional knowledge since then.

Cakes were a luxury food until the end of the nineteenth century. "A Nice Useful Cake," recipe number 2414, calls for new-fangled baking powder. Seven recipes for Plum Pudding appear in *BOHM*, catering to the pocketbooks of the various economic situations of her readers. Isabella also includes recipes for Australian, Indian, French, German, and Italian dishes.

Jean Anthelme Brillat-Savarin's comments about the English being the *worst* cooks in the world drew a sniff from the proper Isabella, sure that her book would right that situation.

Despite it all, the moralizing tone, and the plagiarism, *BOHM* became a runaway bestseller. Readers and critics considered the soup, fish, and sauce chapters the best.

Quantities of food served at dinners during the nineteenth century now seem phenomenal. But Isabella emphasizes strict economy, sometimes distressingly so, especially with family meals. She tackles the problem of leftover joints of meat, indexed in *BOHM* under "Cold Meat Cookery." For surely, as you well know, leftovers signal prosperity and abundance, a luxury not possible for the poor, whose next meal may just be a dream and a wish.

Sam Beeton, crafty businessman as he was, decided to take advantage of that situation. In 1863, he and Isabella created and published *The Englishwoman's Cookery Book*—a compendium of cold meat recipes and economical dishes. Leftover meat presented enormous problems for households, and readers clamored for ideas on how to use up the large joints of meat.

BOHM remains pertinent today for many reasons.

Cooks still mine *BOHM* for recipes because the book reveals social and cultural history. According to Aylett and Ordish in *First Catch Your Hare*, "It is still in print today, though modernised. First editions are extremely valuable properties; all nineteenth-century editions are collectors' pieces."

The book brings to light an invaluable portrait of Victorian English domestic life, especially eating habits. People gorged themselves, at least among the upper classes, and whenever there was enough money for food. Obesity became a problem then, too. *BOHM* reflects the urban life of most of its readers, in that no one appears to have raised their own food.

Isabella also focuses on the marketing/purchasing of goods for the household, including food. At the time, houses boasted official "back doors." Tradesmen came to the door and sold their wares, thus relieving the housewife of going out to do the marketing. Female servants did go out to shop if necessary. Isabella includes copious information on servants, their ranks in the household, and the pay they received. All food was cooked, nothing eaten raw, understandably so because of the dangers of contamination by poor water and dirty hands. Afterall, Isabella's book appeared before Pasteur confirmed his germ theory discoveries around 1862. And the legendary Sweeney Todd, the evil barber of Fleet Street, killed his customers to make meat pies of them.

Keywords characterizing the times of Isabella Beeton include Industrial Revolution, growing female literacy, the appearance of new consumer goods, breakdown of social class, and democratic movements. Charles Darwin had published *The Origin of Species* two years before *BOHM*.

So, Sam's magazines filled an important niche and fed his readers' hunger for knowledge propelled by the burgeoning intellectual life and growing literacy of the times. The contents of *BOHM* include items arranged according to the manner and order in which they appeared or eaten at large dinner parties:

Sauces
Meat
The Sheep and Lamb
The Common Hog
The Calf
Birds
Games
Vegetables
Puddings
Creams
Preserves

Milk and Eggs
Breads and Cakes
Beverages and
Invalid Cookery

Sample recipes:

CAPER SAUCE FOR FISH.

383. INGREDIENTS - 1/2 pint of melted butter No. 376, 3 dessertspoonfuls of capers, 1 dessertspoonful of their liquor, a small piece of glaze, if at hand (this may be dispensed with), 1/4 teaspoonful of salt, ditto of pepper, 1 tablespoonful of anchovy essence.

Mode.—Cut the capers across once or twice, but do not chop them fine; put them in a saucepan with 1/2 pint of good melted butter, and add all the other ingredients. Keep stirring the whole until it just simmers, when it is ready to serve.

Time.—1 minute to simmer. Average cost for this quantity, 5d.

Sufficient to serve with a skate, or 2 or 3 slices of salmon.

CAPERS.—These are the unopened buds of a low trailing shrub, which grows wild among the crevices of the rocks of Greece, as well as in northern Africa: the plant, however, has come to be cultivated in the south of Europe. After being pickled in vinegar and salt, they are imported from Sicily, Italy, and the south of France. The best are from Toulon.

A SUBSTITUTE FOR CAPER SAUCE.

384. INGREDIENTS - 1/2 pint of melted butter, No. 376, 2 tablespoonfuls of cut parsley, 1/2 teaspoonful of salt, 1 tablespoonful of vinegar.

Mode.—Boil the parsley slowly to let it become a bad colour; cut, but do not chop it fine. Add it to 1/2 pint of smoothly-made melted butter, with salt and vinegar in the above proportions. Boil up and serve.

Time.—2 minutes to simmer. Average cost for this quantity, 3d.

Granted, Eliza Acton pioneered several of the features found in Isabella's book. But Isabella adapts them in such a unique way that her book went on to be reprinted and revised many times, unlike Acton's. This virtually guaranteed that other cookbook authors would utilize the same successful techniques, including Fanny Farmer of the Boston Cooking School in the United States.

Excited about the upcoming delivery of her fourth child, Isabella worked on *Mrs. Beeton's Dictionary of Cookery*, an abridged version of *The Book of Household Management*, up to a week before she died. She also started a magazine called *The Queen* (later called *Harpers & Queen*).

She died of puerperal fever at age twenty-eight, one day after the birth of her fourth son, Mayson, in January 1865. Sam's broken-hearted eulogy read:

USQUE AD FINEM (Forever At Rest) Her hand has lost its cunning, the firm, true hand that wrote these formulae and penned the information contained in this little book...exquisite palate, unerring judgment, sound common sense, refined tastes, all these had the dear Lady, who has gone, ere her youth had scarcely come...her duty no woman has ever better accomplished than the late Isabella Mary Beeton.

And when they had finished the fish, Mrs Beaver brought unexpectedly out of the oven a great and gloriously sticky marmalade roll, steaming hot, and at the same time moved the kettle onto the fire, so that when they had finished the marmalade roll the tea was made and ready to be poured out.

~ C.S. Lewis

DISH OF FIGS.

DISH OF APPLES.

BASKET OF GRAPES.

DISH OF MIXED
SUMMER FRUIT.

DISH OF NUTS.

ALMONDS AND RAISINS.

STEWED PEARS.

COMPÔTE OF FIGS.

COMPÔTE OF ORANGES.

DISH OF MIXED FRUIT.

COMPÔTE OF APPLES.

ORANGE CROQUENBOUCHE.

DESSERT DISHES.

Figure 19. Desserts, *Book of Household Management*

COOKING AND DINING IN THE ENGLISH COUNTRY HOUSE: DOWNTON ABBEY COMES TO LIFE

THE TINKLE OF THE TINY BRASS BELL breaks the morning silence.

Cook cocks her head at the scullery maid. And points to the ceiling.

"Herself is awake...."

With that, the scrambling begins, and the decibel level shoots up.

Thus begins another day in an English manor house kitchen.

In this post-Downton Abbey world, I see that house through rose-colored glasses.

I envision towering red-brick walls. So too a winding driveway, a coach-and-four idling in the porte-cochère as the glossy black horses snuffle. A vast dining room, bearded gentlemen dressed in white ties and tails, puffing on fat cigars. A splendid parlor done up in bright yellows, pale ladies in lacy gowns sipping afternoon tea, nibbling on thin tomato sandwiches before dressing to the nines for dinner at eight. Drinking tea likely became popular, thanks to the influence of Catherine of Braganza, a Portuguese princess who married Charles II in 1662.

The English manor house didn't suddenly appear *sui generis* with the Edwardian era portrayed in Julian Fellowes's TV series, "Downton Abbey." Filmed at Highclere Castle, south of Oxford, the series offered insights into the lives of Edwardian nobility. Built in 1679, Highclere—like many others of its ilk—presents various architectural conjunctions, reflecting the whims of various occupants over the centuries. Country houses meant employment for hundreds of local people.

But history dealt these palatial homes several near-fatal blows.

World War I greatly affected the country-house life, as servants left and didn't return. During World War II, the British government requisitioned many houses, such as Bletchley Park, returning properties to owners in bad condition afterward. Many of these places fell out of their owners' hands because of Britain's taxation laws, too. Nowadays, the National Trust manages a significant number of them, allowing owners to continue living on the premises but still opening their houses to the paying public.

In 1827, poet Felicia Dorothea Hemans labeled these edifices "stately houses." However, unlike Downton Abbey, feudal lords and other owners of these early so-called "stately houses" usually fortified them.

Over time, however, these houses evolved into large estates surrounded by parkland and agricultural land. Built and designed to entice the king or queen to visit, they came to be called "prodigy houses." Thanks to architect Inigo Jones, the Palladian style predominated until close to the end of the eighteenth century. For example, Elizabeth I traveled through southern England in annual summer "progresses," bunking in the houses of wealthy courtiers. She brought along an entourage numbering in the hundreds. If things—lodging, food, attention—weren't up to her expectations, she never hesitated to say so, much to her hosts' dismay. Her father, Henry VIII, often entertained up to a thousand people at Hampton Court, arriving by boat from London via the Thames. Initially a hunting lodge fancied up by his former adviser, Cardinal Wolsey, Hampton Court offers the only sixteenth-century kitchens still operational in all of Europe.

To feed royal guests and others, cooks required an army of assistants, as well as a vast knowledge of foodstuffs, their properties, and where to procure fresh ingredients. Later, hothouses such as the one erected at Chatsworth in 1836 by Joseph Paxton enabled hosts to serve all manner of out-of-season delicacies.

According to Clarissa Dickson Wright, a typical dinner menu served at Henry VIII's table included:

Salads: Damsons, artichokes, cabbage, lettuce, purslane, and cucumbers

First Course: Stewed sparrows, carp, capons in lemon, larded pheasant, duck, gulls, forced rabbit, pasties of venison from fallow deer, and a pear pasty

Second Course: A stork, ganner, heron, pullets, quail, partridge, fresh sturgeon, another pasty of venison (this time from red deer), chicken, and fritters

Third (final) Course: Jelly, blancmange, apples with pistachios, pears with caraway seeds, filberts, scraped cheese with sugar, clotted cream with sugar, quince pie, and marchpane.

The meal ended with wafers and hippocras.

I thought, "I could eat that," until I spied "stork," obviously popular at the time, large birds being a thing. A big thing.

A proliferation of popular household manuals guided landholders in managing these stately houses. They turned to books such as Thomas Tusser's 1557 *A hundreth good pointes of husbandrie* and Gervase Markham's *The Countrie Farmer* of 1616, with their treatises on animal husbandry, agriculture, and such.

Aside from the kitchen, these estates required hundreds of people to perform all the daily tasks necessary to keep the household running smoothly. That labor force came from the local village and surrounding areas.

Peter Brears's *The Petworth Book of Country House Cookery* relates the culinary story of an English country house in West Sussex dating to 1150. Queen Adeliza, the second wife of Henry I, presented Petworth House to the Leconfield family in 1150. One of their descendants, Lord Egremont, grew up in the house in the 1950s, although after 1947 it belonged to the U.K.'s National Trust. The house functioned with the assistance of a full staff: butler, cook, housemaids, kitchen maids, and a footman. And no doubt groundsmen and other help.

Recipes in *The Petworth Book of Country House Cookery* testify to the skill and profound knowledge of the cooks. A Petworth retired cook, Mrs. Elizabeth Lane, wrote her recipes on scraps of paper, later salvaged by Lady Leconfield. These recipes make up most of the book. As was the fashion, Mrs. Lane wrote the recipe titles in French. Still, the dishes were usually anything but French.

William Tayler, a footman in the London household of a Mrs. Princep, of 6 Cumberland Street, now the Cumberland Hotel, Marble Arch, kept a diary during the entire year of 1837. Although Mrs. Princep's town house doesn't fit the description of a traditional country house like Petworth, the food served came close. He relates a typical day's repasts thus:

> For the parlour breakfast they have hot rolls, dry toast, a loaf of fancy bread and a loaf of common and a slice of butter ... they make their tea themselves. They have chocalate which is something like coffee but of a greasey and much richer nature. This is all they have for breakfast ... Lunch is at one ... They generally have some cut from ours or have cold meat and some vegitibles. Dinner at six which is considered very early. This day they had two soles fried with saws (sauce), a leg of mutton, a dish of ox, pullets, potatows, brocolo (broccoli), rice and a rhubarb tart, a tabiaca (tapioca) pudding, cheese and butter ... tea at eight o'clock with bread and butter and dry toast, never any supper – its not fashionable.

Brears states that the Victorian and Edwardian periods resulted in some of the "world's most complex, varied and high-quality cuisines because of the Empire." Lizzie Collingham hones this theme in *The Hungry Empire: How Britain's Quest for Food Shaped the Modern World*. Kenneth Graham hints at the opulence in *Wind in the Willows*, as Ratty and Mole head out for a Victorian-style picnic, a common activity among residents of manor houses, as were weekend shooting parties:

Ratty replies, "There's cold chicken inside it [the basket] ... coldtonguecoldhamcoldbeefpickledgherkinssaladfrenchrollscresssandwichespottedmeatgingerbeerlemonadesodawater ...."

I caught a few more glimpses into the manor house kitchen via Fortune Stanley's *English Country House Cooking* from 1972 and *Arabella Boxer's Book of English Food: A Rediscovery of British Food From Before the War*, from 1991. Stanley writes, "[D]rawn from the memories of several English hostesses and cooks who lived and worked in distinguished country houses ...." The book outlines a vivid portrait of pre-war English cooking. The sauce section alone left me drooling. Sauce Nénette? Wemyss Tomato Sauce? Sauce Landaise? And Boxer says, interestingly enough, that "Although the dishes Mrs. [Wallis] Simpson served at her table were hardly typical, being a highly sophisticated version, American food was not widely divergent from our own."

Then there's *The Official Downton Abbey Cookbook*. As a testament to the TV series, it does the job. But as a cookbook, it pales in comparison to the manor house cookbooks mentioned here. The list of recipes includes all the stereotypical English dishes. Bread Sauce? Check? Mint Sauce? Check. Yorkshire Pudding? Check? Beef Roast? Check. The context of the country house gets lost in the glamor, the trappings.

That said, "Downton Abbey" opens windows to the past. Showing vistas of history, what life at Highclere Castle or Hampton Court really meant, the endless toil of the people who made that luxury possible.

The servants.

If more of us valued food and cheer and song above hoarded gold, it would be a merrier world.

~ J.R.R Tolkien

Figure 20. Illustration from *Punch*

WHO WERE THE COOKS?
WHAT WE KNOW—MORE OR LESS—
ABOUT KITCHEN SERVANTS

WHILE STUDYING FLORA ANNIE STEEL'S *The Complete Indian Housekeeper and Cook*, I found the instructions concerning servants to be a fascinating insight into the authors' mindset and—by extension—a reflection of their times.

Servants were servants, usually treated with a hands-off and dismissive, superior attitude.

The intense interest in the British TV series "Downton Abbey" provides some answers to "the servant problem." Through their rigid roles and constant presence, servants made possible many things taken for granted in the history of England.

Cooking, for one thing. And not just the one-pot meal hung over a smoking fire in rustic peasant huts, a scene eliciting sighs of contented nostalgia among certain proponents of the simpler life.

One tremendously important source of information for us about servants lies in popular household manuals. Chiefly prescriptive, the genre emphasizes the ideal way of doing things, much as viewing the "House & Garden" network does for us today. As a result, these manuals supply invaluable information not often found in diaries, letters, or other contemporary literature.

Household manuals also dictate the behavior of servants who made those rarefied, wealthy lives possible. Of the multitude of nineteenth-century household manuals, Mrs. Beeton's *BOHM* probably stacks up as the most familiar of the lot. But household manuals did not suddenly surface in the nineteenth century. These books meant to aid the wealthy classes began appearing during the Renaissance, aimed at stewards of large noble households competing with each other, like more sophisticated versions of males-only pissing contests. The person who threw the largest party won!

Well-trained and well-behaved servants were always in great demand. That demand grew even greater in the nineteenth century as the nouveau riche built country homes throughout England. Supply didn't quite meet demand, as any reader sees in Wilkie Collins's mystery novels from the 1860s. There, he described servants as stupid or sullen. Complaints undoubtedly originated from conversations with mistresses of those ever-proliferating manor houses.

That women played no role as cooks for large manor houses goes without saying. According to Stephen Mennell, French chef Menon in *La cuisinière bourgeoise* believed women in the professional kitchen to be an abomination. Mennell writes, "only the less well-to-do members of the middle class would, by that date, make do with a woman cook in charge of their kitchen."

Not only were household manuals available for the benefit of the ladies of the manor. Publishers brought out books aimed at the servants as well. Hannah Woolley's *The Gentlewomans Companion* of 1673 led to many others, including *A Present for a Servant Maid* of 1745, by Eliza Haywood and *Madam Johnson's Present* of 1754, penned by Mary Johnson. The subtext of these books attests to an attitude toward servants that was quite rigid. As historian Gilly Lehmann puts it: "They [household manuals] were a response to the vociferous complaints about laziness and lack of subservience which characterized contemporary comment."

Given the prevalence of these household manuals in Britain, I wonder about the organization of kitchens in the American South. How much influence did these manuals have on the plantation households from early colonial days to the American Civil War? Because of the English Civil War, English Cavaliers brought the English country house tradition to the South. For example, Sir William Berkeley, a scion of the very wealthy and powerful Berkeley family, built Green Spring, just outside Jamestown,Virginia.

The hierarchy and the exclusion of people of lower status came with them. Those attitudes and sense of propriety extended to enslaved people as well.

Consider this scenario: Isaac, a formerly enslaved person owned by Thomas Jefferson's family, recounted in his later years how Martha Jefferson stood at the door of Monticello's kitchen, reading off recipes to the enslaved female cooks. Since the law forbade enslaved people from learning to read, how else would the cooks know how to cook scones or sweet fluffy layer cakes, for example? Neither came from West African culinary traditions. Kelley Fanto Deetz acknowledges this in *Bound to the Fire: How Virginia's Enslaved Cooks Helped Invent American Cuisine* by stating, "... the [enslaved] cook's role was to produce the sophisticated plantation fare, influenced by British and French cuisines and managed by the plantation's mistress."

Many culinary historians still overlook or ignore this fact. To the point of not examining the vast culinary treasure trove of digitized historic manuscript and printed cookbooks now available.

That is not to say that we can just willy-nilly take as gospel truth information in the manuals, or even oral histories, no questions asked. Far from it. Getting a grip on the day-to-day facts of servants' lives requires a lot more. Fiction and art provide us with material, as do memoirs, diaries, letters, and oral history. Ditto newspaper positions-wanted/positions available ads, etc. The architecture of the grand houses also hints of the logistics needed for preparing meals for hundreds of people a day.

Might some insights into early New World kitchens come from an unexpected place?

Victorian kitchen servants, and we know quite a bit about them, followed a hierarchy that looked something like this:

Cook: in charge of kitchen and supervisor of the kitchen staff

Kitchen Maid: The cook's assistant; prepared simple dishes and cleaned the kitchen

Still-Room Maid: Attended the room where preserves were located(cordials, jams, pickles, etc.)

Scullery Maid: Lowest on the hierarchy of household servants (usually the youngest)

Kitchen Boy: Ran errands for the cook

Other servants involved with food production included gardeners and those who raised and butchered livestock. Regardless of their duties, servants faced a tremendous number of rules governing their every move during the day. And night.

In Elizabethan and Renaissance times—and earlier—kitchen life played out very differently. Royal and other grand households needed many servants besides those listed above, such as bakers, brewers, yeomen of the buttery and pantry.

For example, Henry VIII's Hampton Court boasted several outbuildings dedicated to feeding the king and his hangers-on. In *All the King's Cooks*, Peter Brears lists the various task-oriented buildings: boiling house, bread delivery room, spicery office, pastry yard, pastry office, confectionery, pastry bakehouse and workhouse, dry fish house, paved passage (fish court), dry larder, wet larder, hall-place kitchen, lord's-side kitchen, great wine cellar, beer cellar, and great buttery. A staff of over 200 servants performed the duties associated with each of these spaces. Modern people forget just how much work it is to prepare food for cooking. In the absence of grocery stores, running water, electricity, and time-saving mechanical devices, formidable amounts of labor and time went into every dish.

So, cooks and their assistants counted among the most essential servants in country houses and the emerging middle class, both in England and America. But these people could not perform their kitchen magic without the help of what seemed like platoons of underlings. Even in Victorian times, the sheer number of people needed to keep vast amounts of food on the dining tables of the wealthy and well-placed required well-trained staff moving with the preciseness of crack troops. As Mr. Graham-Palmer of Cefn Lea Park remarked in *The Daily Mail*, preparing the recipes in Margaret Alice Fairclough's *The Ideal Cookery Book* required an army of cooks.

So, behind the scenes in Downton Abbey, upstairs and downstairs, life churned to a different rhythm. The servants kept it all running like well-greased wheels.

I sell dreams, small comforts, sweet harmless temptations to bring down a multitude of saints crash–crash–crashing among the hazels and nougatines....

~ Joanne Harris

TO BAKE A WILDE GOOSE OR MALLARD.

PArboyle them, and breake the brest bone of a large Goose, or take it quite out and all the other bones also, but not out of a Mallard. Season them, and Lard them, and put them into deepe Coffins, with store of Butter: when you draw them out of the Ouen put in more, and doe as before is shewed.

— John Murrell, *A new booke of Cookerie*, 1615 —

Figure 21. William Shakespeare

WARTS AND ALL: COOKS AS WITCHES, WITCHES AS COOKS

PICTURE A BIG, BLACK, SMOKING CAULDRON, symbol of cooking, food, nourishment.

And a metaphor for the basest, most primal horrors imaginable, the power of the Dark Arts, magic, blasphemy. Anyyone who's ever read Shakespeare's "Macbeth" recalls THE scene, the one with the three witches stirring the pot, chanting.

FIRST WITCH:
Round about the cauldron go;
In the poison'd entrails throw.
Toad, that under cold stone
Days and nights has thirty-one
Swelter'd venom sleeping got,
Boil thou first i' the charmed pot.

ALL:
Double, double toil and trouble;
Fire burn, and cauldron bubble.

Macbeth, Act 4, Scene I

I ponder the "ingredients" cast into the cauldron by these three. I also cannot help but recall that many, many early cookbooks so lavishly praised by food writers almost always contain a series of recipes for various health and medical cures. While they were not grimoires, these books share some characteristics peculiar to grimoires or spellbooks. For instance, the *Petit Albert*, likely inspired by Albertus Parvus Lucius. However, until the medical profession became predominantly male by the end of the nineteenth century, healing was the prerogative of women, a divide driven by class and status. Barbara Ehrenreich and Deirdre English discuss this well-known fact in *Witches, Midwives, and Nurses*. It forces me to wonder about cooks as healers in general, not just wise women.

"Bitch" and "witch," ever notice how close the two words seem?

Cooking, the hearth, women, and the sacred all became bound up together early on.

That the cauldron evolved into an emblem of witchcraft, one that you may still tune into at Halloween, says a lot, I think, about how our society still views women. Underneath it all, perhaps, images of the cauldron still emit a frisson of fear, of poisoning, of Sirenic enchantment, and dark moonless nights in a thick and impenetrable forest.

Regarding the flurry of witchcraft accusations in seventeenth-century England and Salem, Massachusetts, I must point my finger at a king. James VI. His book of 1597, *Daemonologie*, cast many poor souls into dark dungeons or fanned the flames of many burning pyres. James, along with many others of like mind, believed witches made pacts with the Devil, a creature still very much alive in Christian dogma at the time. And where one witch lurked, so did many others.

James began his hunt against witches in Scotland, from whence he came. His fear and hatred of them bubbled up when he convinced himself that women such as Mary Napier conjured up injurious, violent storms, like the one that beset his Danish bride Anne off the coast of Denmark in 1589.

Not all witches wore skirts, for some men also found themselves labeled as witches. For example, the chef Richard Roose—a poisoner and graphically brought back to life in an episode of the TV series "The Tudors"—might not have been tarred with the thick brush of witchcraft. Yet he lived at a time when the fear of witchcraft permeated English society. His gruesome death occurred by being boiling while alive in a giant black cauldron.

Death by poisoning, though, remained one of the greatest fears of prominent people. So much so that many notable people hired tasters to ensure their food remained pure and safely edible. For example, King Henry VIII employed tasters for his young son, Edward VI.

It seems to me that a hint of this fear lingers in the current distrust of highly processed foods, especially in the urgent need to ascertain just where one's food is grown and who grows it. So too the many ideas similar in nature to humoral theory.

Let your Food be simple, and Drinks innocent
and learn of Wisdom and Experience how to prepare them aright.

~ Thomas Tryon

Figure 22. Portrait of Elizabeth Raffald

COOKING WITH FIRE:
A PRIMER AND A MEDITATION

I FORGIVE YOU IF COOKING WITH FIRE conjures up visions of grilling hamburgers. Don't forget S'mores, the extent of my experience with fire and cooking for most of my childhood. I forgive myself for that, too.

It's winter now. A wood fire burns in my fireplace, a take-off on a Count Rumford design. There's something primeval about the smell of smoke, isn't there? Remembering those lazy bygone days of summer calls up many fire- and smoke-related food memories. I swear, there must be something to the idea of cellular memory because of the aroma of smoke or the crackle of flames as they lick the raw, fatty side of a piece of meat. Well, that's all it sometimes takes to be transported to another place.

That place usually signifies greater simplicity and innocence, an idyllic time with fewer cares and worries. Nostalgia. Romanticism.

But it was not idyllic at all to cook with fire, day in and day out. So, to truly understand just how our ancestors managed to feed themselves, it is crucial to "get" just what cooking fire really means. Moreover, contemplating cooking with fire throws light on how we moderns view such an ancient practice.

To understand English cooking, indeed any cooking anywhere, it's necessary to understand fire.

Real cooking with fire takes a lot more than squirting some lighter fluid on some "charcoal" and whipping out a green-tipped match the length of a Chinese chopstick.

Early humans worshiped fire. And feared its power as well. They cherished its beauty and utility in making food more edible and nourishing. For them, fire symbolized elements of magic and myth. So, epics and legends and fairy tales emerged to explain the alliance between fire and humans.

Take Theodor de Bry's engravings dating from 1591. He portrays the Timucua Indians of Florida as savages, smoking iguanas, snakes, and small mammals over raging fires. Andrew Warnes elaborates on how barbecue became associated with savagery in his book, *Savage BBQ*. Many reviewers, though, seem to take issue with his findings. Chefs such as Francis Mallmann of Argentina also search the past for inspiration, seeking a culinary ancestry essentially lost because of modern cooking methods and equipment. Mallmann roasts whole animals in enormous pits lined with heated stones, harking back to a pre-European Patagonian heritage, reinforcing the belief that somehow the past was ever so much better. Barbecue, but not Southern U.S.-influenced. I know, as years ago I almost choked to death on a piece of beef at a barbecue outside of Posadas, Argentina.

Today, in the minds of many people in the West, the idea of cooking with fire evokes those visions. Soft flickering light emanating from a stone hearth, the door barred against wolves howling in tune with the wind, and the looming darkness of the forests, thick with wood for cooking, there for the taking, it seemed, until far-off Judgement Day.

Cooking with fire now begets romanticism. We believe it brings us closer to the natural world, fraught as the so-called real world is with artificiality and a reality divorced from that yearned-for nature. Some writers allege that cooking with fire is not unlike poetry. Building a fire, and cooking on it, stands for skills that, until recently, just about everyone mastered early in life. A hesitant move, distracted attention, too hot a flame, and scarce food quickly burns, becoming inedible, wasted and lost. The specter of Death loomed even larger than usual when that happened. A cook who could judge the embers, sense the readiness of the flame, and coax nourishment from it all was a valuable and essential part of society.

Many people fail to understand that serious cooking fires do not require "leaping flames" as Goldenson and Simpson make clear. The type of wood for the fire also merits considerable attention. Hardwoods such as apple, ash, cherry, hickory, sugar maple, and red oak work best. Softwoods—such as willow, pine, spruce, and fir—don't work so well. Not because they don't burn. They do burn and ignite faster than do hardwoods. But because they burn so fast, softwoods don't yield enough long-lasting coals and require constant attention. Another drawback to cooking with softwoods—pine, for example—is the resins imbue food with peculiar flavors, despite the quick speed with which the fire burns.

And cooks needed to be sure "bank" the fire a few hours before any serious cooking could occur. This gives the fire a chance to produce the much-desired coals doing most of the cooking. One interesting tidbit about fires is this: many fireplaces were so large that homeowners placed a huge "backlog" of green wood—often the size of a tree!—up against the back wall of the fireplace. This practice kept the intense heat of the fireplace from damaging the wall. The back log also kept coals and embers going until morning so that the day's cooking fire could be started fairly rapidly. With all the recent talk about enslaved Africans enjoying a holiday over

Christmas, it must be said the English Yule log tradition played an important role, since the tradition apparently began with the concept of the back log. Goldenson and Simpson suggest that "The custom arose for the large plantation owners to grant a holiday from chores to their slaves as long as the back log continued to burn during the Christmas season."

Thus, fire played a starring role in everyday life, over and over, becoming the diva in the opera of the quotidian.

Richard Wrangham's groundbreaking book, *Catching Fire: How Cooking Made Us Human* pays homage to the idea of the centrality of cooking in humanity's evolution. He suggests that with the advent of cooking, early humans catapulted themselves beyond an existence based on raw foods.

Just when humans began cooking with fire is still controversial, ranging from 400,000 years ago to possibly over a million. Evidence of controlled use of fire at a South African cave site—Wonderwerk—dates to approximately one million years ago. Who knows exactly when the first human put two and two together and surmised that cooked food tastes better than raw food, and ever so much easier to chew, too?

Unfortunately, the only survival manual owned by early humans rested between their ears, not just because of their proverbially large brains, but due to knowledge passed down verbally in the dearth of literacy or the lack of writing all together. Deaths of wise elders, both men and women, meant a tremendous loss in this absence of writing, unless their society passed down that knowledge via stories or art. Even after the appearance of writing, diaries and journals, letters, and manuscript cookbooks rarely provided details about cooking with fire or anything about the role of various types of embers or coals. Legends, myths, and fairy tales featuring fire as a major character testify to fire's vital importance to humans, providing all the more reason to look long and hard at the myths that escaped the axe of memory.

Iconic foods in many world cultures originated in the clouds of smoke used as a preservative. People revere these foods now for springing from the land, reminders of the ancient past. Virginia ham—salt-cured and cold-smoked—exemplifies methods early American settlers used to preserve the flesh of pigs on the frontier. They based their smoking techniques on what they knew from curing meat in England, as in Yorkshire. Grimsby smoked fish is another iconic food from the English fishing town of Grimsby. Ditto Finnan Haddie. Smoked fish adds vital protein and flavor to West African "sauces," or stews eaten with various mashed tubers or other sources of carbohydrates. I believe that the smoked/salted pork of English cuisine replaced smoked/salted fish in the diets of enslaved Africans brought to the southern United States. But the English knew how to smoke meat long before they ever stepped foot in the New World.

Some foods smoked over fire create a smoky essence. There's also the Maillard Reaction, or browning, due to the interaction of proteins and sugars during heating. Don't forget that Mary Randolph mentions adding browned flour to sauces for increased flavor in *The Virginia Housewife*. A list of other iconic smoked foods would take pages to complete.

Invented in the late 1700s, the iron stove helped cooks a great deal, despite cooking still being powered by wood. Another factor propelling the invention of non-wood or charcoal-burning stoves came from smoke pollution, a problem that still plagues people, not to mention the depletion of forests. Finally, clever inventors such as Englishman James Sharp came up with a working gas stove around 1826. And with those inventions, cooking with fire receded into the past, becoming more a romantic hobby than a daily necessity replete with danger and drudgery.

Fire, powerful and fearsome, protecting and nurturing. Fire, one of the four elements of classical thought throughout the world, the one that tipped the scales and made us human. What we cook today, what we love to eat today, still bears the marks of flame and smoke, handed down through the ages, forged in the crucible of millions of fires.

The English men understand almost better than any other people the art of properly roasting a joint, which also is not to be wondered at; because the art of cooking as practiced by most Englishmen does not extend much beyond roast beef and plum pudding.

~ Pehr Kalm

TO MAKE FRITTERS.

Take halfe a pint of Sack, a pint of Ale, some Ale-yeast, nine Eggs, yolks and whites, beat them very well, the Egg first, then altogether, put in some Ginger, and Salt, and fine flower, then let it stand an houre or two; then shred in the Apples; when you are ready to fry them, your suet must be all Beef-suet, or halfe Beef, and halfe Hoggs-suet tryed out of the leafe.

— W. M., *The Queens Closet Opened*, 1658 —

GAME.

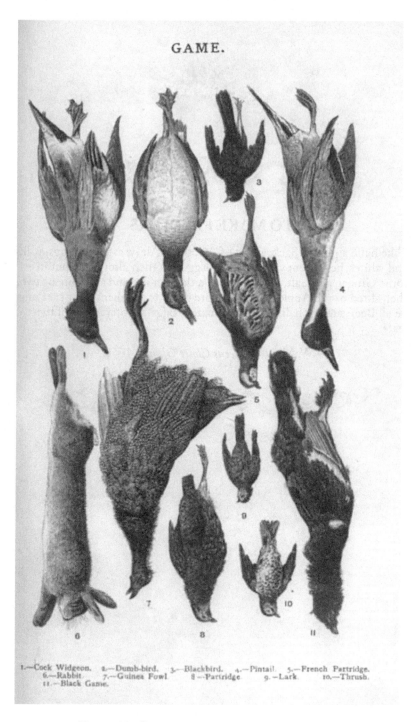

1.—Cock Widgeon. 2.—Dumb-bird. 3.—Blackbird. 4.—Pintail. 5.—French Partridge.
6.—Rabbit. 7.—Guinea Fowl 8.—Partridge. 9.—Lark. 10.—Thrush.
11.—Black Game.

Figure 23. Game, *Book of Household Management*

DAME ELIZABETH DAVID, CBE

READERS EITHER HATE HER OR LOVE HER.

Elizabeth David, according to a 2012 blog post by The Dabbler in the U.K., deserves a lot more kudos than she's getting:

> I confess to having fallen just a little in love with David since I first discovered her books a few years ago. She was willful, adventurous, determined and uncompromising. But for more than anything, I love her for significantly improving the quality of my life.

If you've never read Ms. David's books, run to the nearest bookstore or fire up your Kindle, or indulge in however you buy books these days. My favorite of her books is her 1960 tome, *French Provincial Cooking*. The title bears a sneakingly close resemblance to M.F.K. Fisher's *The Cooking of Provincial France*, which appeared eight years later.

My stained and dog-eared copy dates to 1978. I discovered it in a second-hand bookstore in Gainesville, Florida, just before I returned to Haiti after the ouster of Baby Doc Duvalier. Life in Haiti at that time revolved around hoping to avoid being shot by Duvalier's Tonton Macoutes and hunting for scarce gasoline. Without that precious liquid, worth more than gold, I couldn't drive my seven-year-old son to school nor buy food for daily meals. Or so it seemed. And then there was Le Brown Bag, my lunch-delivery business, running on fumes, not an option. The original street-food truck?

Anyway, inside the back cover of this wretched copy of *French Provincial Cooking*, welded together by a wide strip of clear packing tape, I wrote, "Wouldn't I love to move to a small house in France for six months, and escape from Haiti—I am so weary of the violence and anarchy here, I long for elegance, order, consistency, sanity...."

In Ms. David's book, I found escape.

Some people don't like Ms. David's *oeuvre*. They rest their claims on the fact that David's nostalgia for better times—in her case, pre-war England and Europe—colors her work and renders it less authentic.

As for me, Ms. David's book kept me positive, and at the stove, during a time when a trip down the mountain from Laboule to Port-au-Prince clenched my guts with apprehension and fear. The soulless sound of gunfire day and night never stopped. Or so it seemed.

When I lost myself in her prose, I could deal with my temporary exile, my "Otherness."

How could I not love a writer who gave me that?

Foxed, spotted, acid-rich, the paper crackles under the slightest touch of my hands. The book's an old Penguin paperback, worth only seventy-four cents on Amazon a few years ago, now ten times that. At least.

As I turn the pages of another of David's books, *French Country Cooking*, I vaguely recall a comment I once read by food activist and restaurateur Alice Waters in *The Chez Panisse Menu Cookbook*. There she talks about how she got started in the whole business of food and cooking:

> I bought Elizabeth David's book, *French Country Cooking*, and I cooked everything in it … . I admired her aesthetics of food, and wanted a restaurant that had the same feeling as the pictures on the covers of her books.

Later, after David's death in 1992, Marian Burros of *The New York Times* wrote an obituary of David and quoted Waters, " 'When I go back and read her [David's] book [*sic*] now,' Ms. Waters said, 'I feel I plagiarized them. All of it seeped in so much, it's embarrassing to read them now.' " Some might call it culinary appropriation ….

So, a book catapulted Alice Waters into becoming a crusader for better, fresher, slower, more authentic food?

Yes.

More recently, Alice Waters told interviewer Dave Weich of Powell's Books, "I'm always going back to Elizabeth David. I continue to be a fan. I can read and reread and find something important in there. I love her *French Provincial Cooking*."

There's this, too, what Alice Waters says on her Facebook Page, "Elizabeth David writes so vividly and sensually about food in the markets that you understand the absolute necessity of seasonal, fresh, and locally grown foods."

Think about that.

Does the current American nostalgia for, and the awareness of, a tastier past really stem from the work of an English food writer? In her own words, Alice Waters, now the doyenne of fresh sustainable food in America, locavore of all locavores, suggests that she owes just about everything she is today to Elizabeth David.

David herself based her early books, the very ones that captivated Alice Waters, on nostalgia for pre-World War II European cooking. Including English cooking. She loathed deep-freeze food and said as much numerous times in her many books.

A chain reaction of nostalgia for food reflecting a reality that never existed?

In her introduction to *French Provincial Cooking*, David relates a little story about what might as well be called the "tiny cookbook heard from sea to sea." David succumbed to the charms of a cookbook cover, just as Waters did:

> It was a tattered little volume, and its cover attracted me. In faded pinks and blues, it depicts an enormously fat and contented-looking cook in a white muslin cap, spotted blouse and blue apron, smiling smugly to herself as she scatters herbs on a *gigot* of mutton. Beside her are a great loaf of butter, a head of garlic and a wooden salt box, and in the foreground is a table laid with a white cloth and four places, a basket of bread, a cruet and two carafes of wine.

The promise of the cover was, indeed, fulfilled in the pages of this delightful little book, called *Secrets de la Bonne Table, 120 Recettes inédites recueillies dans les provinces de France*, by Benjamin Renaudet, published around 1900. How seductive a book's cover can be!

And "they" say never judge a book by its cover ….

Elizabeth David's books did (and do) make plain simple food accessible to people. How could anyone not be swept off their kitchen clogs by the following one-long-sentence passage from *French Country Cooking*?

> Every scrap of food produced is made use of in some way or another, in fact in the best way possible, so it is in the heart of the country that one may become acquainted with the infinite variety of charcuterie, the sausages, pickled pork and bacon, smoked hams, *terrines*, preserved goose, *pâtés*, *rillettes*, and *andouillettes* ….

In "Saucier's Apprentice," a 1976 article in *New Society*, Angela Carter adds to the worshipping chorus about David's writing, saying, "This is cookery as pure witchcraft, invocatory cooking in which both the process of cooking and the comestible produced transcend the here and now."

Yes, indeed. Before Alice Waters, there was Elizabeth David. An English cook.

We're all reaping what she sowed, what she shared.

If I could create an ideal world, it would be an England
with the fire of the Elizabethans, the correct taste of the Georgians,
and the refinement and pure ideals of the Victorians.

~ H. P. Lovecraft

DISPLAY THAT CRANE.

Unfold his Legs, and cut off his wings by the joynts, then take up his wings and his legs, and sauce them with powder of ginger, mustard, vinegar, and salt.

— Robert May, *The Accomplisht Cook*, 1660 —

Figure 24. Soldier and His Wife

PATIENCE GRAY, MOORED IN THE MEDITERRANEAN

ELIZABETH DAVID PUBLISHED THE FIRST WIDELY POPULAR English book on Mediterranean food in 1950. But another English author, the lesser-known and free-spirited Patience Gray, wrote more poetically. Her *Plats du Jour*, despite its French title, netted recipes from all the lands of the Mediterranean, mostly gleaned from books and other sources. Years later, she followed up that enticing work with *Honey from a Weed*, in many ways one of the most engaging and tantalizing cookbooks I have ever read. Because *Honey* reflects her lived experience, it is now a classic, first editions commanding high prices among booksellers.

I've owned Gray's bewitching book for years.

My copy is a first-edition hardcover of the American edition. I'd love to own the very first English edition printed by Prospect Books! As well as her other works. *Ring Doves and Snakes* and *Work Adventures, Childhood Dreams*, both memoirs, plus another cookbook, *The Centaur's Kitchen: A Book of French, Italian, Greek, and Catalan Dishes for the Blue Funnel Ships*, all quite rare these days.

Gray would be a blogger today. That I am sure of, for *Honey* reads both like a diary and a series of letters to intimate, food-loving friends.

The lure of the book lies in its hints of life on the road, the eternal ties to people and places that traveling knits and binds. As Angela Carter writes of Gray and David in 1987 for the *London Review of Books*, "... these are women to whom food is not an end in itself but a way of opening up the world."

Like M.F.K. Fisher's ambrosial texts, Gray's words transport us, modern readers and technology addicts that we are, back to a time and place when ringtones and instant messaging did not exist. Away from the distractions of what passed for modern life, she sank into the daily rituals of cooking from scratch. For there simply was no other choice where she lived, in out-of-the-way places near marble quarries her lover, Belgian sculptor Norman Mommens, demanded for his art.

Her sketches of life with Mommens read completely unlike the British travel writers she no doubt read and maybe even interacted with during her time as the women's-page writer for the English newspaper, *The Observer*. In her obituary, Tom Jaine, editor of Prospect Books, wrote of her work at *The Observer*: "There was little consensus among the tweed-jacketed editorial staff as to what sort of thing might appeal to women …. Handed *carte blanche,* Patience filled it to good effect. … And she set about instructing them in European art, design, thought and habits."

Once she met Mommens, though, she blossomed into the woman you hear speaking from the wild and sensual pages of *Honey.* She writes, "Living in the wild, it has often seemed that we were living on the margins of literacy. This led to reading the landscape and learning from people, that is to firsthand experience. This experience is both real and necessarily limited."

On and on, the experiences come.

Recipes float in and out of the narrative. Gray's keen observer's eye connecting with her writer's hand serves forth delectable and daunting descriptions of a vagabond life. Here's her kitchen in Carrara: "In the kitchen at La Barozza above Carrara … marooned on the saddle of an Etruscan hill, there was still the built-in tiled charcoal installation which had to be lit with little sticks of charcoal and paper."

But Gray doesn't just relate the joys of cooking. She also weaves in stories about all the thrilling places, *terroir.* Thus, the environment formed culture and food and politics. All, as it turns out.

There's no better ending to a book like this than how Gray deals with it:

> The recipes in this book belong to an era of food grown for its own sake, not for profit. This era has vanished. If cooking and eating were all I had had in mind when writing them down, the pleasure they might afford would be largely nostalgic. … It seemed to me appropriate to show something of the life that generates this indispensable element at a time when undernourishment bedevils even the highest income groups.

… see whether you can by words give anyone who has
never tasted pineapple an idea of the taste of that fruit.
He may approach a grasp of it by being told of its resemblance
to other tastes of which he already has the ideas in his memory, imprinted there
by things he has taken into his mouth; but merely raising up in him other simple
ideas that will still be very different from the true taste of the pineapple.

~ John Locke

Again, The Food of most Children, of late Years, is so enriched with *West* and *East-India* Ingredients, that is, with Sugar and Spices, that thereby their Food becomes so hot in operation, that it does not only breed too much Nourishment, which generates Obstructions and Stoppages, but it heats the Body, drying up and consuming the Radical Moisture, and infecting the Blood with a sharp fretting Humour, which in some Complexions and Constitutions causeth Languishing Diseases, contracting the Breast and Vessels of the Stomach, and hindering the Passages of the Spirits, so that the Joynts and Nerves become weak and feeble: in others, with the help of bad Diet, and other Uncleanliness, does cause Botches, Boils, and various sorts of Leprous Diseases. Also many that have wherewithal, will frequently give their Children Sack, strong Drinks, and fat Meats, as long as they will eat, which is abominable, and absolutely contrary to the Nature of Children.

— Thomas Tryon, *The Good House-wife Made a Doctor*, 1692 —

Figure 25. Oyster Stall

SEE JANE COOK: A FEW WORDS
ABOUT
SOPHIE GRIGSON'S MUM

ANY AMERICAN OVER THE AGE OF FORTY might well recognize this title's allusion to the horrendously boring tiny readers featuring the stifling little lives of the children Dick and Jane and their dog Spot.

It's a wonder anyone ever wanted to read a book ever again!

And it's no wonder I felt a bit green.

I've always wanted to attend the annual Oxford Food Symposium in Oxford, England. Especially in 2010, when the theme was "Cured, Fermented, and Smoked Foods." Now, for foodists, foodies, gastronomes, and just plain folks, this Symposium takes on the same aura as the Super Bowl for those inclined to love American football or, if soccer is more your cuppa, the World Cup.

This was the big one, in other words. You see, the Jane in question had much to do with the Symposium.

The 2010 program sounded fantastic.

Since I couldn't be sitting in a pub quaffing Guinness that year, I decided to dig out a few of my British cookbooks and think of England. Thinking of England, especially if you're a food-crazed food writer, means recalling food writer Elizabeth David, of course. But Alan Davidson, too, who started the whole Oxford Food Symposium thing with Theodore Zeldin.

And Jane Grigson, too.

Not as well known here in the U.S. as Elizabeth David, who incidentally was responsible for propelling Grigson into the public eye in the first place, Jane Grigson, born in 1928, wrote eleven books, as well as numerous articles for *The Observer*. When she died in 1990, one day shy of her sixty-second birthday, Alan Davidson said of her:

> She won to herself this wide audience [of millions of people]
> because she was above all a friendly writer, equipped by both frame
> of mind and style of writing to communicate easily with them.

Davidson considered each of Grigson's books to be classic. As do I.

In *The Wilder Shores of Gastronomy*, a collection of twenty years' worth of articles from *Petits Propos Culinaires*, Davidson includes a chapter entitled "Jane Grigson: A Celebration in Three Parts." Isobel Holland, Lynette Hunter, and Geraldine Stoneham compiled a thirty-three-page bibliography just of Grigson's thirteen books' sundry editions and printings. In their introduction, reprinted in *Wilder Shores*, they write:

> Her books glow with a warm awareness of history, of the myriad
> tangled skeins of connection which link a kitchen of today with
> kitchens of the past, of the gradual evolution of recipes and
> customs, of how some things have got better and others, many
> others, worse. ...

As for a complete bibliography of Grigson's many articles and such, dream on. No such thing yet exists.

However, here's a list of her books, only one of which is in my local public library, although the nearby university library sports several. I own four:

Charcuterie, Mushroom: Vegetable: and English.

Charcuterie and French Pork Cookery (1967)
Good Things (1971)
Fish Cookery (1973, recently reissued)
English Food (1974)
The Mushroom Feast (1975)
Jane Grigson's Vegetable Book (1978)
Food With The Famous (1979)
Jane Grigson's Fruit Book (1982)
The Observer Guide to European Cookery (1983)
The Observer Guide to British Cookery (1984)
The Cooking of Normandy (for Sainsbury's) (1987)
The Enjoyment of Food—The Best of Jane Grigson (1992, posthumous)

Grigson's charcuterie book attests to her underlying sense of humor and ever-conscious awareness of the hand of history sweeping over the dinner table.

That book came in very handy for me in Haiti. A development project focused on rearing goats from the central plateau hired me as a consultant. My mission? To make goat liver *paté* for a marketing effort aimed at the Haitian elite. Testing took place in a local upscale supermarket and at a local butcher shop owned by a French-Canadian butcher.

The recipe I chose for the base, Grigson's *Pâté de Foie de Porc*, turned out well enough. However, with pungent goat liver as a base, I needed to add more wine with a splash of brandy and *quatre-épices* to pep things up.

That project certainly qualified as a local endeavor.

Jane Grigson, more than Elizabeth David, might well be one of the first modern food writers to tout the glories of local food. As Isobel Holland, Lynette Hunter, and Geraldine Stoneham comment in *Wilder Shores*, "She [Grigson] emphasizes the need to husband our own agricultural heritage and to understand that of others."

Grigson won both the Glenfiddich Writer of the Year Award and the André Simon Memorial Fund Book Award twice. The International Association of Culinary Professionals created an award—the Jane Grigson Award—which "honours distinguished scholarship and depth of research in cookbooks." *Charcuterie* was translated into French, an astonishing turn of events for an English writer on food!

Her other legacy includes her daughter, Sophie Grigson, also a renowned British food writer and cookbook author, a celebrity on the same scale as many American Food TV stars.

Since most of us will not soon be in England, why not seek out one of Jane Grigson's books and get acquainted with a talented writer? Given the heat of summer days, you might prefer *Jane Grigson's Vegetable Book* or *Jane Grigson's Fruit Book*, of which Jane Davidson says:

> Brilliant... A lovely cover evoking thoughts of idyllic summer
> ensures that the *Fruit Book* is rapidly picked up. Its contents ensure
> that it is not rapidly put down ....

As a matter of fact, when librarians in England were asked why none of Grigson's books seemed to be available on the shelves, they answered that the books are so good that people continuously "nicked" them all.

Now that's quite a plug for a writer, isn't it?

In my experience, clever food is not appreciated at Christmas. It makes the little ones cry and the old ones nervous.

~ Jane Grigson

SIR WILLIAM PASTON'S MEATHE

Take ten Gallons of Spring-water, and put therein ten Pints of the best honey. Let this boil half an hour, and scum it very well; then put in one handful of Rosemary, and as much of Bay-leaves; with a little Limon-peel. Boil this half an hour longer, then take it off the fire, and put it into a clean Tub; and when it is cool, work it up with yest, as you do Beer. When it is wrought, put it into your vessel, and stop it very close. Within three days you may Bottle it, and in ten days after it will be fit to drink.

— Sir Kenelme Digby, *The Closet of the Eminently Learned Sir Kenelme Digbie Opened*, 1699 —

Figure 26. Lady Curzon, Vicereine of India

Always Tea Time Somewhere:
The Women Who Fed
the British Empire

My first entry into India was in a masulah boat through the surf at
Madras. It was exhilarating. Something quite new; something that held
all possibilities. A boat that had not a nail in it; dark-skinned boatmen
with no clothes on, who did not look naked, a surf such as I had never
seen before, thundering on yellow sands. ... my energy would be an upas
tree overshadowing all my life.
~ *The Complete Indian Housekeeper and Cook*

THUS, FLORA ANNIE STEEL shares her magical introduction to India
in 1861. At once I identified with her, my first impression of United Fruit's compound in La Lima, Honduras much the same.

Flora, brisk and efficient and very English, later arranges a magnificent
Christmas dinner for the Indian devotees of "Wahhabee-ism," as she calls it, the
religious kind, not the political. Hair tied back, a stiff white collar pinching her
neck just under her jaw, overseeing the work of her houseboys and cooks, she presents her guests with a meal of "fish curries, red *pullaos*, and roast mutton instead of
beef." But the glorious finale of plum pudding shines more brightly than any of the
other dishes. Concocted somehow without suet and brandy, served cold along with
watermelon—also cold, thanks to the ice brought in daily from Lahore—the exotic
pudding stays firmly in the minds of Flora's guests for years to come.

Reading of Flora's party and her food, I put *The Complete Indian Housekeeper*
and Cook down, my mind drifting to a magnificent gala at the Watsons' mansion.
It was one of those hot, sultry tropical nights so common during the rainy season in
La Lima, Honduras. As we pulled up to the circular driveway, lit only by flickering
torches, houseboys ran to open doors, bowing slightly as all the guests stepped from
their cars, starting the long walk up the curving staircase. I felt as if I'd hurtled back
into the past, and in a way, I had been. Life at United Brands's research compound
remained virtually unchanged from the days when United Fruit Company dictated
to dictators throughout Central America.

Parties such as this one, and those described by Flora during the British colonial era, demanded a great deal of ingenuity and steadfastness on the part of foreign women, whether they found themselves in India, Africa, Latin America, or the Far East. To survive the many unknowns of daily life in most tropical areas, they relied on nineteenth-century household manuals. Mrs. Beeton's' *Book of Household Management* and others such as *The Complete Indian Housekeeper and Cook* by our Flora and her friend Grace Gardiner were de rigueur.

Household manuals of this sort became popular during the Renaissance, aimed at stewards of large noble households. Women played no high-placed roles in these households until later, thanks to attitudes like those of French chef Menon. The Industrial Revolution siphoned off many people who might otherwise have gone into service. So well-run households in Britain and elsewhere relied more and more on the knowledge of the housewife. She, in turn, counted more and more on the help of household-management manuals.

In Honduras and elsewhere, I depended on a battered copy of the *Joy of Cooking*, plus the well-thumbed pages of *Where There is No Doctor* and the *Physician's Desk Reference*.

Back in the day, thousands of women followed their husbands and lovers and fathers and brothers to the colonies. They'd never eaten anything like a fresh mango before or maybe not even a bowl of rice topped with a fiery shrimp curry or a hunk of boiled cassava. They lived in culinary exile, except for the Europe shops that sprung up at nearly every station where expats lived and worked. Their main goal culinarily was to keep a kitchen like that of their mothers' back in England, to follow the directives and prescriptions of authors like Mrs. Beeton. What else could they do when faced with the enormity of living away from the familiar and the predictable?

To look at the cookbooks published for the use of British women in India, for example, you would truly wonder how curry ever became popular. The British who actually lived in India did not include many curry recipes or other local foods on their tables. The English frowned upon "going native." Especially after the Sepoy Mutiny of 1857, leading to the eventual ouster of the British East India Company and the creation of the British Raj, or the ruling of all India by the British government. As a result, making sure that English standards prevailed everywhere became the norm, in the kitchen as well, even if the cooks were native men, which for the most part they were.

At the height of the British Empire, the sun never set, so went the old adage. The vast landmass ruled by the British stretched from sea to sea, continent to continent. Regardless of the hour in London, somewhere an English woman like Flora arranged for tea to be served in the late afternoon, rigidly holding on to the trappings of what she considered to be civilized behavior, while lions roared outside her door or parrots squawked in frilly palms leaning over the graveled driveway.

Unlike French women living in French colonies, English women like Flora wrote prolifically about their experiences in the colonies where the Union Jack flew, particularly India and parts of Africa. It didn't matter if a woman married a minor civil servant or if her husband served as the Viceroy: the pen saved them from falling into forgetfulness.

Traveling the empire entailed a certain degree of hardship, whether from place to place as the Viceroy's wife like Lady Curzon or as the wife of a lowly British civil servant stationed in the bush. Consider, for example, the wife of the eighth viceroy to India, Harriet Georgina Hamilton-Temple-Blackwood, Marchioness of Dufferin and Ava. She compiled a journal about her experiences, covering the period of 1884–1888: *Our Viceregal Life in India*. Harriet's comments about food, menus, and dinners supply ample evidence that women of her social class and station did not sully the burners of a stove.

But without experience and without their mothers at their sides, these women needed cookbooks to help manage their households. To read these cookbooks, unless you knew they'd been published in Zimbabwe or Kenya, you'd never know that very few local or "native" recipes appeared by perusing the recipes. Even though curry was nothing new, the occasional curry recipe does appear. Hannah Glasse includes such a recipe in her famous cookery book of 1747, *The Art of Cookery, Made Plain and Easy*. As early as 1826, Margaret (Meg) Dods published "Bills of Fare" in her *The Cook and Housewife's Manual*, including Mulligatawny and curried chickens. She mentions the word "currie" twenty-eight times. Occasionally a local dish shows up in later cookbooks, such as the West African Stew recipe that E.G. Bradley includes in her 1939 *A Household Book for Tropical Colonies*. That is highly unusual.

WEST AFRICAN STEW
A meat stew with tomatoes, okros [*sic*], and garden eggs [*Solanum aethiopicum*] is made as follows in West Africa:
Boil the meat until it is tender, add onions, garden eggs, okros, salt, and pepper. When the vegetables are cooked, they are taken out and mashed, and returned to the stew. Serve with cassava boiled and mashed.

These invaluable cookbooks relay much more than recipes and hints about medical cures. They also outline cultural beliefs and hint at the overall agenda of Empire, where women were expected to create a little England amidst the dust and the heat and the teeming masses of India. In a 1989 article, "How to Make a National Cuisine: Cookbooks in Contemporary India," Arjun Appadurai comments, "The spread of European ideologies of household management in the colonies in the nineteenth and twentieth centuries is an important topic for comparative research."

Indeed, it is.

There's an unforgettable scene in the film, "Out of Africa," which epitomizes the British way with food in their colonies, in this case, Kenya. And their focus on the cooks, mostly male, who worked for them.

Actress Meryl Streep, as Baroness Karen von Blixen (Isak Dinesen), insists her servant Esa wear slippery white gloves while serving at table. Esa nearly drops a wine bottle, all because of colonial British ideas about propriety in cooking and dining. In the kitchen, Blixen's cook Kamante immerses his wooden spoons into puddings and sauces more suited to the damp cold of Denmark or England. But he doesn't seem to mind, for he happily recounts his life with the Baroness in a quaint, handwritten book, *Longing for Darkness: Kamante's Tales from Out of Africa*, with stories collected by Peter Beard and photographs and captions by Isak Dinesen. The tone and the text of this book reflect the colonial myth of the happy native.

Cooking in India and Africa presented quite a challenge to nearly all early European settlers and colonialists. An examination of some of the cookbooks produced during later colonial days, after the Sepoy Mutiny of 1857, reveals few recipes celebrating any of the staples found in traditional Indian or African cooking.

English women going out to colonial India or Kenya or other places in the Empire likely stowed several cookbooks in their steamer trunks. In the mid-nineteenth century, among the many possible tomes available, Mrs. Beeton's brick-sized *Book of Household Management* took up little room but packed a powerful wallop on the lives of these English women. Valuable not only for its culinary instructions and ties to home, the *Book of Household Management* also includes much medical advice, valuable to those living in isolated stations without medical help nearby.

Mrs. Beeton jumped on the speeding curry bandwagon by including a few curry recipes and one for a curry powder touted by Dr. William Kitchiner in *The Cook's Oracle*, published in London in 1829. In *The Road to Vindaloo: Curry Cooks and Curry Books*, David Burnett and Helen Saberi suggest that Mrs. Beeton's "Curried Salmon" recipe probably originated in Dr. Riddell's 1841 *Indian Domestic Economy and Receipt Book*. Before the watershed year of 1857 when the disastrous Sepoy Mutiny took place. Mrs. Beeton's inclusion of this recipe for curry powder reflected the desire of old India hands to enjoy the tastes they first enjoyed while serving in India.

An examination of British cookbooks published before the Sepoy Mutiny suggests that no one thought it odd that people wished to eat the local food, hence the number of titles published prior to *The Complete Indian Housekeeper and Cook*. However, British colonial policy changed after the Mutiny, reigning in the easier, more casual relationships between Indians and British representatives. The cookbooks reflect this change, seen through the increasing paltriness of recipes for local dishes. Nonetheless, Mrs. Beeton's borrowing of Dr. Kitchiner's recipe created no waves, no cries of "plagiarist!" until much later:

INDIAN CURRY-POWDER, founded on Dr. Kitchener's [*sic*] Recipe.
449. INGREDIENTS.–1/4 lb. of coriander-seed, 1/4 lb. of turmeric, 2 oz. of cinnamon-seed, 1/2 oz. of cayenne, 1 oz. of mustard, 1 oz. of ground ginger, 1/2 ounce of allspice, 2 oz. of fenugreek-seed.

Mode. — Put all the ingredients in a cool oven, where they should remain one night; then pound them in a mortar, rub them through a sieve, and mix thoroughly together; keep the powder in a bottle, from which the air should be completely excluded.

Note. — We have given this recipe for curry-powder, as some persons prefer to make it at home; but that purchased at any respectable shop is, generally speaking, far superior, and, taking all things into consideration, very frequently more economical.

By the 1888 edition, Mrs. Beeton—actually her editors, as she died of childbed fever in 1865, four years after publishing her bestselling cookbook—shared information about Indian servants and their habits. Mostly derogatory and based on conjecture, rumor, and assumptions taken from memsahibs, the name given to English women in India.

But Mrs. Beeton's wasn't the only cookbook in the memsahibs' larder.

A whole spate of such cookbooks, many geared specifically toward the Anglo-Indian housewife, cropped up later in the nineteenth century, most written by women who actually knew what they were talking about. The women had done it all themselves, following their husbands from one lonely posting to another, suffering through the brutal heat of the tropical sun and trials of feeding families on slim provender.

Some were also written by men who knew about culinary situations in the colonies.

But now it's time to talk about Flora and Grace

Their *Complete Indian Housekeeper and Cook* became one of the best culinary guidebooks for Englishwomen headed to India. Dedicated "To THE ENGLISH GIRLS to whom fate may assign the task of being house-mothers in our eastern empire this little volume is dedicated by Grace Gardiner and Flora Annie Steel," the book leaves nothing out. It is no surprise that Flora and Grace decided to write a household manual and cookbook for women faced with "going out to India." Their cookbook/household became the bible of existence for many young English women in India. And elsewhere.

The authors assumed that their readers possessed little or no experience in household management. Most certainly, very few of these women cooked, even if they came from a middle-class background in England. Flora and Grace's book followed not only the footsteps of Mrs. Beeton and Dr. Riddell, particularly the latter, but also took leaves from a few other books, too. Since the first book written for British housewives in Britain's African colonies did not appear until the early 1900s, many women there made do with Flora and Grace's *magnum opus*.

The Complete Indian Housekeeper and Cook promises to turn English women into astute managers perpetuating the idea of Empire. By creating the essence of England in their households, yes, even if those households abut up to steamy jungles or vast plains on the Indian subcontinent. Parts of the book were also published in Urdu, a language in which Flora was fluent—unusual for an English woman of the time.

Chapter I starts right off by delineating "The Duties of the Mistress." Followed by "The Storeroom," "The Accounts," "The Duties of the Servants," and "Table of Wages, Weights, &c.," not until page 220 (out of 352) did the authors even begin to address the issues of cooking.

Why?

The best answer lies in the fact that nearly every task in the household required a lot of labor and much basic knowledge about gardening, animal husbandry, and the like.

Chapter XXI, "Advice to Cook," speaks directly to the native cook and includes such salient advice as:

The next point is to keep yourself clean. Cooks must use their hands a great deal. Some things are better done with the hand than with spoon or fork, but not with dirty hands; so keep a piece of soap and a towel handy by the sink for constant use, and don't use your hands unnecessarily. Don't, for example, stir eggs into a pudding with your fingers. They do it very badly.

Flora and Grace include only two recipes for curry and eight native dishes in their book, plus a few chutneys and pickles. Their rationale seems to be summed up by the following comment: "It may be mentioned that most native dishes are inordinately greasy and sweet, and that your native cooks invariably know how to make them fairly well." On the other hand, Dr. Riddell includes four recipes for curry powder alone. Many of Flora and Grace's recipes reveal deep French roots, not at all surprising given the role of French cuisine in English diplomatic and power circles of the day. Chapter XLII, "Native Dishes," provides a recipe for a vegetable curry, often the leavings from an earlier meal, in sync with the prevailing obsession with kitchen economy:

> 2. **Chitchee Curry** – This is a vegetable curry. Slice some fresh onions, fry them in plenty of butter, mix the curry powder to a paste with a little gravy. Add to the butter, fry slightly, then put in an olla podrida of vegetables – the greater variety the better – and simmer the whole till done. Serve with rice.

Most British women in India did not cook, for a lot of reasons, status and class being paramount. But the state of the kitchen facilities in most of their houses also dictated the delegation of cooking tasks to Indian servants. To understand just how different kitchens in India of the time were from the kitchens in your modern house, consider George Francklin Atkinson's comments on the subject.

In 1859, George Francklin Atkinson, a captain of the Bengal Engineers and a writer of some imagination, as well as artistic skill, published *"Curry & Rice" on Forty Plates: Or the Ingredients of Social Life at "Our Station" in India*, a series of plates depicting British life in India. Of the kitchen, or "Our Cook Room," he wrote:

> Look into that Oriental kitchen, if your eyes are not instantly blinded with the smoke, and if your sight can penetrate into the darkness, enter that hovel, and witness the preparation of your dinner. The table and the dresser, you observe, are Mother Earth; ...

Observe the kitchen range, I beseech you; a mud contraption, with apertures for the reception of charcoal, upon which repose pans of native mould, in which the delicacies are cooked.

A question remains: In the British Empire, what of the cooks? Who were they? Were they just invisible, not meriting more than a line or two in all those Victorian diaries?

The story of how British women interacted with their male cooks makes for fascinating reading. Books like *The Complete Indian Housekeeper and Cook* burst with clues about English imperial power, the creation of the Other, and national identity—both English and Indian.

Like these British women, I was expected to employ servants, too. The servant question loomed as a major issue even for modern women in the tropics. However, finding the right nanny, cook, and gardener made all the difference in places where dust nestled in your refrigerator during the dry season or when the rain mildewed everything during the rainy season, and the market ladies sold nothing but stunted carrots and a few soft onions.

As mentioned before, Harriet Georgina Hamilton-Temple-Blackwood, Marchioness of Dufferin and Ava, the wife of the eighth viceroy, refers to these servants, mostly the cooks, when she describes the meals served in *dak* bungalows, constructed along the roads British families traveled on their way to Indian hill stations like Simla, where they escaped from the ravaging summer heat of the low-lying plains:

> Perhaps you would like to know what we have for dinner in
> a dak bungalow, and as each day's bill of fare is much the same
> as the last, it is very easy to tell you. Indeed, I may as well begin
> with breakfast, which is as substantial as all our other metals.
> Mutton-chops, chicken-cutlets, omelette, and chupatties are what
> we begin the day on; these support us till lunch-time, when the
> mutton of the day before becomes lamb, and is eaten with mint-
> sauce; cold chicken also graces the tablecloth round which we sit
> on the ground, and biscuits and very good butter finish the meal
> nicely. Dinner is a very solid one. First there is soup, and then
> follow a joint of mutton, curry, roast chickens or pheasants, and
> pudding. We have tried hard to see wherein lies the roughing it
> and can only discover that we have to do without champagne and
> without cheese, and that for three days out of the five we have had
> no coffee after dinner. What destitution!

Gad, all that mutton. But it makes sense, at least in England, where wool became a major trade commodity in medieval and Renaissance times. So someone surely needed to invent recipes to use up all the meat.

Like Harriet Georgina, I enjoyed respite from the heat offered by United Fruit Company's cabins strung along the shore of Lago Yojoa in the mountains of Honduras. The patterns of behavior among the company's old-timers reflected a keen knowledge and understanding of colonial attitudes long after the end of colonialism.

In *The Complete Indian Housekeeper and Cook*, instructions concerning servants afford fascinating insights into the authors' mindset and, by extension, their time period. And the interest shown in the popular British TV series "Downton Abbey" emphasizes how servants, with their various roles and constant presence, made possible many things taken for granted in the grand sweep of history.

One important source of information about the colonial British relationship with servants lies in the popular household manuals just like Flora and Grace's.

Although chiefly prescriptive, the genre identifies the ideal way of doing things—much as viewing the House & Garden Network counts for us today—these household manuals offer insights into what ambitious people aspired to and what they desired their lives to look like. Of course, fiction and art provide more material, as do memoirs, diaries, letters, oral histories, and newspaper positions-wanted/positions available ads. A glance at the architecture of the grand houses also suggests just how the logistics of meals feeding hundreds of people a day took place.

Household manuals like Flora Annie Steel's also dictated the behavior of the servants who made those rarefied lives possible.

Once in-country, British women found other patterns of servitude imposed upon their households. Local customs, caste beliefs, and tribal relations demanded a great deal of sensitivity. Writers like Flora and Grace recognized this and included tables of wages and lists of servants, their titles in the local language, and their duties.

Later, into the 1930s, other authors, building on Flora and Grace's work, continued the ongoing dialogue about the difficulties of dealing with the servant question in the colonies, from gardeners to nannies. Strict rules especially applied to the hiring and keeping of cooks, as the following statement from E. G. Bradley's aforementioned *A Household Book for Tropical Colonies* suggests. Bradley's book concerned colonists living in Africa and the so-called "bachelor" class, unmarried officers and the like. The tone of the passage reflects the rather condescending attitude held by many of the colonists toward the "natives" and to other servants across the Empire, including Africa:

The most competent cook will need a good deal of coaching before you are sure he can be trusted to do things as you like them done, without constant reminding and correction.

1. He must: (a) Keep his kitchen scrubbed and the towels and oven cloths washed daily. ...

(e) Keep his cap and apron clean. Don't employ a boy who is not clean. Good boys are most fastidious about their hands. A persistently odorous boy must be dismissed if he does not respond to frequent baths with carbolic soap.

2. A good cook should be able to make bread, soup stock and a good white sauce at least; to cook vegetables carefully (no soggy over-cooked potatoes and cabbage!); to roast meat so that it is brown on the outside, soft and juicy on the inside, and not greasy; to understand the method of making:

...

He should also be able to devise a variety of breakfasts, and to make good coffee and tea.

This is the foundation of a good cook. If you can find a boy who understands two-thirds of the above, take him on and gratefully set about bringing the other third up to standard. When he knows that much he will be able to follow the briefest in more elaborate dishes.

Flora and Grace write that if a memsahib found herself lucky enough to enjoy the culinary skill of a good Indian cook, she should "do anything to keep him—short of letting him know that you are anxious to do so." Stories abounded of mishaps with cooks. Many spring from letters home and diaries. Julia Curtis portrays a particularly difficult moment in her memoir, *Mists and Monsoons*, from 1935. Early in the day, a jackal killed and ate her Christmas turkey, which had been fattening up in the yard in preparation for the Christmas feast. Her cook killed an old goose as a last resort, requiring far more preparation than planned. Two hours before dinner, Mrs. Curtis discovered her cook drunk in the kitchen bungalow, splayed out on the floor, dead to the world. No details about the meal follow, but it's not hard to imagine the chaos!

Such was the daily life, and fare, in the colonies.

Certainly, Flora and Grace's book helped to mold the mindsets of the many women who read through it, far from their mothers and the comforts of England. A cookbook in the style of household management books dating as far back as the late Middle Ages, *The Complete Indian Housekeeper and Cook* reinforced the idea of British superiority and romanticized empire at the same time.

A cup of tea? Yes, please.

In any town in India the European Club is the spiritual citadel, the real seat of the British power, the Nirvana for which native officials and millionaires pine in vain.

~ George Orwell

Figure 27. Vintage Engraving of Mushrooms

MUSHROOMS, MUSHRUMPS

I GREW UP BELIEVING THAT MUSHROOMS came out of a small flat can or a squat glass bottle, both usually adorned with a picture of a bald guy dressed in a tight white T-shirt. Or maybe that was another brand? Most people dared not eat the mushrooms popping up on the lawn after a summer night's hard rain. It stood to reason that the mushrooms on pizza or in Thanksgiving green-bean casserole reminded me of rubbery pink erasers on my No. 2 pencils, the ones I chewed on at school.

Until I walked into a gourmet food shop in Aix-les-Thermes in France's Arriège region, I'd never given a thought to mushroom powder, either. Although by that time, dried mushrooms filled many shelves in my tiny town's Asian markets or hung in small (and expensive) cellophane sacks in the produce department of the local grocery store. It is obviously a small step from dried whole mushrooms to a more easily transported and dissolved powder, no?

Yet, in perusing historic cookbooks, even those from so-called mycophobic culinary cultures in the West, it becomes clear that mushrooms played a role in the kitchens even of the British elite. Thanks to the influence of French culinary culture, preserving an abundance of foraged wild mushrooms required centuries-old methods commonly used until commercial canning took root in the late nineteenth century.

Drying and pickling allowed households the luxury of using mushrooms throughout the seasons of the year when fresh mushrooms were not at hand.

English author Flora Annie Steel, that old India hand and a force to be reckoned with as I have said before, wrote of tinned mushrooms in *The Complete Indian Housekeeper and Cook*. She implied that they lacked a great deal of flavor but in a pinch, by all means, use them:

9. Mushroom Soufflé.--*One unit of butter, 1 unit flour, 5 of thin cream. Mix the flour with the butter, add the cream, and boil till thick, stir in 4 units yolk of egg well beaten, and five large mushrooms finely minced. Add 5 units well-beaten white of egg, season with salt and pepper, and bake in a soufflé case. If fresh mushrooms are not be had, mince half a tin of mushrooms, and with the other half make a purée with the cream. This is necessary, because tinned mushrooms will not* *soften and give out their flavour. The best substitute for fresh mushrooms is mushroom powder. Made with this, mushroom soufflé is delicious.*

And what of that mushroom powder?

Given the transitory nature of fresh mushrooms in the kitchen, mushroom powder was something everyone likely knew how to make. Crucial for umami flavor in the pot in the dead of winter and through the scarcity just before spring burst into flower. Mushroom powder shows up in historic cookbooks such as E. Smith's *The Compleat Housewife*. This version stems from the sixteenth edition of 1758:

To make the Mushroom Powder.

TAKE a Peck of Mushrooms, wash and rub them clean with a Flannel Rag, cutting out all the Worms; but do not peel off the Skins; put to them sixteen Blades of Mace, forty Cloves, six Bay leaves, twice as much beaten Pepper as will lie on a half Crown; a good Handful of Salt, a Dozen Onions, a Piece of Butter as big as an Egg, and half a Pint of Vinegar: Stew these as fast as you can; keep the Liquor for Use, and dry the Mushrooms first on a broad Pan in the Oven; afterwards put them on Shelves, till they are dry enough to pound all together into Powder. This Quantity usually makes half a Pound.

Long before either of these two culinary paragons picked up a pen, a housewife in Oxfordshire opened a small leather-bound notebook. She inscribed it "Lady Elinor Fettiplace 1604" and recorded the ins and outs of her seasonal kitchen in "fine, clear, cranky Shakespearean English," as Hilary Spurling quips in her introduction to *Elinor Fettiplace's Receipt Book: Elizabethan Country House Cooking*. Passed down through the centuries until it ended up in the estate of an aunt of Mrs. Spurling's husband, Lady Fettiplace's manuscript includes a late seventeenth-century recipe, not written in her hand, for "Pickled or Marinaded Mushrooms," quite similar to many others of the same ilk:

To Pickle Mushrooms

Take your Buttons [one of the few instances that the mushrooms are even remotely identified], clean y^m with a spunge & put y^m in cold water as you clean y^m, then put y^m dry in a stewpan & shake a handful of salt over y^m, y^n stew ym in their own liquor till they are are a little tender; then strain y^m from ye liquor & put y^m upon a cloath to dry till they are quite cold. Make your Pickle before you do your Mushrooms, y^t it may be quite cold before you put ym in. The Pickle must be made with White-Wine, White-Pepper, quarter'd Nutmeg, a Blade of Mace, & a Race of ginger.

Does her use of mushrooms reflect a recipe stemming from the 1390s, *The Forme of Cury?*

Take Funges and pare hem clere and dyce hem. take leke and shred him smal and do him to seeþ in gode broth color yt w3t safron and do þer inne pouder fort and serve hit forth.

There's something about old (and new) cookbooks like these that I simply adore. They open up worlds I would never experience otherwise, broadening my horizons far beyond the walls of my own kitchen, far beyond the present time. In many cases, cookbooks serve as vectors for culinary change. While old, historic cookbooks cast a somewhat nostalgic air over my thinking, I must stop for a moment as I turn the pages and realize, as I did when I bumped against the phrase "White-Wine" mentioned by Mrs. Fettiplace, and say out loud, "Thank goodness I do not have to make my own wine or vinegar or raise my own chickens to make a soufflé!"

Mushrooms spring up everywhere these days. Just about every day, a new story about these mysterious entities appears somewhere. Neither animal nor vegetable, and still poorly understood, mushrooms seem to be relative newcomers to the American kitchen.

But they're really not.

Before and after the Revolutionary War, they graced the tables of many of Virginia's gentry.

Take George Washington's wife, Martha Custis Washington, for example.

Her family cookbook—*Martha Washington's Booke of Cookery*—is a manuscript cookbook dating to Elizabethan and Jacobean days. Passed down to her in 1749, it includes just one recipe for mushrooms on their own, "To Dress a Dish of Mushrumps."

But another recipe, "To Make the Pasty [Royall]," mentions "mushrumps."

Mary Randolph, well-known for *The Virginia Housewife* and a distant cousin of Thomas Jefferson's, urges her readers forward with four distinct recipes for mushrooms. However, "mushroom" appears thirty-six times in her book, including mushroom catsup added to such dishes as Gravy Soup and Mock Turtle Soup of Calf's Head, indicating a greater tolerance of the lowly toadstool. Back in the motherland, mushrooms and the English seem to mix like oil and water.

Compared to, say, the Russians or the French, the English believed mushrooms to be noxious, not to be trifled with. This mindset stemmed in part due to certain writings.

Botanists such as John Gerard, as well as folk culture, associated mushrooms with the devil and witches. Here's what Tobias Venner of Bath says about them in 1630:

> Many phantasticall people doe greatly delight to eat of the earthly
> excrescences called Mushrums; whereof some are venemous,
> and the best of them vnwholsome for meat: for they corrupt the
> humors, and giue to the bodie a phlegmaticke, earthie, and windie
> nourishment … Wherefore they are conuenient for no season, age,
> or temperature.

This attitude undoubtedly crossed the ocean on sailing ships bringing the English to the New World. Added to that was the fact that Native Americans, for the most part, didn't eat mushrooms either. However, some groups used shelf mushrooms in healing and ingested "magic" mushrooms in certain religious and spiritual rituals.

Until 1796, with Amelia Simmons's *American Cookery*, no truly American cookbooks existed. So, housewives turned to cookbooks from England and France, primarily the latter. As has been noted previously, the English elite lionized French cuisine and sought to hire French cooks—male—whenever possible.

English cookbooks in the American colonies during the 1700s included E. Smith's *The Compleat Housewife*, Hannah Glasse's *The Art of Cookery, Made Plain and Easy*, Elizabeth Raffald's *The Experienced English Housekeeper*, Martha Bradley's *The British Housewife*, and possibly Elizabeth Moxon's *English Housewifery*. Moxon mentions mushrooms sixty-four times.

Smith's book offers four distinct recipes for mushroom powder, pickled mushroom, and five different variations, potted, and stewed.

She exhorts her readers to:

> Gather your mushrooms in the morning, as soon as possible after
> they are out of the ground ; for one of them that are round and
> unopened, is worth five that are open ; if you gather any that are
> open, let them be such as are reddish in the gills, for those that
> have white gills are not good....

Smith pushes her technique for mushroom powder as well, which we have seen previously.

On the other hand, Glasse includes a few recipes for "Mushroom-sauce" for white fowls. She also describes exactly how households might grow their own mushrooms, "To raise Mushrooms." Raffald mentions mushrooms twelve times in her book and includes a recipe for "Mushroom Catchup" that reads suspiciously like the recipe from Mary Randolph's *The Virginia Housewife*. Amelia Simmons did not include mushrooms at all in her oeuvre.

Another book, found in households boasting French speakers—such as Thomas Jefferson at Monticello—proves the point that French cuisine, despite the protestations of various cookbook authors like Glasse, still held sway over the English and American kitchen. Menon's *La cuisinère bourgeoise* has eighty-eight references to *champignon*. A copy resided in Thomas Jefferson's library.

So, there you have it, a very abbreviated survey of the written record on mushrooms in early American cuisine, influenced by English antecedents. As Karen Hess rightly states, written recipes lag behind actual hands-on practice in many cases.

Of course, most cookbook authors in the more remote past enjoyed the comfort of armies of servants and the leisure to think, read, and write. These activities were not available to all women. Or even now. I find it remarkable that in a couple of books recently published on cooking and preserving foods in old ways, the authors omitted recipes for mushrooms entirely.

Maybe as children, they too thought of erasers when eating mushrooms. And never evolved beyond that stage.

Dress them with care, then to the dunghil throw'um
A hogg wont touch um, if he rightly know um.

~ 17th-century poem about mushrooms

TO FRY OYSTERS FOR GARNISH, FOR FISH OR HASH

Wash them in their own liquor, and dry them very well ; then have some Yolks of Eggs beat up, with Spice and Salt finely beat, and flower to make it thick enough to hang on the oysters. Fry them quick in clarified Beef-suet.

— Mary Kettilby, *A Collection of above Three Hundred Receipt in Cookery, …,* 1714 —

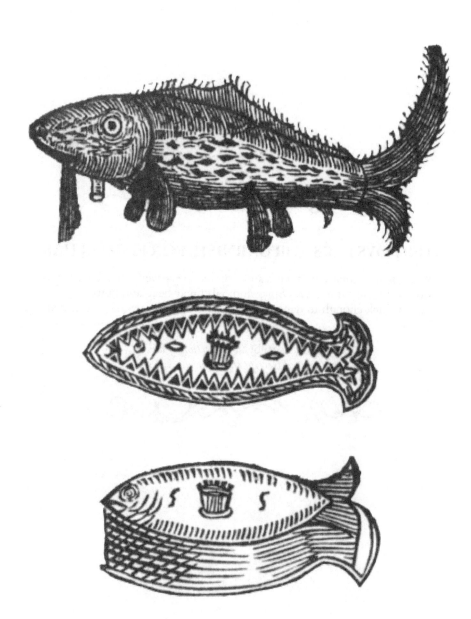

Figure 28. Fish Pies, Robert May's *The Accomplisht Cook*

THE FISH WHISPERER

MY COPY OF ALAN DAVIDSON'S *Mediterranean Seafood: A Comprehensive Guide with Recipes* surfaced in a bookshop in Rabat, Morocco. Selling English-language books imported from England, its owner quickly became my favorite person. Small, though well-lighted, crammed with books from floor to ceiling, the shop stood within a crow's caw of the Oudaias. An immense maze of medieval houses glued together by mortar and whitewash so brilliant that it hurt to look at it in the noonday sun, the Oudaias resembled a village on a Greek island. Complete with aquamarine-blue doors and windowsills.

My reason for buying this book, aside from my propensity for coveting books in general, was not unlike Davidson's reason for writing it in the first place. In Tunis with the British Foreign Service, Davidson served as head of the chancery. The confusing names for all the fish in the market perplexed his wife Jane, so Alan Davidson offered to compile a list of fish for her. With the help of Giorgio Bini, the famous Italian ichthyologist and an explosive situation involving Sicilian fishermen in the Gulf of Tunis, Alan Davidson unwittingly stumbled onto a subject that would lead him to his life's work. Not diplomacy, though it would be years before he left that field of endeavor, but instead studying and writing about food.

A few blocks away from the Berber-era Oudaias, like a siren on the rocks, a fish market lured me, much like Tunis's markets enthralled Jane Davidson. Thronged with djellabah-wrapped older men, younger men in tight blue jeans and T-shirts reading "Omaha Firefighters" or "University of Illinois," and a few veiled women, that early-morning market vibrated with the energy of a beehive on a hot summer day. The fish lay, well, like sardines in a can. Row after row of shimmering flesh, their bright eyes signaling a freshness I'd never seen before.

But what were they? How did they behave in the presence of olive oil or butter or breadcrumbs? Were they fatty, lean? Did they curl up when heated?

That's why, when I discovered Davidson's book, I snatched up the only copy left on the shelf in that bookshop, almost running to the cash register, waving my rumpled red Moroccan dirhams in front of me. There, in my hand, lay the answers to my many questions.

I thanked Alan Davidson from the bottom of my heart for his work.

His first book on seafood, *Mediterranean Seafood*, begins with a detailed catalog arranged by generic names and families. Each entry includes scientific names, remarks on the fish in question, common names in languages other than English, and a listing of recipes found in the last third of the book.

In other words, like the gifted food writer he would become, Davidson made buying and cooking the puzzling fish a pleasant task, not to be feared or avoided. He later wrote *Seafood of South-East Asia* and *North Atlantic Seafood*.

Thanks to Davidson, I cooked monkfish, John Dory, and fresh anchovies for the first time.

And much, much more.

Knowledge does not keep any better than fish.
~ Alfred North Whitehead

HELPS TOWARDS THE PRESERVATION OF FISH

If you would keep fish long, kill them as soon as they are out of the water, and take out their gills ; fill their Heads as much as may be with Pepper, and wipe them very dry, and pack them in dry Wheat-Straw.

— Richard Bradley, *The Country Housewife and Lady's Director*, 1732 —

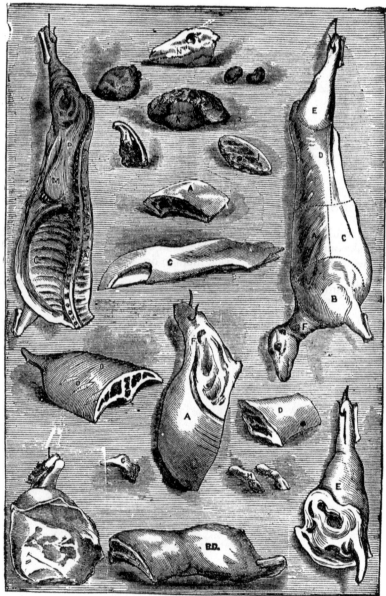

A. Neck; B, Shoulder; C, Breast; D, Loin; D D, Saddle; E, Leg; F, Scrag end of Neck; G, Tongue; H, Feet; I, Loin Chop; J, Chump do.; K, Liver; L, Heart; M, Kidneys; N, Head; E D, Haunch.

Figure 29. Mutton, *Book of Household Management*

A Potful of Mutton

THE FOODS WE EAT TIE US TO THE PAST, true. But I believe our food also separates us from that past.

Mutton is one such food.

Mutton held sway at the English dinner table, at least among certain classes. But as the years passed, that practice faded in the New World. Instead, the United States evolved into a major cattle culture for several reasons.

Thus, I can name several breeds of cattle. I cannot do the same when it comes to sheep breeds, of which there are many, many more than I ever dreamed of. It's not surprising that I grew up ignorant of these animals, among the first domesticated, descended from Asiatic *mouflons*.

But I am getting ahead of myself here.

My family never ate mutton or lamb when I was a child. Never.

And my ignorance of mutton became painfully apparent one night in the communal cafeteria at the small college I attended as an undergraduate. I chose one of the three entrées available—playing-card-size slabs of brown meat with an enticing-looking green sauce. Beef with some sort of parsley sauce, I figured. Imagine my disappointment when I took a large bite of meat, dipping it first in the green sauce. I spat it out onto the plate, hawking over and over to clean my mouth of the thick lanolin coating my palate. My friends at the table stared at me, rightfully disgusted.

One murmured, "Don't you like mutton with mint sauce?" In reply, I stuck my napkin in my mouth to wipe out the rest of the thick, gluey taste of mutton fat.

Unfortunately, the dining-hall rules stipulated that if you wanted more food or seconds, tough luck—you ate what the servers gave you the first time. No going back. So, I managed to eat some potatoes and creamed corn and to drink some milk. Later that night, I dug into my thin wallet and bought a Hershey bar and a Coke. And I spent the night in the equivalent state of going to bed without my supper. Shame on me.

Testimony, yes, to the power of food habits and food aversions. I doubt that there are finicky eaters when death lurks outside the door, threatening starvation. But still, countless stories abound of people refusing to eat unfamiliar food even during famine conditions.

My real introduction to mutton and lamb came when I spent two years in

Morocco. There, of course, I could only buy pork clandestinely, from a French woman running an unmarked shop not far from the central market. The only way you'd know the shop even existed was if someone in the U.S. Embassy or ex-pat crowd showed you the door, hidden as it was by a cascading wall of green English ivy. Buyers scurried in and out, like kids buying illegal cigarettes or booze.

At certain times of the year, the streets of Morocco echoed with the voices of sheep, crying out as knives slit their throats. Butchers moved from house to house, slaying the animals in preparation for Aid-el-Kebir and other feast days. Numerous times, I followed herds of sheep down narrow dirt roads, the sheeps' heavy tails swinging as they ambled along, caked with dirt and manure, hefty with the unctuous fat so prized by Moroccans.

I ate mutton and lamb, but without relish, as much as I wanted to like it all.

Yet, I knew that I was depriving myself of something wonderful because of my prejudice against mutton.

So just what is mutton? Irish food writer Darina Allen offers the following definitions:

Suckling: milk-fed lamb available only in the spring

Spring lamb: born before Christmas and ready for cooking by Easter

Lamb: between Easter and the following Christmas

Hogget: lamb that survives through its second Christmas (about 1 year old or more)

Mutton: more than two years old, also known as "wether"

A great deal wiser, I stand by my original comment: I loathe mutton.

Why did a perfectly good source of protein become sidelined in American culinary culture? That mutton formed a vital part of the English diet becomes clear when skimming through early cookbooks and other sources

At first blush, it appears that people chose to slaughter sheep—sheep being smaller than cattle or pigs—to cook and eat them in their entirety for feasts or in times of famine. There was a larger chance that there'd be no need to preserve any fresh flesh, because a significant portion could be eaten in one go. There was, of course, haggis. Despite my solid Scots ancestry, I have never eaten haggis. The basic principle of that gem's production follows techniques similar to pork preservation, particularly sausage-making.

People applied many of the methods used for preserving pork to mutton, including something called Macon, which cooks substituted for bacon in Britain during the Second World War.

Many other ways for preserving mutton stem from the British Isles.

Dry curing was one way, in much the same manner as pork hams. Well-known cookbook author Hannah Glasse provides detailed instructions for dry-curing mutton hams. She suggests placing the meat in a dry cure with salt and sugar for three weeks, then cold-smoking it over oak and juniper, followed by a maturation period of eight months, a practice stemming from Cumbria in the northwest of England. According to Jennifer Stead, this practice apparently dated from Elizabethan times or earlier.

Drying lamb flesh, observed in the Faroe Islands by G. Landt in 1810 in *A Description of the Feroe Islands*, entailed splitting lambs in half and spreading them out, "butterflying" them if you will, and leaving them to hang in the cold dry air for several months. Mutton could undergo the same treatment but took much longer to dry properly. A similar product was reestit mutton, hung on rafters called reestit in croft houses with open peat fires in the Shetland Islands.

Another technique, quite ancient, was potting. Peter Brears devoted a whole chapter to this topic in his article "Pots for Potting." Interestingly enough, the process of boiling or frying meat to rend out fat and then packing the meat into a pot, covering the meat with the rendered fat, is practiced in Lebanon, France, and England. Brears quotes the Bedford Mss. 432/4, from Leeds University's Brotherton Library, where a Mr. Wood of Slaidburn says that all mutton—except legs—was packed in pots, topped with melted butter, even as late as the early twentieth century. Many Lebanese still consider Qawrama, or spiced mutton preserved in fat a jar, a real treat. And what would France's signature cassoulet be without duck confit, duck legs preserved in the same manner in duck fat?

Rarely do you find accounts of the experiments that people no doubt conducted as they searched for procedures for best preserving their food, for hoarding the excesses of harvests and hunts. The following newspaper articles summarize early attempts of Australians to ship fresh sheep meat to England. A Professor Gamgee suggested the following method, as written in *The McIvor Times and Rodney Advertiser* on Friday, 17 July, 1868:

> The animal is made to inhale carbonic oxide gas, and when it has
> become insensible is bled to death in the usual way. The carcass
> is dressed, and then suspended in an air-tight chamber; the air is
> exhausted, and the receiver is filled with the gas before mentioned.

After remaining exposed to the vapour for from twenty-four to forty-eight hours it is removed and hung in a dry atmosphere; that is all.

It sounded plausible to a number of businessmen, and so they tried it, with quite unsatisfactory results, as reported in the *Rockhampton Bulletin and Central Queensland Advertiser* on Monday, 18 July, 1870:

A NUMBER of gentlemen interested in meat-preserving assembled at the custom-house, Melbourne, on the 30th June, for the purpose of inspecting a parcel of meat consigned to Messrs. McCulloch, Sellar, and Co., by the ship "Crusader," and preserved by Professor Gamgee's process. The Telegraph reports that the meat, which consisted of mutton and pork, had been placed in wooden cases, barrels, and some in a vessel made of boiler plates with a hermetically-fitting lid. Portions of the preserved-meat were packed in tallow, some in oat husks, and the remaining joints were sewn in canvas, and also packed in oat husks. On opening the wooden case the tallow was found to be mildewed and emitted a decidedly unpleasant odour. The meat, as well as that in the barrels and iron vessel, was either tainted or quite bad. Of the two the pork was in the better condition; but it, as well as the mutton, was quite unfitted for human consumption. The trial cannot be regarded other than unfavourable.

As I consider these methods of preservation, I cannot but think of the joy people must have felt, the profound sense of relief when food sat in pantries and root cellars, ready for the barren days and months to come. Then I consider what a disaster it would be to have food go off, what difficulty another attempt would mean, with the potential waste of food that entailed. Plus, the cost.

At Jamestown, John Smith mentioned that cattle and sheep would not do well in the New World, at least not at first, because of the lack of pasturage. But cattle importation took place anyway, including in Williamsburg, Virginia. And we all know about the cowboys of the American West, the Sheep Wars, the clashes over fencing versus open ranges.

As I read more about the place of sheep (lamb, mutton) in the history of American cuisine, I found that mutton shows up regularly in American cookbooks throughout the nineteenth century, beginning with the late eighteenth-century work of Amelia Simmons's *American Cookery*. Later, at the end of the nineteenth century, Fannie Farmer's comprehensive tome carried far fewer recipes for mutton. Still later, lamb appears in twenty-three recipes in *Gourmet*'s 2004 cookbook edited by Ruth Reichl. Index entries under "beef" utilize almost two columns and "lamb" half a column, with no entries at all for "mutton."

In Martha Washington's manuscript cookbook, handed down by generations of female relatives, with some recipes dating to the early seventeenth century, I read of an ancient recipe titled "To Roste a Shoulder of Mutton with Blood." The cook wraps the blood-soaked meat with a caul, a sort of meaty take on the original recipe for coq-au-vin. In the same book, I came across a recipe similar in many ways to English cookbook author Joseph Cooper's 1654 recipe for boiling mutton, which is as follows:

How to Boyle a Joint of Lamb:

Boyle your Lamb in Water and Salt: For the Sauce, take some of the Broth which boyled it, and put it into a pipkin with Verjuice, Mace, three or foure Dates, and handful of Raisins ... and sweet herbs, these being boyled together enough, beating up with Butter, a handful of scalded Gooseberries, and a little Sugar, if you finde it too sharp; dish the Lambe, and sippit it. [Note: Sippits were small pieces of toasted bread used as sops.]

It would take the Westward movement to revive the sheep culture of the early English settlers, many of whom came from sheep-raising clans on the northern border of England. But by then, it was too late for the meat to bounce back on a large scale. Moreover, wolves and Indians moved in on the sheep, decimating the flocks, as did the lack of pasturage mentioned by John Smith. And the Sheep/Range Wars of the American West, heavy with issues surrounding fencing and grazing rights, also discouraged the continuation of the sheep culinary traditions of the early English colonists.

The Zen-like story of mutton—so ancient, so tied up with Western spirituality, too—exemplifies how humans attempt to provide food for the lean days that always came. Many, many cuisines place this meat at the center of traditional dishes. Just consider India's Mutton Rogan Josh or Morocco's *Kefta Mkaouara*, the latter a gorgeous dish thick with lamb meatballs smothered in a rich and fragrant tomato sauce. Think of Christian imagery, Jesus with the lost sheep.

I must try again, for perhaps I will eventually become enlightened enough to love mutton. Or at least a lamb chop or two.

Roste or sodden wholesome is mutton
And of the bones be madea broth full restorative
And a jellye right royalle.

~ 12th-century commentary on sheep and mutton

TO PRESERVE RASBERRIES.

Take the Juice of red and white Rasberries; (if you have no white Rasber-ries, use half Codling-Jelly) put a Pint and half of the Juice to two Pound of Sugar; let it boil, scum it, and then put in three Quarters of a Pound of large Rasberries; let them boil very fast, 'till they jelly and are very clear; don't take them off the Fire, for that will make them hard; a Quarter of an Hour will do them after they begin to boil fast; then put them in Pots or Glasses: Put the Rasberries in first, then strain the Jelly from the Seeds, and put it to the Rasberries. When they begin to cool, stir them, that they may not all lye upon the Top of the Glasses; and when they are cold, lay Papers close to them; first wet the Paper, then dry it in a Cloth.

— *Mrs. Mary Eales's receipts*, 1733 —

Figure 30. Berkshire Pig

THE BARBARISM OF BARBECUE?

"BARBECUE" SOUNDS UNCANNILY LIKE "BARBARISM."
But behind that word lies a long story.

When warm nights and hotter days rev up cooks' tempers, when summer suddenly seems interminable, cooks turn to the trusty (and maybe rusty) BBQ grill. And seek solace in the primeval technique of searing raw, bloody meat over an open flame. Age-old, these methods are, to a degree, indeed barbaric. At least to the Western mind anyway. Even if there is no link linguistically between the two words. "Barbarian," by the way, owes its origin to the Greek word *bárbaros*, "the sound foreigners make."

Barbecue's origins may be mysterious, but most linguistic experts cite Haiti as its birthplace.

Based on an Arawak technique of cooking meat laid over grids of branches, the Spanish conquerors of Hispaniola—comprising present-day Haiti and the Dominican Republic—quickly adopted barbecue. The Indians named the technique "barbicoa," meaning "sacred fire pit" in Taino, their native language. Others interpret the original word as "barbacoa," meaning something like "four sticks in the ground, to cook meat over fire." Later, French pirates arrived in Hispaniola, taking up the tradition of barbecue as well. Their description of barbecue, *de la barbe a la queue* (from the beard to the tail), may have also influenced our current word for grilling over coals or wood or gas.

Most linguists believe this last version to be false. Other wags have it that BBQ, shorthand for barbecue, derives from "Beer, Burgers, and Cue (pool or billiards)" or "Beer, Burgers, and Que (shorthand for "barbecue").

Who knows?

Grilling, or burning, animal carcasses on fire began naturally when humans began hunting and cooking their kill. Later, holocausts—"sacrificial offerings consumed entirely by flames"—underpinning many religions emphasized the spiritual aspect of eating the flesh of once-breathing animals.

Barbecue, long touted as an invention of enslaved people in America, might not be quite what it seems. Elizabeth Raffald, in *The Experienced English Housekeeper* of 1769, was one of the first culinary writers to mention barbecue, according to the *Oxford English Dictionary*.

The English roasted whole animals in massive fireplaces. Hannah Glasse tells us so:

> That prosess'd Cooks will find Fault with touching upon a Branch of Cookery which they never thought worth their Notice, is what I expect: However, this I know, it is the most necessary Part of it; and few Servants there are, that know how to Roast and Boil to Perfection.

> I don't pretend to teach prosess'd Cooks, but my Design is to instruct the Ignorant and Unlearned (which will likewise be of great Use in all private Families) and in so plain and full a Manner, that the most illeterate and ignorant Person, who can but read, will know how to do every Thing in Cookery well.

> I shall first begin with Roast and Boil'd of all Sorts, and must desire the Cook to order her Fire according to what she is to dress; if any Thing very little or thin, then a pretty little brisk Fire, that it may be done quick and nice: If a very large Joint, then be sure a good Fire be laid to cake. Let it be dear at the Bottom; and when your Meat is Half done, move the Dripping-pan and Spit a little from the Fire, and stir up a good brisk Fire; for according to the Goodness of your Fire, your Meat will be done sooner or later.

Christopher Columbus, the "discoverer" of the New World, stayed with Andrés Bernáldez in Seville and showed him his journals from his second voyage. Columbus noted what he'd seen on a beach in what is now Guantánamo Bay, Cuba: Indians cooking four "quintals of fish," along with two rabbits and two serpents (iguanas), which Columbus described as fearsome with diamond-shaped scales running along their spines. This cooking method ensures the preservation of highly desired meat by both smoking/cooking meat and driving away flies, whose eggs spelled hunger for humans if maggots infested fresh flesh.

Andrew Warnes, in his controversial book *Savage BBQ: Race, Culture, and the Invention of America's First Food*, covers the topic in detail, focusing on the inherent violence of the act of grilling. "Invented and exaggerated, held tight in perennial repulsion, *barbecue* belonged to this new cultural compulsion to pit English gentlemen against the barbaric world beyond Europe," Warnes states. And he refutes *The Oxford English Dictionary*, too, along the way.

No matter the niceties of the term, barbecue really is an American thing, despite the English practice of coating roasted meat with mustard. The Flemish artist Theodor De Bry created interesting, if not a hundred percent exact, renditions of Caribbean Indian life in a series of copper engravings. One of those illustrates barbecuing or grilling. Unfortunately, he also portrays acts of cannibalism, igniting deep-seated European fears of what they perceived as Native Americans' inherent "barbarism."

Cooking foods over fire obviously began with the dawn of humankind. Even as late as the Age of Discovery/Conquest, cooking over a direct fire was hardly something extraordinary. However, the native residents of the Caribbean, as well as those living in what is now Virginia and Massachusetts, perfected the pit method of barbecuing, a technique that Europeans no longer practiced. Or at least not much.

Think of the New England Clambake.

Europeans continued to cook over fire in immense hearths, at least in the great houses of royalty and nobility. Most people who could do so built houses with hearths meant for serious cooking.

In *The Art of Cookery, Made Plain and Easy*, Hannah Glasse features a recipe for roasting whole pigs cooked on a spit, similar in function and practice to the grilling taking place on the beaches of the Caribbean. Nearly a hundred years before, William Dampier, an English pirate, witnessed native Arawaks cooking in a similar manner. The *Oxford English Dictionary* states that Dampier's description signified the first time the word "barbecue" (or nearly so) was used in the English language: New Voyage round the World of 1699: "And lay there all night, upon our Borbecu's, or frames of Sticks, raised about 3 foot from the Ground".

Barbecuing, like baseball, quickly became an American pastime. The Jamiesons state in *Born to Grill* that most American cookbooks failed to mention barbecue straight out. However, an English cookbook, the *Encyclopedia of Practical Cookery* of 1890, discusses American barbecue and approaches the topic primarily from a social point of view, focusing on gatherings for various community purposes, including church and political meetings. Kate Moss and Kathryn Hoffman in *The Backcountry Housewife*, as well as other authors, suggest that grilling added an important aspect to daily menus. *The Williamsburg Art of Cookery* quotes a recipe from Toano, Virginia, for "Barbecued Squirrel." In *The Virginia Housewife*, Mary Randolph goes a step further with "To Barbecue Shote":

> This is the name given in the southern states to a fat young hog, which, when the head and feet are taken off, and it is cut into four quarters, will weigh six pounds per quarter. Take a fore quarter,

make several incisions between the ribs, and stuff it with rich forcemeat ; put it in a pan with a pint of water, two cloves garlic, pepper, salt, two gills of red wine, and two of mushroom catsup, bake it and thicken the gravy with butter and brown flour ; it must be jointed and the ribs cut across before it is cooked, or it cannot be carved well ; lay in the dish with the ribs uppermost ; if it not be sufficiently brown, add a little sugar to the gravy; garnish with balls.

Fannie Farmer, American doyenne of culinary measurements, includes a recipe for Barbecued Ham in the 1919 edition of *The Boston Cooking-School Cook Book*. In my copy of the same edition, passed down to me by my grandmother, I read:

Soak thin slices of ham one hour in lukewarm water ; drain, wipe, and cook in a hot frying-pan until slightly browned. Remove to serving dish and add to fat in pan three tablespoons vinegar mixed with one and one-half teaspoons mustard, one-half teaspoon sugar, and one-eighth teaspoon paprika. When thoroughly heated, pour over ham and serve at once.

Once Ellsworth B. A. Zwoyer of Pennsylvania patented his design for charcoal briquettes in 1897, barbecuing—as in grilling over coals—took off in a spectacular way.

But another form of "barbecuing" soon became popular, cooking foods in a sauce, "barbecued" in the oven or with sauce added, as recipes from Mrs. Randolph and Fannie Farmer suggest.

Southerners tended to think of barbecue with sauces and emphasized pork, while Americans in the southwest focused on grilling beef, often over mesquite coals, a trend that became popular again in the 1990s. The Australians dub grilling meat as cooking on the "barbie," a practice familiar to anyone who eats at Outback restaurants, a chain restaurant everywhere in the U.S. South Africans hold their "*braais*" tradition dear, too. Hordes of people attend the American Barbecue Society's events each year.

As with any mode of cooking, in a place as huge as the United States, you'll find several barbecuing styles, mostly related to the various sauces slathered on the meat: Kansas City Sweet Sauce, South Carolina Mustard Sauce, East Carolina Mop Sauce, West Carolina Piedmont Dip, Texas BBQ Sauce, Alabama White Sauce, Kentucky Black Barbecue Sauce, Tennessee Whiskey Sauce with Jack Daniels, and on and on.

Cooking over smoke and fire evokes a sense of primitiveness, a sense of reverting to the past, when pioneers and explorers and hunters squatted on their haunches near campfires, cooking the day's kill in the crackling flames. Hearing a pig's flesh sizzling in the heat or seeing the huge carcasses slowly cooking over red embers arouses primal emotions, an almost visceral feeling of power, of gratitude for the sacrifice made by the pig. But at the same time, there's gladness that the shoe is not on the other foot, so to speak....

"Barbecue" does sound uncannily like "barbarism." In its own way, it is. And that has always been so.

"Gravy to make Mutton eat like Venison" : Pick a very stale woodcock, or snipe, cut it to pieces (but first take out the bag from the entrails), and simmer with as much unseasoned meat gravy as you will want. Strain it, and serve in the dish.

~ Maria Rundell

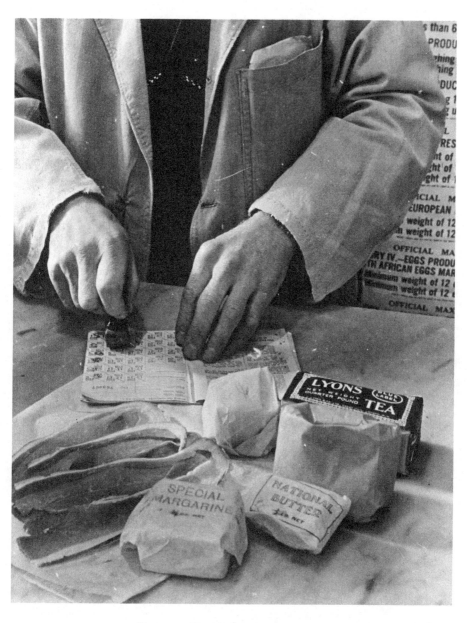

Figure 31. World War II Rationing

FOUR CHICKEN LEGS AND TWO EGGS: RATIONING AND COOKING DURING WARTIME

WAR IS THE HUMAN CONDITION. Or so it seems when reading the reams of words in which history is writ.

And with war comes terrible hunger.

To write of hunger and war is to write of all human history.

With food in the pot and bread in the mouth (or rice or corn or potatoes), people thanked the gods for good fortune during times of relative peace. No wonder rain gods, thunder gods, and wind gods sprang forth in the mythology of so many cultures.

War gods joined those pantheons as well.

Armed conflict upset the balance of life, as armies ravished everything in their path, as with a plague of locusts rampaging through fields, destroying everything edible, everything worth living for. Killing farmers and burning fields, looting food stores—if any even existed—these acts ensured a weakened populace less able, or at least disinclined, to fight back. Attacking supply lines and blockades worked, too, in undermining daily life.

Here I briefly touch on the problem of eating and survival, primarily during World War II, and not just in Britain. To give some perspective on rationing, I begin with the situation in Russia and German during World War II.

Consider the vast amounts of food available today in grocery stores, vending machines, fast-food restaurants, and farmers' markets. It's almost impossible for most people to visualize a world where there're only 125 grams of bread every day. And that bread likely contains an inedible filler like sawdust. Or worse.

Yet, the average housewife in Stalingrad faced that as she woke on a cold crisp morning in November 1941, the day the authorities reduced the rations yet again. Not only did she live with such a small amount of food, she also needed to guard her ration card, and those of her children, with her life. No lost or stolen cards could be replaced. Ever. And that meant sure death in the end.

Imagine living for 872 days, frantic for food, peeling wallpaper paste off the walls, and licking it with relish to calm the stomach's screams. She feared losing her ration card, but the specter of cannibalism hovered over all those still breathing once all other living creatures of the city succumbed to the knives of the starving.

But still, every day in the news, headlines broadcast wars, "small" conflicts, power struggles, and civilians killed in the crossfire. I know that behind the scenes shown on TV screens, women strive to find food, to keep their families alive and whole, much as did their sisters in Stalingrad during that long, relentless siege.

Ideally, rationing meant that scarce commodities could be available to everyone, not just those who could afford them. Rationing also ensured that food shortages would not lead to angry crowds and bread riots. France and Germany, and the rest of combatant Europe, contended with severe food shortages, especially in the cities, as the war ended. In Germany, the government rationed everything. Those living in the country fared somewhat better when it came to food.

Consider the words of a German woman who, as a teenager, scavenged for coal from trains: "The milk was thinned with water. I remember my dad saying that they fried (or reheated) leftover potatoes in leftover coffee, as they didn't have any lard or anything else to fry in."

Although in the beginning, civilians benefited from the fact that the German Army requisitioned goods, crops, and animals from local conquered people. But toward the end, it seemed as if the four horsemen of the apocalypse rode at breakneck speed through what remained of Germany, Russia, and Poland. Before May 1942, civilian rations per month in Germany include:

- 10,600 grams of bread = 353.33 grams/day or 12.5 oz
- 2000 grams of general food stuffs = 66.66 grams per day or 2.3 oz.
- 900 grams of sugar = 1.06 oz. per day

After May 1942, rations in Germany per month amounted to:
- 8000 grams of bread (about a half loaf a day)
- 1200 grams of meat (less than 45 grams of meat per day)
- 600 grams of general foods
- 130 grams of sugar

These figures, of course, do not reflect reality, nor do they account for the rations allocated to Jews. Prewar figures suggest that Germans had access to an average of 3000 kcal. per day. By the war's end, that figure dropped to around 1415. Or less.

Britain and the United States, on the other hand, experienced rationing on entirely different levels.

Rationing began in Britain in November 1939 and ended on July 4, 1954. The British Ministry of Food, in 1940, with the help of Jack C. Drummond, later "Sir Jack," a biochemist and specialist in vitamins and nutrition, designed a rationing plan meant to ensure the health and stamina of the British people throughout the duration of the war. The plan succeeded far better than expected, for the British people as a whole ended the war healthier than before. Lord Woolton, head of the Ministry of Food, lent his name to a much-maligned vegetable pie dubbed "Woolton Pie."

A typical story, the following comes from an English woman I know:

Several friends of mine grew up in WW2 England. Apparently, everyone who was able to plant a Victory Garden did so, even though not many of them had access to a variety of seeds and not everything would grow. Carrots did grow. Everybody had carrots to trade and grew sick of eating them. My uncle still won't eat a carrot that he can recognise, though he gave my aunt permission to hide pureed carrots in soup/stew/mashed turnips/etc. My friend Peter reported that the BBC would broadcast recipes and so on, to be helpful for home cooking. One evening a radio show with a live audience had one of the hosts dash in a little late, and he took a microphone, saying: 'I've just learned the most marvelous thing -- do you know what you can do with carrots?' 'Yes,' said the other host, flatly." *The audience laughed uncontrollably, sick to death as they were of lollipops made of carrots.*

Another English friend told me an interesting story about the English writer Auberon Waugh:

Evelyn Waugh, according to son Auberon, wrote of how his father gathered all the children into the dining room to watch him, head of table, elegantly peel and eat three banana's [sic] - the first they'd ever seen. Bron later disclosed he'd made the story up because it seemed a good tale in character with his crusty yet funny father.

A typical week's worth of adult rations in Britain looks rather sparse when laid side by side with what people eat today:

Bacon and ham: 4 oz

Other meat: to the value of 1s 2d (about 3/4 pound of minced meat, or close to four chicken legs)

Butter: 2 oz
Cheese: 2 oz
Margarine: 4 oz
Cooking fat: 4 oz
Milk: 3 pints + 1 packet dried skimmed milk per month
Sugar: 8 oz
Preserves: 1lb every 2 months
Tea: 2 oz
Eggs: 1 shell egg +1 packet dried egg per month
Sweets: 12 oz

To aid British women in coping with changes wrought by rationing, Marguerite Patten, a major food celebrity at the time, starred in a radio program hosted by Stuart Petre Brodie. Patten focused on cooking with rations and later wrote *We'll Eat Again*, a compilation of recipes from the war years.

Rationing began in the U.S. with the Food Rationing Program in 1942, although the government created The Office of Price Administration in April 1941, hoping to ensure that runaway inflation would not affect food prices. For Americans, rationing turned out to be relatively benign—they could get two eggs a week as opposed to the British one. The mother of yet another friend wrote:

A lot of the time we just did without. Hamburger was stretched
with milk and egg and breadcrumbs for hamburgers. We ate a lot
of macaroni, spaghetti, stew. If your butcher had a friendly farmer
who butchered cattle at the farm and supplied the butcher with
extra meat ... then the butcher supplied you more generously. Hot
dogs were popular.

To encourage British and American housewives, government-issued cookbooks and pamphlets proliferated. These focused on the need to stay plucky, make do, and sacrifice for the troops, presupposing cooks actually had something to cook with. And, if missing an ingredient, the wherewithal to easily substitute something else. Dig for Victory, in Britain, and Victory Gardens, in the United States, inspired people to grow much of their own food. Localities created allotments for those who lacked access to garden space.

What I think is so hard to comprehend about war and food is the swiftness with which life becomes upended.

As English writer J. G. Ballard states:

> One of the things I took from my wartime experiences was
> that reality was a stage set .... The comfortable day-to-day life,
> school, the home where one lives and all the rest of It ... could be
> dismantled overnight.

The veneer of civilization spans no more depth than the varnish on an oak table, or so it seems. William Golding's *Lord of the Flies* underscores that sentiment well.

Bread and milk delivered by horse and cart. being sent out with a bucket
to pick up the manure to put onto the rhubarb. Very humiliating when your
friends were watching.

~ BBC WW2 Archive

Figure 32. Trussing Birds, *Book of Household Management*

COOKING ONE'S GOOSE

THE TRADITIONAL ENGLISH CHRISTMAS GOOSE didn't really make it over the Big Pond, or the other side of the Atlantic. Instead, the native (and meatier) turkey prevailed. Unfortunately, neither did the other traditional flesh dish of the English Christmas season—roasted boar—with its tusked furry head, its toothy mouth stuffed with an apple. A pagan custom, incidentally, handed down since the Druids, or so some authors claim.

That, the Druids, is another story for another day.

Come to think of it, I've never eaten goose. But I have cooked with goose fat. And duck fat. Sauté chunks of potatoes in that golden fat, and you'll never toss a French fry into canola oil again.

Yet frozen geese occasionally show up in the cases of fine food purveyors in America. Wrapped in shiny white plastic, bony legs poking out at one end, reminding me of skinny legs on display on the beach in summer.

What of the goose in English cooking?

Therein lies yet another story.

A fourth-century saint (and former Roman soldier), Martin of Tours, and his legend made the lives of geese miserable in most of Christian Europe. His saint's day, Martinmas or November 11, dates to the Middle Ages. He came to be the saint of vintners and beggars. Through an apocryphal tale, the goose is symbolically associated with him. When offered the position of bishop of Tours, a city then racked with strife, Martin hid in a goose pen rather than take up the scepter. The honking and hissing of the startled geese gave him away.

History took its course. St. Martin became the third bishop of Tours. Perhaps as punishment, geese faced the oven on Martinmas Day, more so in Germany than in England and—ironically—France.

In times past, saints such as Martin of Tours became the celebrities of the day.

In England, geese did not roust would-be saints. No, they foretold the weather. At least, according to an old English saying that goes thus, "If the geese at Martin's Day stand on ice, they will walk in mud at Christmas."

Goose flesh then meant more than prickled, clammy skin.

Medieval manor houses raised multi-purpose geese for many reasons: they packed on weight quickly with minimal amounts of feed. Feathers for beds and pillows proved to be another reason for their constant presence. And one other important role for feathers? Not hats. No.

Arrows.

Goose feathers helped "to flight the arrows that were so crucial to England's success in the wars of the period," according to Clarissa Dickson Wright.

Don't forget writing quills, fashioned from goose feathers as well.

Geese came close to being the two-footed equivalent of the American buffalo, in a way.

The following fourteenth-century recipe comes from the court of King Richard II, as rendered in C.B. Hieatt and S. Butler's *Curye on Inglysch.* But I question just how galingale and cubebs—from West Africa—arrived so very early on. What fascinating backstories therein of migration, trade, marriage, war, and travel, hidden in mere mentions of ingredients.

SAWSE MADAME. XXX.
Take sawge. persel. ysope. and saueray. quinces. and peeres, garlek and Grapes. and fylle the gees therwith. and sowe the hole that no grece come out. and roost hem wel. and kepe the grece that fallith therof. take galytyne and grece and do in a possynet, whan the gees buth rosted ynowh; take an smyte hem on pecys. and that tat is withinne and do it in a possynet and put therinne wyne if it be to thyk. do therto powdour of galyngale. powdour douce and salt and boyle the sawse and dresse the Gees in disshes and lay the sowe onoward.

Transliteration:
Take sage, parsley, hyssop, and savory, quinces and pears, garlic and Grapes and stuff the geese with therewith and sew the hole so that no fat comes out. Roast them well, and keep the fat that falls fthereof. Take galyntyne and fat and add to a posseynet. When the geese are roasted enough, take them off [the fire] and chop them into pieces and take what is within [stuffing] and add to a posseynet and put wine therein if it be too thick. Add thereto powder of galingale, powder douce and salt, and boil the sauce and dress the Geese in the dishes and pour the sauce over them.

Since Elizabeth I's time, goose flesh appeared on menus and tables, a luxury for sure. The poor found a way around the annual expense of the obligatory holiday goose by forming Goose Clubs, periodically salting money away for the purchase of a fine, fat fowl at Christmastide. Of course, sometimes conniving vendors cheated them, but a goose of some sort would be had in the end.

For me, one of the most fascinating aspects of all things goose lies in a recipe for "powdered" goose from Robert May's *The Accomplish Cook* of 1660, published when May was close to seventy-two years old. Cooking his goose employed what appears to have been a pickling-like brine, commonly used by cooks at the time. He offers no instructions for that:

To boil any old Geese, or any Geese.

Take them being powdered, and fill their bellies with oatmeal, being steeped first in warm milk or other liquor; then mingle it with some beef-suet, minced onions, and apples, seasoned with cloves, mace, some sweet herbs minced, and pepper, fasten the neck and vent, boil it, and serve it on brewes with colliflowers, cabbidge, turnips, and barberries, run it over with beaten butter.

Sauces of varying types provided another alternative for serving goose:

Sauce for a stubble or fat Goose.

1. The Goose being scalded, drawn, and trust, put a handful of salt in the belly of it, roast it, and make sauce with sowr apples slic't, and boil'd in beer all to mash, then put to it sugar and beaten butter. Sometime for veriety add barberries and the gravy of the fowl.

2. Roast sowr apples or pippins, strain them, and put to them vinegar, sugar, gravy, barberries, grated bread, beaten cinamon, mustard, and boil'd onions strained and put to it.

The Victorians, however, flipped the Christmas goose tradition toward turkey, with Charles Dickens's help in "A Christmas Dinner" and *A Christmas Carol*.

In *A Christmas Carol*, the character Scrooge relents in his cruel meanness. He presents a large turkey to the Cratchits as atonement for his sins. But they've already devoured a small goose cooked in their local baker's oven, a common custom in those days when few had kitchen facilities for more than boiling:

There never was such a goose. Bob said he didn't believe there ever was such a goose cooked. Its tenderness and flavour, size and cheapness, were the themes of universal admiration. Eked out by apple-sauce and mashed potatoes, it was a sufficient dinner for the whole family; indeed, as Mrs. Cratchit said with great delight (surveying one small atom of a bone upon the dish), they hadn't ate it all at last! Yet every one had had enough, and the youngest Cratchits in particular, were steeped in sage and onion to the eyebrows!

Poverty-stricken people in Victorian days also banded together to form "Goose Clubs," salivating at the thought of an opulent meal starring a large fatty goose.

Goose has never been on a menu of mine. Bouts of strength with a large white goose in Paraguay left me disinclined to eat such a creature. However, I wonder if the geese population around the miniature lakes in London's St. James Park diminishes during the holiday season?

Poachers, you know. On the King's land. But that's still another story.

For all this good feasting yet art thou not loose
Till though give the Ploughman in harvest his goose.
Though goose go in stubble, yet pause not for that,
Let goose have a goose be shee leane be shee fat.

~ Thomas Tusser

A RECEIPT FROM BARBADOES, TO MAKE RUM; WHICH PROVES VERY GOOD.

In Barbadoes the Rum is made of the Scum and Offal of the Sugar, of which they put one ninth part, or eighth part, to common Water, about eighteen Gallons, all together, in a wooden open Vessel or Tub; cover this with dry Leaves of Palm, or for want of them, with the Leaves of Platanus or the Leaves of Fern in England, or the Parts or Leaves which Flagg-Brooms are made of. Let this remain for nine Days, till it changes of a clean yellow Colour, and it will be then fit to distil; then put it into an Alembic, and you will have what we call the Low-Wines. A Day or two after distil it again, and in the Cap of the Still, hang a small muslin Bag of sweet Fennel-Seeds, and the Spirit will be of a fine Flavour. Some will use Anniseed in the Bag, and some use a little Musk with the sweet Fennel Seeds, or else distil the Spirit twice, viz., once with the sweet Fennel-Seeds, and the next with a little Musk.

— Richard Bradley, *The Country Housewife and Lady's Director*, 1736 —

193

Figure 33. Bee

HONEY, I'M COOKING!

AS AN INFANT, ZEUS, THE GREEK GOD OF GODS, fed on milk and honey. Or so the fable goes.

In the King James version of Exodus 3:8, Moses states, "And I am come down to deliver them out of the hand of the Egyptians, and to bring them up out of that land unto a good land and a large, unto a land flowing with milk and honey ...."

These ancient words teach us the importance of honey for humans, something not just to ferment and drink to the point of intoxication, sacred or otherwise. Sweetness dwells in the honeycomb, high up in trees, or resting in sunken hollows of the Earth.

Centuries-old cookbooks, barometers of taste—whether real or ideal—chronicle the journey of honey beyond the honeypot and brewer's barrel. A few examples illustrate this trek.

In Apicius's cookbook, that first-century A.D. Roman affair, honey graced many recipes far from the comfort of milk and honey. Like many chefs who combine seemingly incompatible exotic ingredients today, Apicius (or the cooks who compiled the recipes) poured honey into dishes redolent with dormouse, crane, ostrich, and fish. *De Re Coquinaria* also presents one of the earliest written recipes for pears and other similar fruits:

> *To preserve fresh figs, apples, plums, pears and cherries*
> *Select them all very carefully with the stems on and place them in honey*
> *so they do not touch each other.*

Honey—or similar sugar syrup—prevents certain molds and bacteria from thriving during the preservation process, thus equalizing the osmotic pressure of the fruit in the solution.

And "Bottle bread," moistened with milk and honey, appeared in Ibn Sayyār al-Warrāq's tenth-century *Baghdadi Cookbook*, while sweet-and-sour meat concoctions like *Sikbāj* utilized honey, too.

A chef to at least one Renaissance pope, Bartolomeo Scappi, wrote a cookbook published in 1570, commonly called *Opera of Bartolomeo Scappi*. He included recipes for sweet *tourtes* splashed with honey. He also expounded on how to tell if honey is good: "To be good, honey should be fine-grained, firm, heavy, of a good smell, and golden color. Above all, it should be clean. It is stored in wooden or earthenware vessels."

But Scappi's fish jelly seasoned with honey? I think I'd pass on that one if he invited me to his table!

In medieval England, honey played a role in ale making.

Take Braggot Ale, flavored with cinnamon, galangal, black pepper, and grains of paradise. Cooks learned that sealing foods in honey helped preserve fruits and other foodstuffs. Nasty, moisture-loving bacteria can't thrive in the presence of honey, thanks to its hygroscopic properties. Early recipes for gingerbread relied on honey for sweetness, as the following recipe from *The Forme of Cury* indicates:

> To make gingerbrede. Take goode honye & clarefie it on þe fere, & take fayre paynemayn or wastel brede & grate it, & caste it into þe boylenge hony, & stere it well togyder faste with a sklyse þat it bren not to þe vessell. & þanne take it doun and put þerin **ginger**, longe pepere & saundres, & tempere it vp with þin handes; & than put hem to a flatt boyste & strawe þereon suger & pick þerin clowes rounde aboute by þe egge and in þe mydes yf it plece you &c.

As the centuries passed and humans being the inventive creatures they are, mead became more than a mere drink, more than a ticket to temporary oblivion. Perhaps in mead, honey found its greatest calling. Mead technically consists of nothing more than honey and water left to ferment. The Anglo-Saxons brewed it, as did monks in various Christian religious orders.

Sir Kenelme Digby elaborates on the best honey for mead production in *The Closet of the Eminently Learned Sir Kenelme Digbie Kt. Opened* of 1669:

> The Honey of dry open Countries, where there is much Wild-thyme, Rosemary, and Flower, is best. It is of three sorts, Virgin-honey, Life-honey, and Stock-honey. The first is the best. ... Hampshire Honey is most esteemed at London.

Honey's importance dropped sharply once Europeans discovered sugarcane. It had been fading in importance in Europe since approximately the sixteenth century. Its popularity began to wane around Scappi's time. Honey obviously was no longer a hot item despite two recipes for mead in Hannah Glasse's *The Art of Cookery, Made Plain and Easy* and E. Smith's for mead in *The Complete Housewife*. Eliza Acton features a recipe for "Herodotus' Pudding" in *Modern Cookery for Private Families*, alluding to honey as the sweetener in the original.

In colonial America, sweetness usually took the form of molasses. But Martha Washington's *Booke of Cookery* touts a few recipes for gingerbread, including one with honey that, for all practical purposes, dates to the earliest written renditions for gingerbread, namely Harleian MS. 279 of 1430. In *The Virginia Housewife*, Mary Randolph records a recipe for Honey Vinegar (To Make). That said, her gingerbread recipes call for sugar or molasses, a commonly used sweetener (and a by-product of sugar production). No honey.

Gargantuan, those gifts of the tiny bee. A drop of honey calms that antediluvian craving, awoken by the sweetness of mother's milk. It heals wounds, lights the nights, appeases deep hungers. So clasp the gold and cherish it. Like King Midas, hold it, hoard it, hallow it. Most of all, relearn its power, its sacred nature.

But, getting back to milk and honey, a cheesecake made with honey epitomizes the divine in honey. With antecedents in Sicily (and Greece, where honey-slathered cheese evokes rapture), cheesecake represents, in my mind, the reason why the ancients designated milk and honey as "food of the gods."

By Zeus!

The sweetest honey is loathsome in its own deliciousness.
And in the taste destroys the appetite. Therefore, love moderately.
~ William Shakespeare, *Romeo and Juliet*, II, vi. 13-15

Figure 34. Vintage Tableware

BISCUITS OR SCONES?: ENGLISH ORIGINS OF AN AMERICAN FAVORITE

NOPE.

I can just see your neurons pointing fingers, your eyes sending signals to your brain, a tiny interior voice whispering, "Oh, yes, those are biscuits, just like my grandma used to make."

But don't be mistaken.

Nope.

Scones. Which I baked one day from a lilliputian new cookbook, a treasure from Britain's National Trust: Sarah Clelland's *National Trust Book of Scones*.

Now, I know this is going to bother some people, but I'm going to voice it regardless: Traditional American cooking, anyway the kind we think of as traditional—roasts, potatoes, gravy, three-vegs, etc.—evolved from British roots. Yes, yes, let's not forget the other influences. I hear you. Native American, German, French, Dutch, West African, and Spanish, yes to all.

But I'm going to flog that old horse once more.

I'm going to say it once more: examine recipes step-by-step, ingredient by ingredient, technique by technique. I don't want to hear any more generalized and unfounded/undocumented claims that Southern food isn't essentially British in origin.

Between 1620 and 1640, thousands of English people sailed for the New World. Do the math.

In my opinion, the only food writer who's tackled this issue of origins in any detail—other than Stephen Schmidt and Damon Lee Fowler—is Adrian Miller. His stellar work of scholarship, *Soul Food: The Surprising Story of an American Cuisine, One Plate at a Time*, Miller dissects the origins of Southern and soul food. He demonstrates that many dishes attributed to African origins, including greens with salt meat, first emerged from kitchens in the British Isles. Actually, the Romans liked to toss smoked or salted meat into pots of beans, etc., too. The Romans occupied Britain, so ....

Yes, many hands stirred the pots in the kitchen.

Still, the structural background—the backbone—derives from the first ethnic group other than Native Americans who sank permanent roots in North America. And lest you think that English cooking is bland, boring, and stodgy, you've not been paying attention to historical cookbooks, among other things.

Scones likely originated as Bannocks, a Scottish oats quick bread that moved with the times and evolved into scones. Thanks to Anna, the Duchess of Bedford, Queen Victoria's friend, scones became a relatively permanent fixture for English tea. She felt faint one afternoon and asked her kitchen staff to send up some refreshments. One such delicacy was scones. From that day on, she demanded scones every day. Or so the legend goes. Coincidentally, commercial baking powder became widely used in the 1840s, due to the inventiveness of Alfred Bird, who combined cream of tartar and baking soda.

But you're still wondering about those scones of mine, I imagine.

Baking powder helped to make these breads—scones, biscuits, what-have-you—lighter, taking the place of pearl ash or just plain beating the dough.

Maybe a little cream of tartar, too.

Mrs. Beeton's 1861 edition of *BOHM* didn't include scones.

So, according to Ms. Clelland, classic scones today consist of the following ingredients:

- Self-rising flour
- Butter
- Lard
- Milk

I decided to give scones a whirl.

The dough turned out to be a bit denser than what I'm used to, e.g., American biscuits, which come in all sorts of permutations. Many recipes in the *National Trust Book of Scones* require an egg, but not this one, the classic recipe. A little note of interest: An Englishman, Henry Jones, invented self-rising flour. In 1849, he patented his "invention" in the United States. This flour became a must-have in English kitchens, as well as kitchens in the American South.

They're scones, true, but you could have fooled me. My eyes told me another tale: biscuits, America-style

Now check out recipes for bannocks, which seem to be ancestors to scones.

More and more clearly as the scones disappeared into his interior, he saw that what the sensible man wanted was a wife and a home with scones like these always at his disposal.

~ P.G. Wodehouse

Figure 35. Frontispiece, John Nott's *The Cooks and Confectioners Dictionary*

NUTTY AS A ... FRUITCAKE

IT'S LIKE LIVER. Either you love it, or you hate it.

What?

Fruitcake, of course.

Just to prove a point, a few years back some enterprising journalists conducted a survey on the most hated Christmas gifts. Guess what people most hated to receive as gifts?

Fruitcake.

Described variously as full of "gooky" candied fruit or heavy enough to break bones when dropped on a foot, glued together only by sheer perversity, fruitcake is definitely not number one on the taste charts these days.

And yet people still regard fruitcakes as symbolic of Christmas. Why, when most people sheepishly admit to detesting them?

Tradition. Fruitcakes are Tradition.

Because most of America's Christmas traditions stem from early English times—with many Celtic and Saxon influences—fruitcake exemplifies one of many rock-bound traditions associated with Christmas celebrations.

However, the Romans also bear some responsibility in this scenario, for they ate a cake called "satura," rich with honey, nuts, and fruits. The Tuscans in Italy, also culpable, created a fruitcake-like tradition with *panforte* with roots dating back to the thirteenth century. *Panettone*, another fruitcake-like concoction, bears little resemblance to the brick-like English version of fruitcake. German *stollen* represents yet another variation on fruitcake. And let's not forget Jamaican Black Cake, soaked in rum with ground-up fruit, a cousin of English Plum Pudding.

Imagine the scenario in jolly old England: cakes became very special because of scarce and costly ingredients required by traditional recipes. Nuts, dried sugary fruits from the Mediterranean, white flour, and liqueurs cost staggering amounts of money. Making a gift of fruitcake symbolized a sacrifice of time and money and food. Fruitcake represented status.

Drying the fruits of summer and early fall, and preserving them in sugar syrup or honey, consumed copious amounts of time and energy. Wood needed to be cut for the wood-burning stove and the fire moderated, or the cakes would burn. Producing precious liqueurs required a time-consuming process. Since people hoarded most of these liqueurs for medicinal purposes, it was yet another hardship to pour these nectars over the cake as a preservative.

Yet the tradition persevered and persisted.

Topped with an almond-based marzipan shell and then frosted with hard white icing, the English Christmas cake thus joined the repertoire of Christmas traditions.

And earned the enduring hatred of many discriminating eaters.

Unfortunately for fruitcake haters, the darn things are practically indestructible as long as they receive a bimonthly brandy bath. *Joy of Cooking* states that cakes can last twenty-five years after baking with proper storage. Russell Baker, syndicated columnist, joked once about inheriting a fruitcake and said, "While an eon, as someone has observed, may be two people and a ham, a fruitcake is forever."

In 1727, J. Pemberton published E. Smith's *The Compleat Housewife*. Smith includes several recipes for "plumb" cakes. Her recipe for a rich Great Cake epitomizes the trend toward boozy, fruit-filled cakes:

To make a rich great Cake.

TAKE a Peck of Flour well dried, an Ounce of Cloves and Mace, half an Ounce of Nutmegs, as much Cinamon, beat the Spice well, and mix them with your Flour, and a Pound and half of Sugar, and a little Salt, and thirteen Pounds of Currants well washed, picked, and dried, and three Pounds of Raisins stoned and cut into small Pieces; mix all these well together; then make five Pints of Cream almost scalding hot, and put into it four Pounds of fresh Butter; then beat the Yolks of twenty Eggs, three Pints of good Ale-yeast, a Pint of Sack, a quarter of a Pint of Orange-flower Water, three Grains of Musk, and six Grains of Ambergrease: Mix these together, and stir them into your Cream and Butter; then mix all in the Cake, and set it an Hour before the Fire to rise, before you put it into your Hoop; mix your Sweetmeats in it, two Pounds of Citron, and one Pound of candied Orange and Lemon|peel cut in small Pieces: You must bake it in a deep Hoop, butter the Sides, and put two Papers at the Bot|tom, and flour it and put in your Cake; it must have a quick Oven; four Hours will bake it: When 'tis drawn, ice it over the Top and Sides. Take two Pounds of dou|ble refin'd Sugar, beat and sifted, and the Whites of six Eggs beaten to a Froth, with three or four Spoonfuls of Orange-flower Water, and three Grains of Musk and Am|bergre•se together; put all these in a Stone Mortar, and beat them with a wooden Pestle, 'til 'tis as white as Snow, and with a Brush or Bunch of Feathers, spread it all over the Cake, and put in the Oven to dry; but take Care the Oven does not discolour it; when 'tis cold paper it; it will keep good five or six Weeks.

As costly as the fruitcake tradition may be, and as disliked, there is still room for "forever fruitcake" in modern gift-giving schemes. Traditionally a butter-rich cake served as a foundation for fruitcakes. Another example of English influence, Southern bourbon pecan cakes fill the need for something less, shall we say, hefty. Bricklike it is not. Raisins stand in as the only dried fruit called for. Southern bourbon pecan cakes require less butter and fewer eggs. Less rich means less expensive. Ease of preparation ratchets this cake up another notch on the "yum" scale, making this cake perfect for gifts. Or as a quick snack on Christmas afternoon.

By the way, the slang term, "nutty as a fruitcake," dates to about 1935.

"Oh, these people's minds work in strange ways, Petunia, they're not like you and me," said Uncle Vernon, trying to knock in a nail with the piece of fruitcake Aunt Petunia had just brought him.

~ J.K. Rowling

Figure 36. Fourteenth-century Sailing Ship

DANDYFUNK, BURGOO, SALT HORSE, LOBLOLLY, DUFF, SKILLYGALEE, LOBSCOUSE, AND LAPSKAUS

THINK OF THE SEASIDE ON A WINDY DAY, waves roiling like a maddened bee-stung donkey. Then envision three small wooden ships cresting on the waves, sighting land after four-and-a-half months at sea. Despite brief provisioning sojourns in the Canary Islands and the Caribbean, all 105 English passengers and thirty-nine crew members on board undoubtedly sank to their knees in prayer when Cape Henry's shoreline bobbed up on the horizon on April 26, 1607.

Land.

The men staggered ashore, leaving those famous English ships: the Susan Constant, the Godspeed, and the Discovery.

But if you've ever been to Cape Henry, Virginia, you'll know it could not have been an encouraging sight. Rocky outcrops, shrubby low-lying bristly trees with shiny beetle-like leaves, stretching for miles and miles. No wonder the men soon reboarded their ships and sailed up the James River, where they settled a site named Jamestown, after James I of England.

A similar verbal portrait could be painted of the scene greeting the Massachusetts colonists in 1620.

The rest of both stories underlie one of the most astonishing sagas in the history of the world.

Say what you might, despite the commercial or religious motivations of the earliest settlers of the future United States, it took guts, a lot of guts, setting out on the open sea, disembarking on those distant and unknown shores, facing a very uncertain future.

One aspect of these stories that's always puzzled me is this: How did these people cook and eat while tossing about on boats smaller than the average modern American family home?

The square footage on the deck of each of these ships measured approximately as follow, according to data from replicas now moored at Jamestown, Virginia:

2,900 on the Susan Constant, with seventy-one people on board
1,496 on Godspeed, with fifty-two people on board

924 on the Discovery, with twenty-one people on board

What follows is an exploration in itself.

Let's start with a dish that likely began as pottage.

Beef stew. A memory jerker, especially if you grew up on a farm. And more specifically a dairy farm, where an old cow did not always end up in a can of dog food.

What does a dish called Lapskaus ("hodge-podge") cooked in my mother-in-law's Wisconsin farmhouse kitchen have to do with the seafarers, explorers, and colonizers who swaggered their way into the New World?

As it turns out, quite a bit.

According to the *Oxford English Dictionary*, the first use of "Lobscouse" in English appears to have been around 1707: "A sailor's dish consisting of meat stewed with vegetables and ship's biscuit, or the like."

The meat most likely started out in the form of mutton.

Of course, beef stew—as with most savory meat-and-vegetable-rich one-pot dishes—dates far back in time, long before 1707. Across the globe, stew is universal. A one-pot meal. Very forgiving of even the worst of cooks.

And current received wisdom points to Norway and possibly the rest of Scandinavia as the probable source of this seaborne "lobscouse." Lillian Langseth-Christensen in *The Mystic Seaport Cookbook* claims that Liverpool deserves the credit. Etymological convolutions seem to bear out Ms. Langseth-Christensen's conclusions, remarked upon as well by Anne Chotzinoff Grossman and Lisa Grossman Thomas in *Lobscouse & Spotted Dog: Which It's a Gastronomic Companion to the Aubrey/Maturin Novels*.

Sailors and other people who found themselves on the high seas also gnawed on tons of ship's biscuits.

Only a hammer could do justice to it, this twice-cooked, rock-hard bread concocted only of flour, water, and salt, this ancestor of the saltine cracker and maybe the beaten Southern biscuit.

Seafarers discovered the known world under its power and denigrated it with names such as tooth dullers and weevil castles in response to its manifold gifts. Settlers, explorers, colonists, and adventurers, ditto.

An Englishman, Captain John Smith compiled a great deal of information about the proper food for seafaring men in his *A Sea Grammar: With Plaine Exposition of Smiths Accidence for Young Sea-Men*. Interestingly, he includes "the juice of Limons for scurvy" in his list, almost 200 years before the British Navy finally issued citrus as a preventive for scurvy.

With good reason, Samuel Pepys once quipped, "Englishmen, and more especially seamen, love their bellies above anything else." Life and limb at risk, every single day, that's what those incredible voyages meant.

We moderns forget age-old travel challenges like scurvy as we hop an airplane on the East coast at 8 a.m., whine about the airline food, arrive in London in time for a late dinner, quaffing a glass of warm beer while downing a plate of stinging-hot curry.

For people today, the sea is a "thing of beauty ... a joy forever," as the poet John Keats so poignantly wrote. White sandy beaches and piña coladas, sipped to the sound of crashing waves and the aroma of coconut sunscreen, that's the closest to the sea we get. Or even want to.

Yet, the sounds of the sea played a vital role in our personal histories, for many of our ancestors arrived here by ship, most willingly, others not so much.

And, in those days, that meant that ship's biscuits starred on the menu. Everyone on board, from the captain to the lowliest deckhand, ate ship's biscuits. Richard Henry Dana described the food situation quite aptly in *Two Years Before the Mast*:

> This day was Christmas, but it brought us no holiday. The only change was that we had a "plum duff" for dinner, and the crew quarrelled with the steward because he did not give us our usual allowance of molasses to eat with it. He thought the plums would be a substitute for the molasses, but we were not to be cheated out of our rights in this way.

> Such are the trifles which produce quarrels on shipboard. In fact, we had been too long from port. We were getting tired of one another, and were in an irritable state, both forward and aft. Our fresh provisions were, of course, gone, and the captain had stopped our rice, so that we had nothing but salt beef and salt pork throughout the week, with the exception of a very small duff on Sunday. *[Duff was another English word for pudding/dessert]*

One of the first industrialized foods, ship's biscuit paired with salted meat, dried peas and beans, oatmeal, weak beer, and other items, including fresh food when available. Cooks stored biscuits in bread barges, or trays, which cooks kept for each mess, a mess usually being a group of four men. A daily ration of one pound of biscuit per man meant approximately four biscuits per man. Weevils and worms eventually found this treasure trove, hence the name "weevil castles," among many others.

The biscuits were too hard to eat without first soaking them in some sort of liquid. Tea or stew supplied the usual softening medium. For men with scurvy, eating became torturous since scurvy eventually results in gum disease and ensuing tooth loss as connective tissue breaks down. Due to a lack of vitamin C, scurvy impairs collagen formation. Scurvy didn't take long to plague the crews of sailing ships, sometimes as soon as a few weeks out, since many crew members were likely malnourished before they even stepped on deck.

Biscuits performed another job as well.

Because water went off quickly along with other fresh provisions, cooks burned old wormy ship's biscuits to make charcoal, which they used to purify the water and reduce impurities. Some writers today use the word "hardtack" interchangeably with ship's biscuit, but hardtack only came into use during the American Civil War. "Tack" is another word used for bread.

The 1773 edition of *Encyclopaedia Britannica* described ship's biscuit thus:

Sea bisket [*sic*] is a sort of bread much dried by passing the oven twice to make it keep for sea service. For long voyages they bake it four times and prepare it six months before embarkation. It will hold good for a whole year.

Cooking on board could be a dangerous act, what with ships made of wood and caulked with highly flammable tar called oakum. A large metal cauldron served as a cooking vessel, placed on deck over a fire box on a sheet of iron when the ocean was calm. When the seas thrashed wildly, the men ate cold food.

Based on my own experiments with ship's biscuits, I conclude that people hated ship's biscuit/pilot bread because of the monotony of eating the same thing every day. By the time of Nelson's navy in 1793, the British Admiralty strove mightily to provision their ships well, and they did, from all accounts. Food on board a navy ship often offered men a better diet than they would have had on land. But, prior to that, shipboard food on British ships left a great deal to be desired.

What of lobscouse?

The version thickened with our old friend, ship's biscuits, shared the table, or bowl as it were, with other dishes boasting touches of those infamous weevil castles and tooth dullers. Ship's biscuits add an interesting texture and flavor to stews like lobscouse.

But the prize winner for one of the most unappetizing-sounding dishes with ship's biscuit, at least for modern tastes, seems to be dandyfunk. Best described as a "slightly sweet, boiled pudding, sometimes likened to a seagoing gingerbread." Similar to Plum Duff without the dried fruit. Another version of dandyfunk requires only a water-soaked ship's biscuit to be topped with molasses. Yet another calls for smashing the ship's biscuit into a flour-like consistency, then adding slush (fat) and molasses, mixing it up, and patting the mass into a pan to bake until crisp.

The molasses suggests a precursor to Boston Brown Bread. Or does it?

There may well be connections between the food cooked on board those ships and some of the dishes we take for granted as being daily fare in parts of the country. Think salted meat in the American South, for one.

Another interesting tidbit: Ship's biscuit crumbs of the larger persuasion remain intact even after going through the wash cycle of a modern washing machine. How do I know this? Well, I wrapped the biscuit in a cloth while making an abbreviated version of lobscouse. Some crumbs clung to the fabric and would not budge even when I shook out the cloth. And so, they did not, after all, come out in the wash. Still rubbery to the touch and likely quite chewy, though I cannot testify to that part, reluctant as I was to pop those odd bits into my mouth.

What about that lobscouse?

The dish always depended on what was on hand, as did the variations cooked on ships. Fresh meat was a rarity on board ships, but sometimes rats sweetened the pot. The go-to meat for lobscouse could only be of the long-lasting salted type. That in itself turned out to be quite a feat, as John Farley's 1783 *The London Art of Cookery* suggests:

Admiral Sir Charles Knowles's Receipt to Salt Meat

As soon as the ox be killed, let it be skinned and cut up into pieces for use, as quick as possible, and salted whilst the meat be hot; for such purpose have a sufficient quantity of saltpetre and bay-salt pounded together and made hot in an oven, of each equal parts. With this sprinkle the meat, at the rate of about two ounces to the pound. Then lay the pieces on shelving boards to drain for twenty-four hours. Then turn them, and repeat the same operation, and let them lie for twenty-four hours longer. By this time, the salt will all be melted, and have penetrated the meat. Each piece must then be wiped dry with clean, corse cloths, and a sufficient quantity of common salt made hot likewise in an oven and mixed, when taken out, with about one-third of brown sugar. The casks being ready, rub each piece well with this mixture, and pack them well down, allowing about half a pound of the salt and sugar to each pound of meat, and it will keep good several years, and eat very well.

According to the *Oxford English Dictionary*, in 1707 satirist Edward Ward wrote, "He has sent the Fellow ... to the Devil, that first invented Lobscouse."

It could be said, could it not, that empires balanced on barrels of lowly ship's biscuits, too?

Yer may talk of yer flummadiddlers and fiddlepad-
dies, but when it comes down to gen-u-ine grub, there
ain't nothing like good old salt hoss that yer kin eat
afore yer turns in and feel it all night a-laying in yer
stummick and a-nourishin' of yen.

~ Samuel Eliot Morison

A HERICO OF A BREAST OF VEAL, FRENCH WAY.

Take a breast of veal, half roast it, then put it into a stew-pan, with three pints of brown gravy; season your veal with nutmeg, pepper and salt; when your veal is stew'd enough, you may put in a pint of green peas boil'd. Take six middling cucumbers, pare and cut them in quarters long way, also two cabbage-lettices, and stew them in brown gravy; so lay them round your veal when you dish it up, with a few forc'd-meat-balls and some slices of bacon. Garnish your dish with pickles, mushrooms, oysters and lemons.

— Elizabeth Moxon, *English Housewifery Exemplified,* 1764 —

Figure 37. Vintage Illustration of Strawberries

STRAWBERRIES, THE QUINTESSENTIAL ENGLISH DELICACY OF THE AMERICAN SOUTH

THEY SAY THAT BEHIND EVERY RECIPE, there lurks a tale.

In the case of strawberries and the American South, that's certainly true. There's a story there, an important one.

You see, Southerners point to strawberry shortcake and claim it as their own. Ditto strawberry pie. But strawberries, All-American perhaps, still come with a long English history behind them. Delve into English cookbooks from the first recipe books. You'll find recipes suspiciously like those served both in the antebellum South and today's South.

All of this strongly suggests that in many, many instances, English cooking served as the backbone for much of traditional American cooking, despite the much-touted influences of other culinary groups.

The truth is this: bless their hearts, but many food writers tend to make assumptions about how Southern cooking came to be what it is today without closely examining all the antecedents, the cookbooks, and the different cultures—not just African—at play. That is, there's a lack of comparing the actual recipes found in the past with what passes as plantation-inspired cooking.

Stephen Schmidt dissects this quandary in his comprehensive article, "When Did Southern Begin?" He hints at the disdain shown toward English culinary antecedents when he says, "But [Karen] Hess, oddly, falls into a trap that popular historians have set. *Rarely bothering to study period recipes*, the popularizers endlessly repeat the tired wisdom that historical English food was 'bland and boring.'" Hess also fell into the trap of generalizing more than she should have about the origins of recipes found in Southern cookbooks. Schmidt states emphatically that "Randolph does call for cayenne frequently, but so do her northern counterparts, for cayenne was beloved in England: Raffald's reliance on cayenne in *The Experienced English Housekeeper* is almost compulsive," questioning the widespread assumption that cayenne or other chiles only entered the pot via the hand of a cook with an African culinary heritage. After all, Hannah Glasse includes a recipe for curry in *The Art of Cookery, Made Plain and Easy*. But more telling is J. Skeat's inclusion of "chian

215

pepper" in *The Art of Cookery Made Easy and Familiar* of 1769. Cayenne.

Before I move on here, I must add that Karen Hess made a name for herself as annotator/interpreter/editor of several historical cookbooks. But I very strongly question some of Mrs. Hess's generalizations in her annotations to *What Mrs. Fisher Knows About Old Southern Cooking.*

Look at what she says: "While the overwhelming basic influence in the various Southern cuisines was English, with strong streaks of French and occasional traces of other kitchens, African aromas were everywhere." She then points to a few okra recipes in Mary Randolph's *The Virginia Housewife* as proof of a widespread African influence. Note that Mrs. Randolph also includes several Spanish recipes in that very same book.... Recall too, please, that Henry VIII's first wife, Katherine of Aragon, was Spanish, with a love of pomegranates, grapes, oranges, and lemons.

Another generalization of Mrs. Hess's is this, "I should note that most of the recipes in *all* [her emphasis] Southern cookbooks are, in fact, largely recipes gleaned by the writers from African American cooks, their own, and others." I ask: how can anyone be a hundred percent certain of this fact? These comments of hers are direct contradictions to those she made in *Martha Washington's Booke of Cookery* and *The Virginia Housewife.* (See pages xiv and 266.)

So, for example, take strawberries, a proper vehicle for examining some of these issues.

Although tiny *fraises des bois* grew in Europe prior to the discovery of the New World in 1492, it wasn't until English and French horticulturalists combined these tiny European berries with the bigger, sweeter, redder *Fragaria virginiana* (scarlet or Virginia strawberry)—indigenous to Virginia and mentioned by William Byrd in his *Natural History of Virginia*, published in 1737, thought by some to have actually been written by John Lawson—that the modern plum-size strawberry began.

It took another New World strawberry cousin—*Fragaria chiloensis* (pine or beach strawberry), discovered by Amédée-François Frézier (1682–1773)—to create the modern supermarket strawberry.

Native Americans created a type of cornbread mixed with crushed strawberries, too. They also dried them. Strawberries figured in a creation legend told by the Cherokees, too. Thomas Jefferson mentions strawberries so often in his *Garden Book* that curators at Monticello surmised that the strawberry ranked as one of Jefferson's favorite fruits, no small feat in the eighteenth century before the large-scale production of improved varieties. But by 1867, newspapers such as *The Prairie Farmer* of Chicago carried advertisements for bedding plants.

But way long before all that birds and bees stuff began percolating in English greenhouses, the English took to strawberries like flies to honey. Recipes dating to 1290 suggest this very long history. An *Oxford English Dictionary* entry claims the words "Frega, streaberige" appeared in a glossary from 1000 A.D. In other words, the strawberry is no Johnny-come-lately to the English table.

One reason for the modern popularity of strawberries rests with Thomas Wolsey, a sixteenth-century Catholic Cardinal, in deep with Henry VIII. Wolsey's Hampton Court palace twenty miles south of London, boasted enormous kitchens. It was there in 1509 that one of his cooks concocted the delicious combination of strawberries and cream, discussed years later by Andrew Boorde, author of *Fyrst boke of the Introduction of knowledge*. Boorde wrote a few sentences about the strawberry,

> Rawe crayme undecocted, eaten with strawberyes or hurtes (whortleberry, billberry) is a rurall mannes blanket. I have knowen such blankettes hath put men in jeoperdy of theyr lyves.

Up to this point, and beyond, humoral theory ruled the British kitchen. Galen's theories greatly influenced these dietaries, written by men, read by men. Note again Boorde's comment: cream "puts men in jeopardy of their lives."

John Russell's *Boke of Nurture* circa 1460 also cautioned against eating cream from cows and goats. Why? Because cream's cooling nature caused ill health under certain circumstances. Many people abandoned the humoral theory of medicine and food when Enlightenment ideas trickled into England's American colonies. But it's important to recall that cooks still followed, and avoided, certain specific food pairings, as demonstrated by Trudy Eden in *The Early American Table*, particularly in her discussion of the work of the Scottish physician, George Cheyne. And Alfred Crosby, better known for his work on the Columbian Exchange, delved into this topic as well in his more controversial *Ecological Imperialism*, discussing the many adaptations of plants, animals, and people to the new environments turned up by colonialism.

What Boorde described is essentially the signature dish now associated with Wimbledon and tennis, a "foolish" dish, as it were.

Or strawberry fool.

This strawberry dessert could well be the grandparent to Wimbledon's strawberries-and-cream and Eton Mess, a name that still tickles my funny bone, as do so many English recipe monikers. Wigs! Stargazy Pie! Humbugs!

So, what is a fool, and more specifically, a strawberry fool? Is it, perhaps, an ancestor of strawberry shortcake?

First, a definition.

"Fool," thought by many to be a name possibly (and loosely) based on the French word *fouler*, to press or trample upon (as in grapes). But it may actually be associated with the more pejorative word for simpleton—"fool"—frivolous and light, without substance. The earliest versions of this dish seem to have been custards with fruit mixed in. WM's *Compleat Cook* of 1658 offers a recipe for gooseberry fool. Take Randle Holme's description in his *Academy of Armory* from 1688 as well: "Foole is a kind of Custard, but more crudely; being made of Cream, Yolks of Eggs, Cinnamon, Mace boiled; and served on Sippets with sliced dates, Sugar, and white and red Comfits, strawed thereon."

"Sippets" signify small pieces of bread or toast and could well be substituted with various bready or cakey items, such as scones or crumpets. Or biscuits …. Or pie pastry ….

Hannah Glasse printed a recipe for gooseberry fool in *The Art of Cookery*, highly popular in the American colonies during the eighteenth century, as we have seen.

A deeper look at this concept, fruit mashed and dispersed in a thick creamy medium, suggests a quick version of pottage. Or posset even.

A fifteenth-century English cookery book, Harleian MS 279 manuscript from around 1435, includes a pottage concocted with strawberries:

.Cxxiij. Strawberye. - *Take Strawberys, & waysshe hem in tyme of ȝere in gode red wyne; þan strayne þorwe a clope, & do hem in a potte with gode Almaunde mylke, a–lay it with Amyndoun oþer with þe flowre of Rys, & make it chargeaunt and lat it boyle, and do þer-in Roysonys of coraunce, Safroun, Pepir, Sugre grete plente, pouder Gyngere, Canel, Galyngale; poynte it with Vynegre, & a lytil whyte grece put þer-to; coloure it with Alkenade, & droppe it a–bowte, plante it with þe graynys of Pome-garnad, & þan serue it forth.*

Translated, this is:

Strawberry. - *Take strawberries and wash them in time of year in good red wine; then strain through a cloth, and do them in a pot with good almond milk, ally it with wheat starch or with rice flour, and make it thick and let it boil, and do therein currants, saffron, pepper, sugar great plenty, powdered ginger, cinnamon, galingale; sour it with vinegar, and*

a little white grease put thereto; color it with Alkanet, and drop it above
with pomegranate seeds, and then serve it forth.

Then E. Smith serves up a strawberry fool in *The Compleat Housewife* of 1727:

To make Strawberry or Raspberry Fool.
TAKE a Pint of Raspberries, squeeze and strain the Juice with
Orange-flower Water; put to the Juice five Ounces of fine Sugar;
then set a Pint of Cream over the Fire, and let it boil up; then put
in the Juice, give it one stir round, and then put it into your Bason;
stir it a little in the Bason; and when 'tis cold use it.

And …strawberry shortcake, the first published recipe possibly appearing in
Miss Eliza Leslie's *The Lady's Receipt Book: A Useful Companion for Large or Small
Families* of 1847. However, some authorities suggest that the recipe surfaced in the
1840s, perhaps first in Michigan. That may be so, but the hints abound that idea of
strawberries with cake could well have existed before that. Indeed, serving strawberries and cream had a much longer history.

Here's more proof.

In *The Good Huswifes Handmaide for the Kitchin*, from the 1590s, you'll come
across what might just be the earliest printed record of "short cake."

Take wheate flower, of the fayrest ye can get, and put it in an
earthern pot, and stop it close, and set it in an Ouen and bake it,
and when it is baken, it will be full of clods, and therefore ye must
searse it through a search: the flower will haue as long baking as a
pastie of Uenison. When you haue done this, take clowted Creame,
or els sweet Butter, but Creame is better, then take Sugar, Cloues,
Mace, and Saffron, and the yolke of an Egge for one doozen of
Cakes one yolke is ynough: then put all these foresaid things
together into the cream, & temper them al together, then put them
to your flower and so make your Cakes, your paste be very short,
therefore yee must make your Cakes very litle: when yee bake your
cakes, yee must bake them vpon papers, after the drawing of a
batch of bread.

So, the next time someone serves strawberry shortcake, gushing about the
ingenuity of cooks in American kitchens, think of England's green and pleasant
land, not the piney woods of South Carolina or the red clay earth of Georgia nor
the Piedmont of Virginia.

Rawe crayme, undecocted, eaten with strawberys or hurtes is a rurall mannes banket. I have known such bankettes hath put men in jeopardy of they lyves.

~ Andrew Boorde

36. TO COLLAR A CALF'S HEAD TO EAT HOT.

Take a large fat head, and lay it in water to take out the blood; boil it whilst the bones will come out; season it with nutmeg, pepper and salt; then wrap it up round with a large lump of forc'd-meat made of veal; after which wrap it up tight in a veal kell before it is cold, and take great care that you don't let the head break in two pieces; then bind it up with a coarse inkle, lay it upon an earthen dish, dridge it over with flour, and lay over it a little butter, with a little water in the dish; an hour and a half will bake it; when it is enough take off the inkle, cut it in two length ways, laying the skin-side uppermost; when you lay it upon your dish you must lay round it stew'd pallets and artichoke-bottoms fry'd with forc'd-meat-balls; put to it brown gravy-sauce; you may brown your sauce with a few truffles or morels, and lay them about your veal.

Garnish your dish with lemon and pickle.

— Elizabeth Moxon, *English Housewifery Exemplified*, 1764 —

Figure 38. Victorian Men Drinking Wine

MULLED WINE, A TIMELESS TASTE OF THE DIVINE?

BLAME IT ON CHARLES DICKENS, the literary trendsetter who blazed the way for the Victorian Christmas.

It?

Mulled wine. You know, the foul stuff Grandmother allowed in the house once a year, at Christmastime. Most people considered that a blessing.

Like fruitcake, mulled wine comes from entrenched and revered Tradition.

You'll find early written recipes for mulled wine in sixteenth-century recipe books. But the practice of spicing and heating wine likely dates far back into the billowy mists of history, creating a way to rescue wine gone bad by heating it and spicing it up to hide off-tastes. Or maybe, just maybe, they *liked* it like that.

The Romans dubbed it *"Calida"* or *"Calda,"* an eerily similar word to the Spanish word, *"caldo,"* or stock. *Caliente*, too.

During the Middle Ages, some people named it *Potus Ypocras* or *Hipocris* after, yes, Hippocrates, the Greek Father of Medicine, because of the healthful properties of this ancient concoction. Since only poor people generally drank plain water, mulled wine offered some assurance of status. Not to mention the unmentionable: no diarrhea caused by bad water. No disease, either. Hopefully not, anyway.

In English dialect from the fourteenth and fifteenth centuries, the word "mulled" signified "muddled" or "mixed up." In earlier times, of course, ale, cider, perry, or mead stood in for wine. And probably tasted better. F.W., in *A Treatise of Warm Beer*, 1641, writes,

> ... when I did always drink cold beer...I was very often troubled
> with exceeding pain in the head...also with stomach-ache, tooth-
> ache, cough, cold, and many other rheumatic diseases. But since
> my drinking my beer (small or strong) actually as hot as blood, I
> have never been troubled with any of the former diseases, but have
> always continued in very good health constantly...

Mulled ale became associated with rambunctious sailors and other disreputable sorts around the beginning of the seventeenth century, opening the way for mulled wine. Another name for the concoction was "flip."

One version of mulled wine, Lamb's Wool, makes a grand appearance as a potion served on Epiphany (January 6) and requires crushed baked-apple pulp, cream, egg yolks, and whipped egg whites. (It's beginning to sound a little bit like eggnog, isn't it? But it isn't.)

Honoré Balzac, in *The Peasants*, captured a certain truth about the popularity of mulled wine:

> In the Morvan and in that part of Bourgogne which lies at its foot on the Paris side, this mulled wine, which La Tonsard flung in Pere Fourchon's face, is a rather dear beverage which plays a great part in the life of the peasants, and is prepared with more or less skill by grocers, or by keepers of cafes where cafes exist. This blessed beverage, compounded of choice wine, sugar, cinnamon, and other spices, is preferable to all the disguised or adulterated forms of *eau de-vie* known as *ratafia, cent-sept-ans, eau-des-braves, cassis, vespltro, esprit-de-solril,* etc. Mulled wine is found as far east as the boundary between France and Switzerland. In the Jura, in the wild regions to which some few enthusiastic tourists find their way, the innkeepers, on the word of travelling salesmen, give the name of Syracuse wine to that manufactured product, an excellent drink, by the way, for which you are delighted to pay three or four francs a bottle under the spur of the canine thirst caused by ascending mountain peaks. In the households of the Morvan and Bourgogne, the slightest twinge of pain, the most trivial shock to the nerves, is an excuse for a draught of mulled wine. The women, before, during, and after their confinement, take sugared toast with it. Mulled wine has devoured many peasant fortunes. More than once, too, the seductive fluid has necessitated marital chastisement.

That holds true for other time periods and places as well.

William Kitchiner expounded on mulling spices in *The Cook's Oracle*:
Essence of Allspice for mulling of Wine.—(No. 412.)
Oil of pimento, a drachm, apothecaries' measure, strong spirit of wine, two ounces, mixed by degrees: a few drops will give the flavour of allspice to a pint of gravy, or mulled wine, or to make a bishop. Mulled wine made with Burgundy is called bishop; with old Rhenish wine, cardinal; and with Tokay, Pope.

Of course, Mrs. Isabella Beeton, that eternal icon of English cookery, took a few liberties and "borrowed" mulled wine recipes from Hannah Glasse and Eliza

Acton. Her recipe for mulled wine doesn't include certain particular touches, such as the orange rind suggested by Acton:

1838.-TO MULL WINE.

INGREDIENTS.- To every pint of wine allow 1 large cupful of water, sugar and spice to taste

Mode.-In making preparations like the above, it is very difficult to give the exact proportions of ingredients like sugar and spice, as what quantity might suit one person would be to another quite distasteful. Boil the spice in the water until the flavour is extracted, then add the wine and sugar, and bring the whole to the boiling-point, when serve with strips of crisp dry toast, or with biscuits. The spices usually used for mulled wine are cloves, grated nutmeg, and cinnamon or mace. Any kind of wine may be mulled, but port and claret are those usually selected for the purpose; and the latter requires a very large proportion of sugar. The vessel that the wine is boiled in must be delicately cleaned, and should be kept exclusively for the purpose. Small tin warmers may be purchased for a trifle, which are more suitable than saucepans, as, if the latter are not scrupulously clean, they spoil the wine, by imparting to it a very disagreeable flavour. These warmers should be used for no other purpose.

And from Eliza Acton's *Modern Cookery in All its Branches*, there's this:

TO MULL WINE.
(An excellent French Receipt.)

Boil in a wineglassful and a half of water, a quarter of an ounce of spice (cinnamon, ginger slightly bruised, and cloves), with three ounces of fine sugar, until they form a thick syrup, which must not on any account be allowed to burn. Pour in a pint of port wine, and stir it gently until it is on the point of boiling only: it should then be served immediately. The addition of a strip or two of orange-rind , cut extremely thin, gives to this beverage the flavour of bishop. In France light claret takes the place of port wine in making it, and the better kinds of vin ordinaire are very palatable thus prepared.

As Beeton implies, one crucial piece of equipment assisting a cook in mulling the wine, or the cider, or the mead, was a "mulling cone." Inserted into the wine, it heated up the liquid faster. Charles Dickens described it quite well in *The Old Curiosity Shop* in 1841,

> "Then," said Mr. Codlin, "fetch me a pint of warm ale..."
> ...the landlord retired to draw the beer, and presently returning with it, applied himself to warm the same in a small tin vessel shaped funnel-wise, for the convenience of sticking it far down in the fire and getting at the bright places. This was soon done, and he handed it over to Mr. Codlin with that creamy froth upon the surface which is one of the happy circumstances attendant upon mulled malt.

> Numerous cookbook authors in the nineteenth century plagiarized Mrs. Beeton's recipe for mulled wine, including Laura Simkins Fitchett. That lady's *Beverages and Sauces of Colonial Virginia, 1607-1907* sports dozens of recipes with catchy names for alcohol-based drinks, such as "Governor Berkeley's Claret Cup," most of which appear in Beeton's best-selling *Book of Household Management*. Fitchett takes a recipe for "Mulled Wine" verbatim from Beeton's book.

All this just goes to show you that perhaps there never really has been anything new under the sun when it comes to food writing!

The big question, one you're probably asking too, is how did poor peasants afford the spices necessary for a proper mulling? What was the role of the monasteries in all this mulling about? Another avenue to explore concerns the question of ritualized drunkenness in the apparent wild abandon of winter solstice celebrations ....

Wyne is made by crafte of good spicery and herbes.
~ Bartholomaeus Anglicus

TO MAKE ONION SOUP.

BOIL eight or ten large Spanish onions in milk and water, change it three times, when they are quite soft, rub them through a hair sieve, cut an old cock in pieces, and boil it for gravy with one blade of mace, strain it, and pour it upon the pulp of the onions, boil it gently with the crumb of an old penny loaf, grated into half a pint of cream, add Chian pepper and salt to your taste : a few heads of asparagus or stewed spinach, both make it eat well and look very pretty : grate a crust of brown bread round the edge of the dish.

— Elizabeth Raffald, *The Experienced English Housekeeper*, 1786 —

Figure 39. Chillingham Cattle

BOEUF À LA MODE: BRITISH BEEF MADE AMERICAN

COOKING AT THE WHITE HOUSE wasn't always the glam job it is today.

Thomas Jefferson's French chef Honoré Julien—who'd cooked for George Washington as well—wanted to quit upon seeing the kitchen at the White House. After he left office, Jefferson wrote to Henry Foxall, his iron supplier:

> The cook which I had in Washington (mr [sic] Julien) and who is now with me for a time, informs me you made for the President's [White House] kitchen some irons of casting for the stoves or stew-holes in the kitchen, in which the box-part & the grille or bars were all solid together, and that you made them of three sizes. I must ask the favor of you to make 8. for me...

Julien taught Jefferson's enslaved cooks Edith Hern Fossett and Frances Gillette Hern how to cook the French food that Jefferson loved so much. Daniel Webster once wrote of a meal he'd eaten at Monticello, "His [Jefferson's] dinners are in the half Virginian half French style, in good taste, and abundant."

And when George Washington placed a want ad for a cook in a Philadelphia newspaper, it read "A cook is wanted for the family of the President of the United States. ... No one need apply who is not perfect in the business, and can bring indubitable testimonials of sobriety, honesty and attention to the duties of the station."

A tavern owner, staunch patriot, and spy with a murky background, Samuel "Black Sam" Fraunces got the job, probably because Washington knew that the guy could really cook. After all, Fraunces cooked for the general during the Revolutionary War when Washington and his troops languished in New York. To cook edible foods under those conditions, well, that took some doing.

Washington no doubt felt that if a cook could satisfy men on the edge of hunger, with bayonets and bullets coming at them, then all would be well in a properly equipped kitchen, at least one thus provisioned for the times. No stove appeared in the White House until the Millard Fillmore (who?) presidency, 1850-1853. That meant, of course, hearth cooking until that point.

So, by the time of Lincoln's second inaugural, the White House was prepared to serve the elaborate coronation-like meals Americans thought necessary for

229

serving foreign diplomats and dignitaries from Europe.

That explains, at least in part, why Lincoln's menu featured Boeuf (Beef) à la Mode.

French, yes, with a long pedigree in England.

In his *Diary*, Samuel Pepys describes visiting "a French house to dinner," where he sat at a table "covered, and clean glasses ... and a mess of pottage first, and then a piece of boeuf-a-la-mode, all exceeding, well seasoned, and to our great liking."

The truth of the matter is that recipes for Beef à la Mode appeared in the many English cookbooks so popular in the new United States for almost 100 years prior to Lincoln's inaugural dinner. Evidence suggests that the recipe went by a less glossy name. Beef stew, popular and pervasive in England and France for centuries. Hannah Glasse includes it in her 1747 classic, *The Art of Cookery, Made Plain and Easy*, that work underlying many of the earliest American cookbooks. E. Smith's *The Compleat Housewife*, first published in England in 1727, contains a recipe for "beef alamode," although her recipe title actually reads as "To Stew a Rump of Beef." In 1742, William Parks—a printer in Williamsburg, Virginiaprinted Smith's book in what we today would call a pirated version. The author of the first truly American cookbook, Amelia Simmons, provides three different recipes for this beef stew in her *American Cookery* of 1796, while Mary Randolph includes "Beef-A-La-Mode" in her well-used 1824 cookbook, *The Virginia Housewife*.

Meanwhile, in England, Mrs. Isabella Beeton included two Beef à la Mode recipes in her *Book of Household Management*, one "economical" and the other full-bore expensive.

An official definition of "à la mode" is in order here. According to Oxford Languages, two meanings encompass this phrase:

à la mode
/ˌä lä ˈmōd/

adjective

1. in fashion; up to date.

2. (of beef) braised in wine, typically with vegetables.

In other words, Beef à la Mode, despite being dressed up with a fancy French name, was nothing more than a glorified pot roast cooked with a splash of wine.

No one knows precisely what Beef à la Mode recipe Lincoln's caterers used for that dinner on March 6, 1865. But the following recipe from Mrs. Beeton's *Book of Household Management* no doubt comes close, because Mrs. Beeton's book may well have been enough of a novelty at the time to entice Mary Lincoln to request the recipe for the dinner:

BEEF A LA MODE.

602. INGREDIENTS.-6 or 7 lbs. of the thick flank of beef, a few slices of fat bacon, 1 teacupful of vinegar, black pepper, allspice, 2 cloves well mixed and finely pounded, making altogether 1 heaped teaspoonful; salt to taste, 1 bunch of savoury herbs, including parsley, all finely minced and well mixed; 3 onions, 2 large carrots, 1 turnip, 1 head of celery, 1-1/2 pint of water, 1 glass of port wine.

Mode.-Slice and fry the onions of a pale brown, and cut up the other vegetables in small pieces, and prepare the beef for stewing in the following manner:-Choose a fine piece of beef, cut the bacon into long slices, about an inch in thickness, dip them into vinegar, and then into a little of the above seasoning of spice, &c., mixed with the same quantity of minced herbs. With a sharp knife make holes deep enough to let in the bacon; then rub the beef over with the remainder of the seasoning and herbs, and bind it up in a nice shape with tape. Have ready a well-tinned stewpan (it should not be much larger than the piece of meat you are cooking), into which put the beef, with the vegetables, vinegar, and water. Let it simmer *very gently* for 5 hours, or rather longer, should the meat not be extremely tender, and turn it once or twice. When ready to serve, take out the beef, remove the tape, and put it on a hot dish. Skim off every particle of fat from the gravy, add the port wine, just let it boil, pour it over the beef, and it is ready to serve. Great care must be taken that this does not boil fast, or the meat will be tough and tasteless; it should only just bubble. When convenient, all kinds of stews, &c., should be cooked on a hot-plate, as the process is so much more gradual than on an open fire.

Time.-5 hours, or rather more.

Average cost, 7d. per lb.

Sufficient for 7 or 8 persons.

Seasonable all the year, but more suitable for a winter dish.

Basically, it's beef stew we're exclaiming over here. But Beef à la Mode *does* sound far more sophisticated, doesn't it?

On polished charger laid,
The bulky chine, with plenteous fat inlaid
Of golden hue, magnificently shines.

~ Joseph William Jenks

AN EXCELLENT TRIFLE

Ingredients

Macaroons and ratifias, ½ lb.

wine and brandy mixed, ¼ pint

rich boiled custard, 1 pint

whipped syllabub

light froth to cover the whole, short ½ pint of cream and milk mixed

sugar, dessertspoonful

wine, ½ glassful.

Method

Take equal parts of wine and brandy, about a wineglassful of each, or two-thirds of good sherry or Madeira, and one of spirit, and soak in the mixture four sponge-biscuits, and half a pound of macaroons and ratifias; cover the bottom of the trifle-dish with part of these, and pour upon them a full pint of rich boiled custard made with three-quarters of a pint, or rather more, of milk and cream taken in equal portions, and six eggs; and sweetened, flavoured and thickened by the receipt; lay the remainder of the soaked cakes upon it, and pile over the whole, to the depth of two or three inches, the whipped syllabub, previously well drained; then sweeten and flavour slightly with wine only, less than half a pint of thin cream (or of cream and milk mixed); wash and wipe the whisk, and whip it to the lightest possible froth: take it off with a skimmer and heap it gently over the trifle.

— Eliza Acton, *Modern Cookery for Private Families*, 1845 —

A CAROL FOR A WASSAIL BOWL.

Figure 40. Vintage Illustration

WASSAILING THROUGH

AN EVEN FOOT OF SNOW PRESSES AGAINST THE FRONT DOOR, presents glimmer under the Christmas tree. Sugar cookies lie temptingly in the old painted tin box, colorful with romantic winter scenes. No slush there. Or black ice.

And Wassail punch simmers gently on the stove, the fragrance of cinnamon wafting through the house.

On a dark, cold winter night, when something visceral stirs like a tiny claw scratching at the wall, a cup of this bright and warm and soothing drink is in order. To banish the darkness away.

Geoffrey of Monmouth's *History of the Kings of Britain*, written in 1135, supposedly explains the origin of the toast:

> While Vortigern was being entertained at a royal banquet, the girl Renwein came out of an inner room carrying a golden goblet full of wine. She walked up to the King, curtsied low, and said "Lavert King, was hail!" When he saw the girl's face, Vortigern was greatly struck by her beauty and was filled with desire for her. He asked his interpreter what it was that the girl had said and what he ought to reply to her. "She called you Lord King and did you honour by drinking your health. What you should reply is "drinc hail." Vortigern immediately said the words "drinc hail" and ordered Renwein to drink. Then he took the goblet from her hand, kissed her and drank in his turn. From that day to this, the tradition has endured in Britain that the one who drinks first at a banquet says "was hail" and he who drinks next says "drinc hail."

The early settlers of Virginia brought many, many culinary customs with them from Britain, including punches at Christmas, yet no one recorded the practice of the "*waes haeil*" bowl. Ironically, when the Bishop of Aberdeen visited Virginia in 1927, he wrote the following:

> These dear Virginians! They are not Americans at all. They are just old fashioned English folk. One keeps wondering what on earth they are doing here. This is old England, old England at its best and kindliest ... Everywhere flow the wassail bowls of that seductive Christmas beverage, "egg nog" which in spite of the

Volstead Act [Prohibition], surely contains more potent ingredients than whipped eggs and cream. (From a 1927 newspaper clipping, Valentine Museum, Richmond)

There is a traditional custom with deep pagan roots, still practiced in some areas of the west of England, where a group of wassailers enters an orchard. Choosing a tree to symbolize the entire orchard, they pour a little hard cider at the base of the tree to encourage fertility and a good harvest. Verification that this tree was-sailing took place in more remote times comes from accounts found from St. Albans dating to 1486 and Kent dating to 1586.

Wassail, with mead:

2 cups fresh apple cider
2 large oranges, cut in half
2 whole cloves
2 large apples, unpeeled, cored, and cut into wedges
4 cinnamon sticks
Pinch of nutmeg
1 small slice of peeled ginger root
¾ (750 ml.) liter bottle of mead

Orange and apple slices

Pour cider into a large nonreactive pot. Add one of the orange halves with two cloves embedded in it. Squeeze the juice from the other halves into the cider. Stir in apple wedges, cinnamon sticks, nutmeg, and ginger slice. Bring to a boil, reduce heat, and let steep for about an hour. Pour in mead, bring to a simmer. Remove cooked fruit, cinnamon sticks, and ginger slice. Serve hot, garnished with slices of orange and apple.

Since the season isn't the season without music, here's a traditional Christmas carol dating back to the Middle Ages, the Gloucestershire Wassail. The lyrics (more or less) follow.

Wassail! wassail! all over the town,
Our toast it is white and our ale it is brown;
Our bowl it is made of the white maple tree;
With the wassailing bowl, we'll drink to thee.

Here's to our horse, and to his right ear,

God send our master a happy new year:
A happy new year as e'er he did see,
With my wassailing bowl I drink to thee.

So here is to Cherry and to his right cheek
Pray God send our master a good piece of beef
And a good piece of beef that may we all see
With the wassailing bowl, we'll drink to thee.

Here's to our mare, and to her right eye,
God send our mistress a good Christmas pie;
A good Christmas pie as e'er I did see,
With my wassailing bowl I drink to thee.

So here is to Broad Mary and to her broad horn
May God send our master a good crop of corn
And a good crop of corn that may we all see
With the wassailing bowl, we'll drink to thee.

And here is to Fillpail and to her left ear
Pray God send our master a happy New Year
And a happy New Year as e'er he did see
With the wassailing bowl, we'll drink to thee.

Here's to our cow, and to her long tail,
God send our master us never may fail
Of a cup of good beer : I pray you draw near,
And our jolly wassail it's then you shall hear.

Come butler, come fill us a bowl of the best
Then we hope that your soul in heaven may rest
But if you do draw us a bowl of the small
Then down shall go butler, bowl and all ....

Figure 41. Early Printers

ALEING HERBS: COSTMARY

ALE-MAKING IN MEDIEVAL AND RENAISSANCE ENGLAND depended upon a number of herbal flavorings, especially before hops became the predominant flavor. One of those herbal flavorings was costmary.

An aleing herb (and a medicinal one, too), costmary (*Tanacetum balsamita*, also *Chrysanthemum balsamita*), is a cousin to Tansy. Thomas Green mentions costmary in his sixteenth-century herbal, *Universal Herbal*. In *The Countrie Farmer*, Gervase Markham refers specifically to Costmary's use in ale making. John Gerard's *Herbal or General History of Plants* and Nicholas Culpeper's *Complete Herbal* both describe maudlin (Magdalene), which might have been similar to costmary.

"Costmary" hails from a Latin word, *costus*, referring to a plant originally from India because costmary wound up in Europe via Asia. During the Middle Ages, people associated costmary with the Virgin Mary. The French name for the plant, *Herbe Sainte-Marie*, reflects this practice. Other popular names include Alecost, Balsamita, Balsam Herb, Bible Leaf, Costmarie, Mace, and Balsamita.

Costmary's flavor resembles mint and lemon. The traditional English Wassail bowl often contained costmary.

Several nineteenth-century works refer to costmary, in quite interesting contexts.

According to *Anglo-Saxon Leechcraft : an historical sketch of early English medicine*, costmary helps people suffering from mental disorders. Note that the herb was added to ale for effectiveness:

> For a lunatic ; costmary, goutweed, lupin, betony, attorlothe,
> cropleek. field gentian, hove, fennel ; let masses be sung over, let
> it be wrought of foreign ale and of holy water ; let him drink this
> thick for nine mornings, at every one fresh, and no other liquid that
> is thick and still, and let him give alms, and earnestly pray God for
> his mercies.

In *Notes and Queries: A Medium of Intercommunication for Literary Men, General Readers, etc.*, John K. Jackson of the Kew Museum says this about costmary:

> HALE-COAST " OR " HALE-CAUST " (5 th S. xi. 468.) The
> herb is alecost, or, as written by Cotgrave, alecoast. It was also

called costmary, balsamine, or balsam herb (Balsamita vulgaris). In French it was known as costamer, cost, coq, sauge romaine (Cotgrave). Alecost occurs in all the old herbals. Its medicinal virtues may be read in extenso in Culpepper's [sic] *English Physitian Enlarged*, ed. 1671, p. 75. Culpepper speaks there of alecost as a very frequent and familiar herb in the gardens of his time, and he continues, "It is an especial friend and help to evil, weak, and cold livers." As to the etymology, the second element may be connected with costus, an Eastern shrub of noted aromatic properties, with which it somehow came to be confounded, though, of course, widely distinct, the balsam of which shrub Horace mentions in a familiar quotation from his Odes as *Achceminium costum*. The Oriental spice root was known in England in 1440, for we find in the *Promptorium*, "Cooste, herbe : Costus, cujus radix dicitur costum,"on which Mr. Way notes that "of the various virtues of coste, which is the root of an Indian plant, the early writers on drugs give long details." As to the ale portion of alecost, Skinner says, "quia forte cerevisise immissa gratum ipsi saorem odoremque conciliat, et est sane jucundissimi odoris planta." And so in Johnson's edition of Gerard, bk. ii. ch. ccviii. (cited by Nares), "Costmarie is put into ale to steep, as also into barrels and stands, amongst those herbs wherewith they do make sage ale."

Costmary seasons poultry and meat, as well as ale, in old English cookbooks. Appearing in England in the sixteenth century, it grew happily in Elizabethan knot gardens, its yellow ornamental flowers clustering in bunches, adding eye appeal for the viewer as well as an aroma close to that of spearmint.

Herbalist Nicholas Culpeper writes of costmary as being:

strengthening to the liver and all other inward parts; and taken in whey works more effectually. Taken fasting in the morning, it is very profitable for pains in the head that are continual, and to stay, dry up, and consume all thin rheums or distillations from the head into the stomach, and helps much to digest raw humours that are gathered therein .... It is an especial friend and help to evil, weak and cold livers. The seed is familiarly given to children for the worms, and so is the Infusion of the flowers in white wine given them to the quantity of two ounces at a time.

Now that hops flavor most ales, costmary simply is one of those culinary items that fades away into the pages of dusty, ancient texts.

*In old English literature, there is reference to costmary leaves
tied up with bundles of lavender and placed on beds
and in linen closets because of their sweet scent.*

~ Edward Mowbray Tuttle

Figure 42. Vintage Illustration of Mustard Greens

THE MYSTERIES OF MUSTARD, WITH THANKS TO THE ENGLISH

FOR ME, AMERICAN BALLPARK MUSTARD—that tart, yellow, unctuous friend of the hamburger and the hot dog—fails to define prepared or "table" mustard.

Oh no, indeed not.

The truth is, the diversity of mustards boggles the mind. Second worldwide only to black pepper in popularity as a seasoning, mustard possesses a reputation for being easy to grow and to prepare.

Best of all, however, cooks like me only need to meander down the aisle of the local supermarket and find those multitudes of mustard. Or at least some of them.

Speaking of multitudes, three-quarters of a pound of black mustard seed or two pounds of white mustard seed will spawn anywhere from 110 million to 500 million seeds on one acre of land. Great self-sowers, mustard seeds needed nothing more than ambulant animals or wind to proliferate in ancient, pre-agricultural times.

Authorities suggest that mustard seeds grew throughout Europe as early as the Stone Age. Before some creative "chef" thought to grind the seeds between two stones, making the first "prepared" mustard, people popped the seeds into their mouths as they chewed their food. Cooks soon began blending and brewing the proverbial multitudes of mustards.

Instant seasoning is nothing new, it seems. Neither is the human love hotness in the mouth.

The first written record of mustard appeared in a Roman manuscript, Lucius Iunius Moderatus Columella's *De Re Rustica. XII 57.* The Bible, too, weighs in on mustard seeds with Matthew 17:20:

> *And Jesus said unto them, "Because of your unbelief: for verily I say*
> *unto you, If ye have faith as a grain of mustard seed, ye shall say unto*
> *this mountain, Remove hence to yonder place; and it shall remove; and*
> *nothing shall be impossible unto you."*

Mentioned in several medieval cookbooks, mustard provided spice and heat for a far lower price than more expensive spices from the Far East. A cold-weather crop with flowers resembling canola, mustard aided the growth of many grain crops, including wheat and barley. Its greens appeared in English pottage long before the settlement of America and the introduction of enslaved African cooks.

A little etymology is in order here: The word *mustard* originated from the Middle English word *mustarde*, or "condiment," derived from an Old French word, *mostarde*. In this root the Latin lingers, *mustum*, the word for grape must, or unfermented wine. Cooks originally made mustard by mixing fresh grape juice with ground mustard seed. Medieval recipes, despite difficult spelling and vague quantities of ingredients, provide a peep into how mustard fit into menus of the times.

From *The Forme of Cury*, a fourteenth-century English manuscript cookbook, comes Lumbard mustard:

> *Take Mustard seed and waishe it & drye it in an ovene, grynde it drye. farse it thrugh a farse. clarifie hony with wyne & vynegur & stere it wel togedr and make it thikke ynowz. & whan þou wilt spende þerof make it thynne with wyne.*

Shakespeare highlighted mustard in *Henry IV*: "His wit's as thick as Tewksbury mustard." No doubt Will built his witty rejoinder on the saying, "He looks as if he had lived on Tewksbury mustard," a compliment actually for a sharp mind.

Possibly the most fascinating fact for me about mustard in England involved cannonballs. Yes, those big, heavy metal things used in war. The ones under consideration here most likely measured about three inches across, not eight inches, like some of the cannonballs I saw at the Citadel in Haiti and at the Tower of London, too.

John Nott urged his readers of his 1723 *The Cooks and Confectioners Dictionary* to grind mustard seeds with "... a Bowl with a Cannon-Bullet ... or in a Mortar with a Pestle." His recipe for mustard ball uses the word "Seamy,"

To make Mustard in Cakes
Take four Ounces of Seamy, an Ounce of Cinnamon, beat them with Vinegar and Hony very fine, in a Mortar, make it into a Paste, and then into little Cakes, dry them in an Oven, or in the Sun, when you would use them, dissolve them in Vinegar, Verjuice, or Wine.

Undoubtedly, he recognized the wisdom in Robert May's earlier words on the subject, wherein May advises readers to use a "... mustard quern, or a bowl with a cannon-bullet ..." when faced with grinding pinhead-small mustard seeds.

Mustard balls, such as those made on Tewkesbury, were composed of ground mustard seeds and spices mixed with horseradish. So dried, they lasted a good long while and could be sold at markets far from the manufacturing site. Cooks then bought them, reconstituting them with vinegar or wine in their kitchens.

Thus, creating prepared mustard!

As Peter Munday says,

> Mustard off this place [Tewkesbury] is much spoken off, Made upp in balles as bigge as henns eggs, att 3d and 4d each, allthough a Farthing worth off the ordinary sort will give better content in my opinon, this beeing in sight and tast Much like the old dried thicke scurffe thatt sticks by the sides off a Mustard pott...

Further changes occurred in 1720, when a Mrs. Clements of Durham milled mustard seeds into a fine yellow powder. When mixed with water, the powder transformed into a most incendiary concoction known for a long time as Durham Mustard. According to folklore, mustard cured sore muscles, colds, upset stomachs, and more. Who knows, maybe it worked? Mustard's chemistry certainly enables it to act as a natural preservative. Certainly, its effects in gaseous form made it the curse of soldiers in World War I.

Today, chefs and cooks add prepared mustards more to sauces and salad dressings than to sore muscles. Types of prepared mustards available include the aforementioned American mustard, French-style Dijon mustard—about which an entire book could be written thanks to the Dukes of Burgundy. There are also whole-grain or rustic mustards, plus brown mustard, a cousin to the whole-grain family. That's just the bare bones of mustard taxonomy.

Add a tablespoon or two of French Dijon-style mustard to meat gravy, along with a few tablespoons of sour cream, just before dinner and, well, you will be amazed at what you have wrought. Try putting a pot of mustard on the table when you serve any sort of roasted or grilled meat. Meat tastes extraordinarily special when spread with a few dabs of mustard before roasting. Collect a multitude of jarred prepared mustards. Or go a step further: blend and brew your own mustards for the mustard pot.

When winter arrives, and persists, a few pots of exotic mustards brighten palates even on the most dismal of days. Of course, in America, I may never send my child to the mustard shop, as they do in Dijon, France, instructed to buy a kilogram (2.2 pounds) of prepared Dijon mustard. Nor will I reach for those Tewkesbury mustard balls. But I just might.

Oh yes, indeed.

*The seede of Mustard pounded with vinegar is an excellent sauce,
good to be eaten with any gross meates, either fish or flesh ....*

~ John Gerard

50. – RATAFIA ICE CREAM

Bruise 1 pound of ratafia biscuits in the mortar. Make a custard of 1½ pints of milk, 10 raw yolks of eggs, and 6 ounces of castor sugar; and when it thickens, pour it over the bruised biscuits, and pass altogether through the tammy or hair sieve. Add half a wine-glass of noyeau syrup, and freeze. The crumbs may be left in the custard if liked. Serve for dinner or dessert.

— Agnes B. Marshall, *Book of Ices*, 1885 —

Engraved for M.ʳ Glasse's Complete art of Cookery.

Figure 43. Frontispiece, Hannah Glasse's *The Art of Cookery, Made Plain and Easy*

Whereupon I Examine Kissing Cousins: Yorkshire Pudding and Spoonbread

I DO BELIEVE THERE'S SUCH A THING AS DÉJÀ VU.

Many times, I've sensed I've experienced something before, details foggy, but nonetheless, there's that strange feeling of having been there, done that.

That sensation came over me when I began reading old and new British cookbooks, seeking mentions of puddings, especially Yorkshire pudding.

Not only did I metaphorically slip into my seat at my grandmother's table, I found myself remembering more tables and more kitchens from my past. The recipes in those British cookbooks could have been lifted verbatim from memory, so similar were they to what I knew from the very first bite of solid food I ever ate.

These comments presuppose that I carry around a definition in my mind as to what constitutes British food, what American food is at its base, and how the two intertwine.

The first thing I think of is the traditional preponderance of beef in both cuisines. Then come potatoes. Peas, too, of all types, not just the green ones. No Yorkshire pudding on this side of the pond, at least not that I recall, it being one of those dishes that disappeared from the mainstream. Unless ... you count popovers. And spoonbread, made with corn, is a dish that seems to have remained stuck in the southeastern region of the United States.

The importance to early colonists of cornmeal as a substitute for wheat flour becomes very apparent, too, when considering the numerous grist mills that sprang up wherever people settled. "Corn," by the way, was the English word for many types of grains, and not just "maize," as they labeled "Indian" corn.

In the early days of England's American colonies, corn was planted before the clearing of heavily forested land, and later with wheat. Wheat gained a foothold beginning in the eighteenth century. George Washington grew a fair amount of it at Mount Vernon, attempting to reduce his reliance on tobacco as a cash crop.

When did Yorkshire Pudding stop appearing on American tables?

It never really did. Think popovers.

Hannah Glasse first called the dish Yorkshire Pudding in her 1747 *The Art of Cookery, Made Plain and Easy*. But before that, the English knew it as Dripping Pudding, because cooks baked it along with roasted meat, catching the drippings as the meat cooked. Sir Alexander William George Cassey included a recipe for it in *The Whole Duty of a Woman* in 1737. A batter pudding usually includes wheat flour,

Spoonbread closely resembles Yorkshire pudding in execution. I'd be willing to bet my last nickel and stick my neck out by saying this: When a trip to the pantry yielded no wheat flour, spoonbread was the colonial housewife's answer to "Where's the pudding?"

And that's an old, old dish.

Early accounts of "Indian" pudding sound suspiciously like spoonbread. At the moment, without documentation, I wonder if Native Americans added eggs on occasion. That said, it is unlikely that they added milk for want of the same and the incidence of lactose intolerance as well.

Amelia Simmons includes three recipes for "Indian" pudding in *American Cookery*, two of which require baking and one boiling. All three call for milk and eggs. Later, Mary Randolph includes recipes for "Indian" pudding in *The Virginia Housewife* and Puff Pudding, the latter definitely a version of Yorkshire Pudding. She could count on it being at her table because of her ability to procure wheat flour on a reasonably regular basis. Many households could not because not everyone during the colonial period could afford wheat flour. Or enslaved cooks. Over seventy-five percent of colonial households did not own enslaved people.

This implies that cooks in said households were housewives or indentured servants who cooked with a decidedly English palette and palate. Later, of course, immigrant cooks from various ethnic backgrounds did the cooking.

The first time I ate spoonbread in the American South, I was sure I'd eaten it before. For it recalled some childhood taste memory of mine. Perhaps the baby pudding my mother fed my little brother, its base sweetened condensed milk. Or perhaps I savored it at my grandmother's table. I don't remember. If my father were still alive, I am sure he'd tell me, yes, his mother made spoonbread.

One sleepless night, thinking of my deceased father, how I can no longer ask him questions, wondering where the Sandman'd disappeared to while I counted countless dozens of sheep, I experienced a "Eureka" moment. You see, I'd baked a Yorkshire pudding the night before, using lard as the fat, for lack of proper suet. It reminded me, first of all, of one of those sweet German pancakes.

But memories of spoonbread kept nudging their way into my consciousness. Sure, several writers suggest a cousinly relationship between Yorkshire pudding and spoonbread. None, however, seem to have followed through on testing that more scientifically, that is, baking these and tallying up the similarities and differences.

That is what I did.

By baking both the Yorkshire pudding and the spoonbread in a shallow pan—specifically a glass Pyrex pie plate/pan—and not a soufflé dish, the physical resemblance between Yorkshire pudding and spoonbread became quite clear. I followed both Jane Grigson's recipe for Yorkshire pudding in *British Cookery and* Jan Carlton's instructions for Mile-High Spoon Bread, in *Richmond Receipts Past & Present.*

Examining these recipes, I noted the following about the recipes:

Requires a base of milk, eggs, flour, salt

Texture is similar

Behaves the same way, rises up—due to the scientific properties of eggs

The reason why cornmeal fails to behave as does wheat flour here in part lies in the difference between corn gluten and wheat gluten, both proteins. In the case of wheat, gluten forms stringy structures that help to trap air and assist in the rising of bread and other products. Corn, on the other hand, does not produce the same results. When a cook sets out to make spoonbread, and first boils the mush, what happens is that starch granules in the cornmeal undergo gelation, a process that softens the granules as they absorb water. The grind, or size, of the corn particles is very important, depending upon what dish the cook wishes to make.

Since the chief contributor to structure in corn is starch, the addition of eggs plays a terribly vital role in creating the culinary architecture sought in dishes such as spoonbread. Egg chemistry, as with gluten, relies on proteins for structure. There's a fine balance involved in heating eggs, because eggs—as any good cook knows—can turn rubbery very quickly, because any water or other liquid (milk, in the case of spoonbread and Yorkshire pudding) is unable to bond with the proteins if the heat is too high. The egg proteins coagulate into a thick mass. As you can guess, adding liquids in the amounts called for in Yorkshire pudding or spoonbread causes egg proteins to become diluted. With sufficient time, and evaporation during baking, the egg proteins bond to form a matrix, but a much less dense one.

That's what happened when I cooked up that spoonbread. Delicious hot, it's also lovely at room temperature or heated up slightly, with a dollop of butter and a squeeze of honey. Personally, I like spoonbread much better than Yorkshire pudding, but that's probably the American in me. This whole exercise points out something of the process that occurs when people find themselves in culinary exile, away from familiar foods and trappings of their natal kitchens.

Innovation is always based on something that's gone before.

Isaac Newton got it right when he quipped that his discovery of gravity came about because he stood on the "shoulders of giants."

Cooks do the same.

Take a Quart of Milk, beat up Six Eggs, half the Whites, mix as above Six Spoonfuls of Flour, a Tea Spoonful of Salt, and one of beaten Ginger.

~ Hannah Glasse

NO. 38. PIG'S FEET.

These are to be well salted for about four days, and then boiled in plenty of water for about three hours; they may be eaten either hot or cold.

— Charles Elmé Francatelli,
A Plain Cookery Book for the Working Classes, 1852 —

Figure 44. Vintage Serving Ware

254

PIE/PYE: ENGLISH TRADITION, AMERICAN ICON

"AS AMERICAN AS APPLE PIE." Well, no. It should be as English as apple pie. Or just plain pie.

The story of pie is an ancient one, for some believe that the ancient Egyptians knew a thing or two about pastry.

It's no surprise that English pies began as meat-filled "coffyns" (another word for box or container). A thick dough ("huff paste") surrounds the meat, allowing it to cook for long hours, keeping the meat moist and delectable, like baking a fish or hunk of meat wrapped in clay. One of the modern holdovers of this practice could be Beef Wellington. Yet, wheat flour, or rye, mixed with water hardly makes for an authentic pastry experience, at least not as we know it today.

The first written recipes in English for proper pastry appeared in the six-teenth century, with fat—lard or butter—mixed into flour just so, to create an increasingly desired flakiness.

Sweet pies tend to be associated with American kitchens, particularly Southern kitchens. But English cooks *did* produce sweet pies, as witness recipes in Gervase Markham's *The English Housewife*, a known cookery text in colonial Jamestown by 1620.

Just as the Pilgrims were getting started in their frigid Massachusetts settlement, cooks in Jamestown could be making cherry, pippin, apple, codling, pudding (custard), yellow (cream), or prune pies/tarts, following Markham's recipes, most of which called for sugar. Fear of eating fresh fruit was common in English culinary circles, based on the old ideas of humoral theory. Not until the eighteenth century did fresh fruit become more welcome in the English diet. It is not surprising that a typical way of incorporating fresh fruit into the menu resulted in prolonged baking with sugar and spices in crusts. Or using dried fruit, as in mince pie, an interesting combination that started out as meat pie combined with sweet ingredients, thus metamorphizing into today's version with suet and no meat.

Herbalist John Parkinson claimed that by 1629, England boasted of many different varieties of fruits: fifty-seven of apples, sixty-two of pears, sixty-one of plums, thirty-five of cherries, and twenty-two of peaches. "Not to mention "gooseberries, grapes, whortleberries, strawberries, quinces, apricots, raspberries, currants, barberries, and melon," as Trudy Eden emphasizes in *The Early American Table*.

C. Ann Wilson suggests that pumpkin pie, a perennial American favorite, graced upper-class English tables during the seventeenth century. But perhaps one of Ms. Wilson's more surprising comments concerns the sweet potato, "imported from Spain during the late summer." She refers to Thomas Dawson's well-known and widely quoted recipe in *The Good Housewife's Jewell*, meant to impart courage to a man or a woman, the sweet potato believed to be an aphrodisiac at the time:

A Tarte to prouoke courage either in man or Woman.
TAKE a quart of good wine, and boyle therein two Burre rootes scraped cleane, two good Quinces, and a Potaton roote well pared and an ounce of Dates, and when all these are boyled verie tender, let them be drawne throgh a strainer wine and al, and then put in the yolks of eight Egs, and the braines of three or foure cocke Sparrowes, and straine them into the other, and a litle Rosewater, and seeth them all with Sugar, Sinamon and Ginger, and cloues and Mace, and put in a litle sweet Butter, and set it vpon a chafingdish of coales betweene two platters, and so let it boyle till it be something big.

Sweet potatoes, of course, were a New World food, for a long while enjoying popularity at the tables of the English elite, including the colonists of Virginia. Only later did the sweet potato transform into food for enslaved Africans, given its resemblance to some root vegetables native to Africa.

And let's not forget the impact of Edward Kidder's pie shops in Cheapside, the first of which opened in 1660. Kidder later started what some might consider the first cooking school. There he taught upper-class English women how to make pastry, claiming toward the end of his life he'd taught over 6000 the art of pastry. His cookbook, *The Receipts of Pastry and Cookery*, no doubt went home with his students. Did those students sail away to America sometime later?

The association between pastry and upper-class aspirations is intriguing, suggesting that perhaps eating pie, particularly sweet pies, conveyed to a person certain social aplomb. The term "humble pie" refers to the use by the poor of umbles or innards instead of choice bits of the animal in question.

Probable explanations for the evident dichotomy between English and American pie lore lie with a few distinct possibilities. The eighteenth-century tendency of the English elite to emulate the French in the kitchen meant less sugar in recipes. As Barbadian plantations churned out sugar for the world market, including the English settlers living along the Eastern seaboard, the price of sugar declined dramatically.

Pie, an immensely complicated symbol of cultural contact, becomes a topic requiring more examination.

As American as Apple Pie? Make that as English as apple pie.

Look at Pork. There's a subject!
If you want a subject, look at Pork!

~ Charles Dickens

Figure 45. View of Early American Household

CHRISTMAS DINNER WITH GEORGE WASHINGTON

GEORGE WASHINGTON'S VIRGINIA PLANTATION, Mount Vernon, served as the backdrop for many scrumptious dinners, cooked by Washington's enslaved cooks. Just reading the following Christmas menu makes my lips twitch, my fingers itch for my wooden spoons. Note that even at the relatively late date of 1790 and independence from England, there's a soup going by the name of King's Soup ....

It took our forbearers a long time to cease thinking of themselves as English. At least when it came to the table.

From 1790 to 1792, President George Washington lived in Philadelphia. The following people worked in his kitchen:

Samuel ("Black Sam") Fraunces, steward and chef

Hercules Posey, enslaved cook, French-trained

Richmond Posey, enslaved, Hercules's son, kitchen scullion and chimney sweep

Katy Lefferts, kitchen maid

Until Washington chose to follow the lead of the disgruntled English colonialists, like most of them, he considered himself English.

His Christmas dinner at Mount Vernon in 1790 features a good number of English dishes:

An Onion Soup Call'd the King's Soup
Oysters on the Half Shell
Broiled Salt Roe Hering
Boiled Rockfish
Roast Beef and Yorkshire Pudding
Mutton Chops
Roast Suckling Pig
Roast Turkey with Chestnut Stuffing
Round of Cold Boiled Beef with Horse-radish Sauce
Cold Baked Virginia Ham

Lima Beans

Baked Acorn Squash

Baked Celery with Slivered Almonds

Hominy Pudding

Candied Sweet Potatoes

Cantaloupe Pickle

Spiced Peaches in Brandy

Spiced Cranberries

Mincemeat Pie

Apple Pie

Cherry Pie

Chess Tarts

Blancmange

Plums in Wine Jelly

Snowballs

Indian Pudding

Great Cake

Ice Cream

Plum Pudding

Fruits, Nuts, Raisins

Port, Madeira

Martha Washington's Booke of Cookery and Booke of Sweetmeats doesn't include the recipe for the King's onion soup, which may or may not be authentic. But, like Hannah Glasse's onion soup, it's thickened with egg yolk. In fact, the recipe touted today by Mount Vernon, Washington's Virginia plantation *is* Hannah Glasse's, from her 1747 *The Art of Cookery, Made Plain and Easy*:

> Take half a Pound of Butter, put it into a Stew-pan on the Fire,
> let it all melt, and boil till it has done making any Noise; then
> have ready ten or a Dozen middling Onions peeled, and cut small,
> throw them into the Butter, and let them fry a quarter of an Hour;
> then shake in a little Flour, and stir them round; shake your Pan,
> and let them do a few Minutes longer, then pour in a Quart or
> three Pints of boiling Water, stir them round, take a good Piece of
> Upper-crust, the stalest Bread you have, about as big as the Top of
> a Penny-loaf cut small, and throw it in; season with Salt to your
> Palate; let it boil ten Minutes, stirring it often; then take it off the
> Fire, and have ready the Yolks of two Eggs beat fine, with half a

Spoonful of Vinegar; mix some of the Soop with them, then stir it into your Soop, and mix it well, and pour it into your Dish. This is a delicious Dish.

Whether or not King George III ever ate this soup is one of those moot questions never to be answered. But George W. seems to have loved it.

Man is a carnivorous production,
And must have meals, at least one meal a day;
He cannot live, like woodcocks, upon suction,
But, like the shark and tiger, must have prey;
Although his anatomical construction
Bears vegetables, in a grumbling way,
Your laboring people think beyond all question,
Beef, veal, and mutton better for digestion.

~ Lord Byron

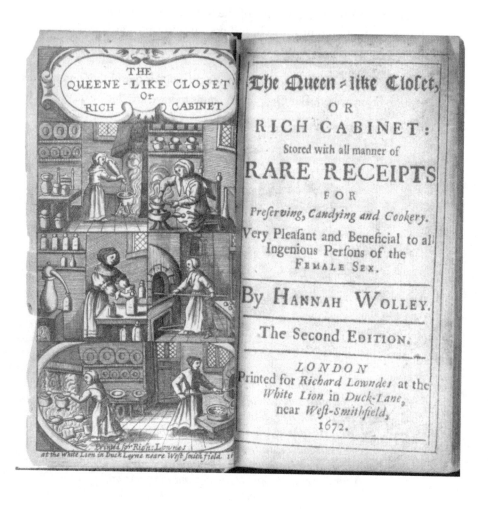

Figure 46. Title page, Hannah Woolley's *The Queen-like Closet*

A "FOUNDING MOTHER" CUISINE: THE INVISIBLE ETHNICITY OF THE ENGLISH

IT WAS ONE OF THE LARGEST AND MOST MASSIVE EXODUSES since the days of the Pharaohs.

Over 350,000 courageous English men, women, and children migrated to America in the seventeenth century. Within just a few generations, England grew to be a distant memory for many of them, a place redolent of nostalgia, a paradise that never was.

Attesting to that truth, my own ancestors hailed from various places in England and were in the New World as early as 1618. They left no significant, family-rich culinary legacy for us, their descendants. There *was* plum pudding at Christmas in my grandmothers' houses, true. And a love of roast beef survived as well. A luxury in England, beef became the prerogative of the wealthy classes, whose large manor houses boasted the enormous hearths crucial for cooking large joints of beef and whose land provided for their sustenance.

The Tudors and their courts influenced the cooking of the first English people in America in innumerable ways. They altered ideas about cooking, cemented the beliefs that sailed with those first settlers on the rickety wooden ships that tossed them about for months on the Atlantic waves.

In the beginning, the people who left the comforts of their English homes and migrated to the New World wouldn't eat Indian corn, or maize. They deemed the New World grain as fit only for hogs and cattle. For Native Americans, too. Eating maize, they believed, would render Englishmen into beings just like the New World savages surrounding them. However, this attitude wasn't peculiar only to the seventeenth century, when humoral theory provided Englishmen with medical theories later debunked.

That way of thinking persisted for many centuries.

Over a hundred years later, Joseph Plum Martins indicated that this attitude was anything but dead in his *Revolutionary War Memoir*: "When they [the British soldiers] could find none to wreak their vengeance upon, they cut open the knap sacks of the [Continental] guard and strew the Indian meal about the floor, laughing at the poverty of the Yankee soldiery who had nothing but hogs fodder, as they termed it, to eat."

When did the English turn to Indian corn? When did they relinquish the ideas behind humoral medicine, specifically concepts such as the "doctrine of similarities" and the "doctrine of signatures?"

The "doctrine of similarities," for example, suggested that a person would imbibe the characteristics of the thing eaten by eating certain foods. Think of testicles. That same theory applied to female ovaries as well as the male organs. The hoped-for result of eating such food would be increased fertility. Eating the heart of a strong animal would give strength to a weak heart, while goat flesh could make you randy. If you caught too many rabbits, you might take on their fearful nature by eating their meat.

With another aspect of the four humors, the "doctrine of signatures," the diner considered the effect of color or shape or both. Red foods added heat when coldness prevailed. Dark red flesh ensured a state of dryness and heat. Light-colored meat, such as chicken and other poultry, promised cold and moistness, to tame the heat of a fever or a hot, dry choleric temperament. Eating the dark flesh of swans led to a melancholic state or exacerbated an already existing one.

But when I read Peter Brears's radiant *Cooking and Dining in Tudor and Early Stuart England*, avid for the telling details that always make the past come alive, something stood out. He emphasizes a critical point that set English food on a path to greater sophistication. With the Dissolution of the Monasteries from 1536 to 1541, the Church's lands fell into the hands of the wealthy class, who then spared no expense when it came to food and entertainment. With dishes from Italy, Germany, Holland, and Turkey making inroads on English medieval cookery, Brears postulates that by around 1600, medieval cooking ceased to exist in "polite households."

All of this, of course, worked subtly behind the scenes to change mindsets.

What I mean by that statement is this: The settlers who arrived on the shores of Cape Henry in 1607 came from a higher social class than did those of Plymouth in 1620. For the people who populated the early Virginia colony, the Tudor years were relatively fresh. You may think that thirteen years difference—the span of time elapsed between the Virginia and Massachusetts settlements—insignificant, but it's an intriguing difference, nonetheless. Memories of food stay with you, as you know. As for the Plymouth colonists, seventeen years and social class separated them from the heritage of Elizabeth I's reign, which ended a mere four years before the settlement of Jamestown.

So many changes, so many enemies, so many challenges faced those intrepid Englishmen (and women)! The climate, from fierce, nose-hair freezing winters in Massachusetts to heat and humidity in Jamaica. The presence of wolves, deep forests, the stuff that led to the creation of so many medieval fairy tales of witches and demons of northern Europe. The specter of hunger, haunting them like so many ghosts, even though fish and fowl abounded around them. Or so John Smith implied.

And then there were the Native Americans, whose land the English felt justified in taking. The English believed the Native Americans failed in their stewardship of the Earth, by wasting resources or misusing them.

No wonder the colonialists aimed to recreate a lost paradise, a nostalgic look at an England that existed only in fantasy. Far from home, over 3,000 miles away, a little bit of England nestled in vast wilderness cheered them.

Their food memories sustained them as they made their way through the wilderness. As chef-turned-culinary-historian Stephen Schmidt remarks in his essay, "What Manuscript Cookbooks Can Tell Us that Printed Cookbooks Do Not": "American cookery began as a dialect of English cookery and was still pervaded by English influences through the antebellum period."

These attitudes, then, explain partly why English cookbooks predominated throughout the colonial period, with no cookbooks written and published by American authors until Amelia Simmons's *American Cookery* in 1796. However, it is likely that every family owned and used handwritten manuscript cookbooks compiled by various generations of English women. Martha Washington's manuscript cookbook comes to mind. Popular English cookbooks did not mention Indian corn, although pumpkin and turkey appeared in Hannah Glasse's book, *The Art of Cookery, Made Plain and Easy*. An American memoirist, quoted by Stavely and Fitzgerald, quipped,

> We had emancipated ourselves from the sceptre of King George, but that of Hannah Glasse was extended without challenge over our fire-sides and dinner-tables, with a sway far more imperative and absolute.

The first American version of Hannah's book appeared in 1805 and included a section titled "Several New Receipts adapted to the American Mode of Cookery." Pumpkin Pie. Cranberry Tarts. Maple Sugar.

Prior to Simmons, Susannah Carter's 1765 *The Frugal Housewife* found a place on the shelves of American households. An American version arrived in 1772, omitting several pages about wines, but including two woodcuts designed by none other than Paul Revere himself. In 1803, the printers added an "appendix containing several new receipts adapted to the American mode of cooking" to boost sales. Ironically, one-fourth of Simmons's book consisted of recipes from Susannah Carter's original book.

The point of delving into cookbook history is this: Food habits tend to change last, if at all, in migrant groups. People adapt to local ingredients, but they also continue to eat familiar foods. That the English in America produced no home-grown cookbooks between 1607 and 1796 testifies to their desire to remain English in matters of the stomach, as well as in law, politics, architecture, and many other aspects of English life. Karen Hess wrote in *Martha Washington's Booke of Cookery*: "Still [in spite of other influences such as African and Native American, etc.], the way of our [United States] cooking is English, much as common remains the basis of our law."

As Malcolm Gaskill says in *Between Two Worlds*, "The men and women of the frontier were combatants bonded by fire, their experience and mentality impossible for outsiders to comprehend." Yet their experience led them to cling harder to a nostalgic idea of England, one that still persists despite the waves of immigrants reaching the shores and borders of what is now the United States. Just think of "Downton Abbey" and the ongoing popular American fascination with British royalty.

Florence White alludes to this kinship between America and England, this motherhood. In *Good Things in England*, she concludes, "Our kitchen has more in common with America than any other country. … one of the great interests of this … has been to come across continual evidence of our common family interests with our cousins across the Atlantic."

Above all, I think it bears saying that courage is the keyword when it comes to the English experiment in the New World and the birth of the United States in all its permutations. As Gaskill writes, "The best way to remember the Pilgrim Fathers, it has been said, is to look at Plymouth Rock, then turn around to gaze at the vastness of the ocean whence they came."

That goes for them all.

I felt the impact of Gaskill's words when I stood on the shore at Cape Henry, thinking of those who landed there in 1607 as cold waves lapped at my feet and sandburs clung to my ankles.

Courage indeed.

They walked on with him until they came to a dirty shop window
in a dirty street, which was made almost opaque by the steam of hot meats,
vegetables, and puddings. But glimpses were to be caught of a roast leg of pork
bursting into tears of sage and onion in a metal reservoir full of gravy,
of an unctuous piece of roast beef and blisterous Yorkshire pudding,
bubbling hot in a similar receptacle, of a stuffed fillet of veal in rapid cut,
of a ham in a perspiration with the pace it was going at, of a shallow tank of
baked potatoes glued together by their own richness, of a truss or two
of boiled greens, and other substantial delicacies.

~ Charles Dickens

Figure 47. Queen Elizabeth I

THE FALLACY OF CULINARY APPROPRIATION

CLAIMS OF CULTURAL APPROPRIATION based on the argument that certain groups of people have "stolen" the culinary achievements of other groups, as well as commentaries suggesting that unless a cook or chef was fetched up in a certain culture, then *they no business cooking the food of another culture.*

Sorry, to this nonsense I can only say this: What poppycock!

But how about if we look at this from another point of view? The English—who of course borrowed many culinary ideas from the French and others over the centuries—yes, the English, are the ones who ought to be grumbling about culinary appropriation.

How so?

Consider a few facts.

Chief among those facts lies the reality that much of so-called American cuisine derives from European, and more specifically, English/British roots. First, let's examine this so-called American cuisine. It evolved from the earliest days of the embryonic nation, but not so much that certain English meal patterns and food types are still very, very recognizable, even now. Especially in Southern cooking, but also in that of the Great Plains states. Meat, gravy, vegetables, cake, pie. The dishes found in the cookbooks of Fannie Farmer, James Beard, Irma S. Rombauer, and most charity and Junior League cookbooks harkened to the food routinely cooked across the nation in most households until fairly recently.

The trend toward more international foods, remember, is a relatively recent phenomenon. Recall as well that "... immigrant families were sometimes targeted by social workers, who tried to expedite the process of acculturation and assimilation by teaching them American cookery," as Alice Ross writes in *The Oxford Encyclopedia of Food and Drink in America.*

Let's just consider beans.

Might it not be possible that soup beans, baked beans, and even Louisiana red beans first saw the light of day in the pot of an English woman standing in her log cabin or lean-to, relying upon her heritage of many types of pottage?

Look at this list from 1622 of suggested provisions for persons setting out for the New World from England. Note the second item under the section labeled

"Victuall":

> Eight bushels of Meale
> **Two bushels of Pease**
> Two bushels of Oatmeale
> One gallon of Aquavitae
> One gallon of Oyle
> Two gallons of Vinegar

A universal food. Beans with bacon, one of the oldest English dishes, long based on the tradition of pottage. After all, a fourteenth-century cookbook mentions this combination. Look at this, too, from the 1390 manuscript, *The Forme of Cury*:

I. For to make Gronden Benes
Take benes and dry hem in a nost or in an Ovene and hulle hem wele and wyndewe out þe hulk and wayshe hem clene an do hem to seeþ in gode broth an ete hem with Bacon.

Not exactly baked beans as we now know them or soup beans, but proof enough that the marriage of beans and bacon (or ham) has been a long one indeed, bacon and beans obviously being one of the oldest of English, nay, European dishes.

As I have mentioned many times before, Hannah Glasse's cookbook appeared constantly in advertising in colonial newspapers in America. Martha Washington owned a copy, now in the Fred W. Smith National Library for the Study of George Washington at Mount Vernon.

Here's Hannah Glasse's take on things beans and bacon:

To dress Beans and Bacon

When you dress Beans and Bacon, boil the Bacon by itself and the Beans by themselves, for the Bacon will spoil the Colour of the Beans. Always throw some Salt into the Water and some Parsley nicely pick'd. When the Beans are enough (which you will know by their being tender) throw them into a Collender to drain. Take up the Bacon and Skin it; throw some Raspings of Bread over the Top, and if you have an Iron make it red-hot and hold over it, to brown the top of the Bacon. If you have not one, set it before the fire to brown. Lay the Beans in the Dish, and the Bacon in the Middle on the Top, and send them to Table with Butter in a Bason.

From time immemorial, humans have been borrowing culinary ideas, doing what they can to survive and to make money. Perhaps it's time to ask just who is appropriating whom. Or maybe, just maybe, no one is appropriating anyone.

Maybe a better word is simply this: sharing.

The late Lord Dudley could not dine comfortably without an apple pie.
~ Abraham Hayward

Figure 48. Vintage Illustration of Geese

SO, JUST WHAT IS AMERICAN CUISINE?

WHO KNOWS?

Jean Hewitt, author of *The New York Times Heritage Cookbook* of 1980 states, "It is unfortunate that a foreign visitor can travel on our superhighways from coast to coast [about 1544 miles], Maine to Florida, and go away with the impression that Americans subsist largely on a diet of hot dogs, hamburgers and soggy French fries."

With that comment, Ms. Hewitt unwittingly joined a large chorus of observers—mostly non-Americans—over the years who stared dumbfounded at the eating habits of "those Americans." Interestingly, Hewitt focuses only on the heritage of immigrants other than the English and includes only four recipes related to the myriad Chinese immigrants of California. Take a look at the jabs of Margaret Hunter Hall, Frances Trollope, Edouard Montulé, and Thomas Hamilton for more evidence of this disdain.

Hall's 1820 comments serve as a prime example of this disdain:

> It goes rather against one's feelings to see a prettily dressed, nice-looking, young woman ladling rice pudding into her mouth with the point of a great knife, and yesterday to my great horror I saw a nursery maid feeding an infant of seventeen months in the same way. I must own the woman deserved credit for her dexterity in not cutting the child's mouth.

American food stands under a large umbrella these days, thanks to the enormous numbers of immigrants still coming here seeking the same things my English ancestors sought in the 1600s. I admit that calling the food of the United States "American" is not entirely correct. After all, we do share the hemisphere with many other countries, but it suits my purposes. I mean, if Budweiser can co-opt the name "America" for their beer, well....

Forget Margaret Hunter Hall's gripes about eating with knives. Forget shriveled hot dogs and hockey-puck hamburgers and flabby slices of pizza. Forget McDonald's.

Hey, I only eat hot dogs about once every five years.

That said, I will own up to the fact that not long ago, I ate every bite of two chili dogs and all the crinkle-cut French fries at The Weiner Stand in the Roanoke City Market. Those hot dogs conjured up everything despicable to today's health-conscious food advocates: salt, grease, questionable meat, mass-produced French fries, and corn-syrup-rich root beer.

Honestly? I loved every morsel.

And I feel the same way about the food of my vast and diverse country. After a few weeks whenever I traveled to France or Africa or the Caribbean or Asia, I'd pine away for the food of home, dreaming of specific dishes that set my blood on fire with longing. Like many exiles, when I lived in various developing countries, I searched for ways to recreate the tastes of home using local ingredients. The recipes I knew served as templates for these dishes, which were not new inventions, just modified versions of old ways of cooking the things I longed for. Peach pie easily became mango pie in Haiti, cream added to a farmer-like soft cheese substituted for ricotta in Morocco, and a local shortening-like industrially produced fat worked well for flour tortillas in Burkina Faso.

So, here's the question again: Just what *is* American food?

It is easy to say what it is not.

Pundits claim a melting pot exists in the United States.

But that's not true.

I suggest that American food rather resembles a composed salad, all the ingredients together but separate and distinguishable. Our cooking is very regional and has been for some time, as Mark Twain so aptly noted. It is true that because of long exposure to British culture, as well as other European cultures, the predominant cooking pattern circled around those for almost 300 years. This makes complete sense, for food habits are among the last things to change when exiles leave their homelands.

David Rosenberg nailed it with a comment in *It's All American Food* in 2003, when referring to the immigrants and others who stepped on these shores, beginning way back when the first Native Americans took possession of their lands: "They worked old ideas into new forms here." In other words, cooks built on pre-existing ways of cooking.

It's a complicated subject, is American cooking, compounded by history, geography, technology, class, and race. It's hard to say exactly when the great shift occurred from a primarily English culinary orientation to an acceptance of other foodways. Certainly, the mass immigration that began after the end of the Civil War affected all aspects of American food, because immigrants wanted to eat their own food. Home economists of the late nineteenth and early twentieth centuries strove mightily to dissuade housewives—not native-born—to leave their old food-ways in the dust and embrace the American way in the kitchen. As Suky Hutton writes in *Tastes of Liberty: A Celebration of Our Great Ethnic Cooking* in 1985, "The individual roots and histories of American citizens would emerge from the four corners of the earth, but America's national ancestry was firmly, unmistakably British."

American ways in the kitchen changed gradually as years passed. It's possible to see this change in the cookbooks that appeared, the types of ingredients available in the markets, the focus of advertising, the loss of servants, etc. Nineteenth-century cookbooks generally read like their English cousins of the day. But all the while, subtle changes, and inroads worked to dilute somewhat the influence of the earliest culinary traditions in the United States.

In the late twentieth century and early twenty-first century, cookbook authors have tried to codify the unwieldy creature that is now American cooking. The latest rendition of *Joy of Cooking*, for many decades nearly every American bride's kitchen bible, stuffs in all manner of international and ethnic recipes into its 1,156 pages. But the basics, the backbone, still pay homage to the English kitchen.

Cookbooks supply what I like to think of snapshots of time. Practices frozen in the time and place when an author wrote, not always carried on in future editions. It takes a thorough sweep through a stream of cookbooks to see the trends, the changes, the differences wrought by the outer world.

Presentism cannot play a role in this process. Yet, that is exactly what has occurred in much culinary writing in the last decade. Examining the past through the lens of the present.

Presentism ignores the very English heritage of American food. Meat, beans, potatoes, cake, and pie appeared on the tables of both the wealthier classes and those of the poorer rungs of society. This dietary pattern still persists in pockets across the country, with the famous "meat and three" of the American South as one example.

Consider Mark Twain's list of what he considered American food. Written in a European hotel room in a moment of deep longing for his homeland and later published in *A Tramp Abroad*.

> It has now been many months, at the present writing, since I have had a nourishing meal, but I shall soon have one—a modest, private affair, all to myself. I have selected a few dishes, and made out a little bill of fare, which will go home in the steamer that precedes me, and be hot when I arrive ....

He then lists dozens of dishes, many preceded by the word "American." But the following dishes are not entirely American in origin:

Baked apples, with cream
Fried oysters; stewed oysters
Fried chicken, Southern style
Porter-house steak
Saratoga potatoes
Broiled chicken, American style
Hot biscuits, Southern style
Hot wheat-bread, Southern style
American toast
Virginia bacon, broiled
Blue points, on the half shell
Cherry-stone clams
San Francisco mussels, steamed
Oyster soup
Philadelphia Terrapin soup
American roast beef
Roast turkey, Thanksgiving style
Celery
Roast wild turkey
Woodcock
Canvas-back-duck, from Baltimore
Missouri partridges, broiled
Boston bacon and beans
Bacon and greens, Southern style
Boiled onions
Turnips
Asparagus
Lettuce
String beans
Mashed potatoes
Catsup
Boiled potatoes, in their skins
Apple dumplings, with real cream
Apple pie
Apple fritters
Peach cobbler, Southern style

Peach pie

American mince pie

All sorts of American pastry

Fresh American fruits of all sorts, including strawberries

And a glance at Edna Lewis's famous posthumously published article, "What is Southern?," follows the same trend as Twain's. Hidden among the various dishes now strongly associated with so-called Southern cooking lie such gems as braised leg of mutton, beets "in a vinaigrette sauce," "English peas in cream," herring, asparagus "served on toast, with a rich cream sauce spooned over," strawberries, turtle soup, yeast rolls, potted shrimp, and "desserts galore," including white groom's cake, a type of fruitcake. All these delicacies would be right at home in an English cookbook. In fact, an Englishwoman once whispered to me that Edna Lewis's wonderful *A Taste of Country Cooking* reads just like an English cookbook! Again, here's an unpopular idea: Might it be said that a great deal of what people today consider peculiar to the American kitchen is actually appropriated from English cooking?

Mizald's cruel instructions to "Take a Goose or a Duck" notwithstanding, this book celebrates the glories of English cooks, cookery books, and cuisine. And indirectly its impact on the food and cooking of the United States. It's best to say that despite attempts to denigrate it, English cooking did, and still does, form the backbone of traditional American cooking.

It is The Mother Cuisine.

No one who cooks, cooks alone. Even at her [sic] most solitary, a cook in the kitchen is surrounded by generations of cooks past, the advice and menus of cooks present, the wisdom of cookbook writers.

~ Laurie Colwin

Figure 49. Joseph Ritson

BIBLIOGRAPHY

Acton, Eliza. *Modern Cookery in all its Branche, Reduced to a System of Easy Practice for the Use of Private Families.* London: Longmans & Co., 1845.

Anderson, Virginia DeJohn. *Creatures of Empire: How Domestic Animals Transformed Early America.* Oxford: Oxford University Press, 2006.

Andrews, Colman. *The British Table.* New York: Abrams, 2016.

Anglo-Saxon Leechcraft: an historical sketch of early English medicine: lecture memoranda. American Medical Association, Atlantic City, 1912.

Appandurai, A. "How to Make a National Cuisine: Cookbooks in Contemporary India." *Comparative Studies in Society and History* 30: 3–24, 1988.

Appelbaum, Robert. "Rhetoric and Epistemology in Early Printed Recipe Collections." *Journal of Early Modern Cultural Studies* 3 (2): 1–35, 2003.

Aylett, Mary and Ordish, Olive. "Mrs. Isabella Beeton, 1836–865." In: *First Catch Your Hare: A History of the Recipe Makers.* London: Macdonald, 1965, 220–239.

A.W. *A booke of Cookre Very necessary for all such as delight therein.* London: Allde, 1584.

Bagnasco, Orazio. *Catalogo del fondo italiano e latino delle opera di gastronomia sec. xiv-xix.* Canton Ticino: Edizione B.IN.G., 1994.

Beeton, Isabella. *Mrs. Beeton's Book of Household Management.* Oxford World's Classics. Abridged Edition. Edited by Nicola Humble. Oxford: Oxford University Press, 2000.

Biebel, Elizabeth M. "Pilgrims to Table: Food Consumption in Chaucer's *Canterbury Tales.*" In: *Food and Eating in Medieval Europe.* Martha Carlin and Joel T. Rosenthal, eds. London and Rio Grande: Hambledon, 1998, 15–26.

Bilton, Sam. *First Catch Your Gingerbread.* Blackawton, Totnes, Devon, U.K.: Prospect Books, 2021.

Bitting, Katherine Golden. *Gastronomic Bibliography.* Mansfield, CT: Martino Publishing, 2004. (Reprint of 1939 edition.)

Bittman, Mark. *How to Cook Everything.* Boston: Houghton Mifflin Harcourt, 2019. (Reprint of 1998 edition.)

Blackwood, Harriet Georgina, Marchioness of Dufferin & Ava. *Our Viceregal Life in India: Selections from My Journal, 1884–1888.* London: John Murray, 1890.

Blencowe, Lady Anne. *The Receipt Book of Lady Anne Blencoe.* Christina Stapeley, ed. n.p.: Heartsease Books, 2004. (Reprint of 1694 edition.)

Boase, Tessa. *The Housekeeper's Tale: The Women Who Really Ran the English Country House.* London: Aurum, 2014.

The Boke of Cokery. London: Richard Pynson, 1500.

The boke of keruynge. London: Enprynted by Wynkyn de Worde at London in fletestrete at the sygne of the sonne, The yere of our lorde god. 1513.

The Book of Sent Soví: Medieval Recipes from Catalonia. Joan Santanach, ed. Barcelona: Barcino-Tamesis, 2008. (From a fourteenth-century manuscript.)

Boorde, Andrew. *Fyrst boke of the Introduction of knowledge.* London: N.T. Trübner & Co, 1870. (Early English Text Society reprint of 1550 edition.)

_____. *Hereafter foloweth a compendyous regyment or a dyetary of helth: made in Mou[n] tpyllier, compyled by Andrew Boorde of physiycke doctour, dedycated to the armypotent prynce, and valyaunt Lorde Thomas Duke of Northfolche.* London: Robert Wyer, 1542. (*Dyetary of helth*)

Booth, Sally Smith. *Hung, Strung and Potted: A History of Eating Habits in Colonial America.* New York: C. N. Potter, 1971.

Boswell, James. *Boswell's Life of Johnson.* Charles Grosvenor Osgood, ed. New York: Scribner's Sons, 1917. (Reprint of 1791 edition.)

Bottéro, Jean. *The Oldest Cuisine in the World: Cooking in Mesopotamia.* Chicago: University of Chicago Press, 2002.

Botkin, Stephen. "The Anglo-American Book Trade before 1776: Personnel and Strategies." In: *Printing and Society in Early America.* William L. Joyce et al., eds. Worcester: American Antiquarian Society, 1983.

Boxer, Arabella. *Arabella Boxer's Book of English Food.* London: Fig Tree, 2012.

Bradley, E.G. A Household Book for Tropical Colonies. Oxford: Oxford University Press, 1948.

Bradley, Martha. *The British Housewife.* London: S. Crowther and H. Woodgate, 1756.

Bradley, Richard. *The Country Housewife and Lady's Director.* London: D Browne, at the Black Swan without Temple Bar, 1736.

Brandon, Ruth. *The People's Chef: Alexis Soyer: A Life in Seven Courses.* New York: Wiley, 2005.

Brears, Peter. *All the King's Cooks: The Tudor Kitchens of King Henry VIII at Hampton Court Palace.* London: Souvenir, 1999.

_____. *Cooking and Dining in Medieval England.* Blackawton, Totnes, Devon, U.K.: Prospect Books, 2007.

_____. *Cooking and Dining in Tudor and Early Stuart England.* Blackawton, Totnes, Devon, U.K.: Prospect Books, 2015.

Bridge, Tom and English, Colin Cooper. *Dr. William Kitchiner: Regency Eccentric—Author of "The Cook's Oracle".* London: Southover Press, 1992.

Briggs, Richard. *The English Art of Cookery.* London: G.G.J. & J. Robinson, 1788.

Brooks, Catherine. *The Complete English Cook; or Prudent Housewife.* London: The Authoress, 1765.

Brown, Eleanor and Bob. *Culinary Americana.* New York: Martino, 1999. (Reprint of 1961 edition.)

Burnet, Regula. *Ann Cook and Friend.* London: Oxford University Press, 1936.

Burnett, John. *Plenty and Want: A Social History of Food in England from 1815 to the Present Day.* London: Routledge, 1989.

Byrd, William. *Natural History of Virginia.* Petersburg: Ruffin, 1840. (Reprint.)

Cagle, William R. *A Matter of Taste: A Bibliographic Catalogue of the Gernon Collection of Food and Drink.* New York: Garland Publishing, 1990.

Carlton, Jan. *Richmond Receipts Past & Present.* Richmond, VA: Donning Company Publishers. 1987.

Carroll, Ruth. "The Middle English Recipe as a Text-Type." *Neuphilologische Mitteilungen* 100 (1): 27–42, 1999.

Carson, Jane. *Colonial Virginia Cookery.* Williamsburg, VA: Colonial Williamsburg, 1968.

Carter, Angela. "Saucier's Apprentice." In: *Shaking a Leg: Collected Journalism and Writings.* London: Vintage, 2013, 104–108.

Carter, Charles. *The Complete Practical Cook.* London: W. Meadows, C. Rivington, R Hett, 1730.

Carter, Susannah. *The Frugal Colonial Housewife, or Complete Woman Cook.* n.p.: Dolphin Books, 1976. (Reprint, annotated from 1772.)

Chaney, Lisa. *Elizabeth David: A Biography.* London: Pan, 1999.

Chateau St. Michelle. *Tastes of Liberty: A Celebration of Our Great Ethnic Cooking.* New York: Stewart, Tabori & Chang, 1985.

Cheyne, George. *An Essay of Health and Long Life.* London: printed for George Strahan; and J. Leake, Bath, 1724.

Clutterbuck, Lady Catherine. *What Shall We Have for Dinner?* London: Bradbury & Evans, 1851 [written by Catherine Dickens]

Cochrane, John. *The Seaman's Guide Shewing How to Live Comfortably at Sea.* London: J. Murray, 1797.

Collingham, Lizzie. *The Hungry Empire: How Britain's Quest for Food Shaped the Modern World.* New York: Basic Books, 2007.

_____. *The Taste of War: World War II and the Battle for Food.* New York: Penguin, 2012.

Collins, John. *Salt And Fishery.* London: Printed by A. Godbid and J. Playford, and are to be sold by Mr. Robert Horne at the Royal Exchange, in St. Pauls Church-yard, Mr. William Bury, Globe-maker ..., 1682.

Colquhoun, Kate. *Taste: The Story of Britain through its Cooking.* London: Bloomsbury, 2007.

Cook, Ann. *Professed Cookery.* Newcastle: J. White, 1754.

Cook, Margaret. *America's Charitable Cooks: A Bibliography of Fund-raising Cook Books Published in the United States (1861–1915).* Kent, Ohio: Cookery Bibliography, 1971.

Cooke, Maud C. *Social Etiquette: or Manners and Customs of Polite Society.* London: McDermid & Logan, 1896.

Cool. H.E.M. *Eating and Drinking in Roman Britain.* Cambridge: Cambridge University Press, 2006.

Cooper, Artemis. *Writing at the Kitchen Table: The Authorized Biography of Elizabeth David.* London: Faber and Faber, 2000.

Cooper, Joseph. *The Art of Cookery Refin'd and Augmented.* London: J.G. for R. Lowndes, 1654.

Cowan, Ruth. *Relish: The Extraordinary Life of Alexis Soyer, Victorian Celebrity Chef.* London: Orion, 2008.

Cox, Robert S. *New England Pie: History Under a Crust.* Cheltenham, UK: The History Press, 2015.

The Court & kitchin of Elizabeth, commonly called Joan Cromwel the wife of the late usurper, truly described and represented, and now made publick for general satisfaction. London: Printed by Tho. Milbourn for Randal Taylor ..., 1664.

Crosby, Alfred E. *The Columbian Exchange: Biological and Cultural Consequences of 1492.* Green Wood, N.Y.: Greenwood, 1972.

_____. *Ecological Imperialism: The Biological Expansion of Europe, 900–1900.*

Crophill, John. *Commonplace Book.* Harley MS 1735, ff 1r-28v., 1485. Cambridge, U.K.: Cambridge University Press, 1986.

Culpeper, Nicholas. *Complete Herbal.* London: Thomas Kelly, 1850. (Reprint of 1653 edition.)

Currah, Anne M., ed. *Chef to Queen Victoria: the Recipes of Charles Elmé Francatelli.* London: Kimber, 1973.

David, Elizabeth. "Isabella Beeton and Her Book." In: *An Omelette and a Glass of Wine.* London: Viking, 1986, 303–309. (Reprinted from *Wine and Food*, Spring 1961.)

Davidson, Alan. *North Atlantic Seafood.* New York: First Viking, 1980.

_____. *The Wilder Shores of Gastronomy.* Berkeley: Ten Speed Press, 2002.

Davis, Jennifer J. *Defining Culinary Authority: The Transformation of Cooking in France, 1650–1830*. Baton Rouge, LA: LSU Press, 2013.

Davies, Jennifer. *The Wartime Kitchen and Garden: The Home Front 1939–1945*. London: BBC Consumer Publishing, 1993.

Dawson, Thomas. *The Good Huswifes Jewell*. London: Edward White, 1585.

Day, Helen. "Isabella Beeton." In: *Culinary Biographies*. Alice Arndt, ed. Houston, Texas: Yes Press, 2006, 57–59.

Day, Ivan. "From Murrell to Jarrin: Illustrations in British Cookery Books, 1621–1820." In: *The English Cookery Book, Historical Essays*. Eileen White, ed. Totnes, Devon: Prospect Books, 2004, 98–150.

Deetz, Kelley Fanto. *Bound to the Fire: How Virginia's Enslaved Cooks Helped Invent American Cuisine*. Lexington: University Press of Kentucky, 2017.

Digby, Sir Kenelm. *The Closet of the Eminently Learned Sir Kenelme Digbie Opened*. London: H. Brome, 1669.

Dodds, Madeline Hope. "The Rival Cooks: Hannah Glasse and Ann Cook." *Archaeologia aeliana*. 4 (15): 43–68, 1938.

Dorling Kindersley. *History of Britain & Ireland*. London, DK, 2019.

Driver, Christopher and Berriedale-Johnson, Michelle. *Pepys at Table: Seventeenth-Century Recipes for the Modern Cook*. New York: HarperCollins, 1984.

Driver, Elizabeth. *A Bibliography of Cookery Books Published in Britain, 1875–1914*. Blackawton, Totnes, Devon, U.K.: Prospect Books, 1989 and 2012.

_____. "Cookbooks as Primary Sources for Writing History, A Bibliographer's View." In: *Food, Culture and Society*. 12 (3): 257–274, September 2009.

Dubois, A. [Analysis of frontispieces in seventeenth-century books from the Rouen libraries collections]. (In French) *Revue d'histoire de la pharmacie (Paris)*. 52 (344): 559–74, 2004.

Eales, Mary. *Mrs. Mary Eales's receipts*. London: R. Montagu, 1733.

Earle, Rebecca. " 'If You Eat Their Food …' ": Diets and Bodies in Early Colonial Spanish America." *American Historical Review* 115 (3): 688–713, June 2010.

Eatherley, Dan. "What Have the Romans Done for Us?" *History Today*. July 2019, 15–17.

Eden, Trudy. *The Early American Table: Food and Society in the World*. DeKalb: Northern Illinois University Press, 2008.

Eisenstein, Elizabeth. *The Printing Revolution in Early Modern Europe*. New York: Cambridge University Press, 1983.

Ehrenreich, Barbara and English, Deirdre. *Witches, Midwives, and Nurses*. New York: Feminist Press at CUNY, 1973. (Reprint 2010.)

Elkins, Caroline. *Legacy of Violence: A History of the British Empire*. NY: Knopf, 2022.

Erol, Burçin. "Food Culture and Food Imagery in Chaucer's *Canterbury Tales*." In: *The Routledge Companion to Literature and Food*. Lorna Piatti-Farnell, and Donna Lee Brien, eds. Abingdon: Routledge, 2018.

Evelyn, John. *John Evelyn, Cook: The Manuscript Receipt Book of John Evelyn*. Blackawton, Totnes, Devon, U.K.: Prospect Books, 1997.

_____. *The Diary of John Evelyn*. London: Boydell, 2004. [Written between 1640 and 1706]

_____. *The Rusticall and Economical Works of John Evelyn: Acetaria, a Discourse of Sallets*. London: B. Tooke, 1699.

Ezell, Margaret J.M. "Cooking the books, or, the three faces of Hannah Woolley." In: *Reading and Writing: Recipe Books 1550–1800*. Michelle DiMeo and Sara Pennell, eds. Manchester: Manchester University Press, 2013.

Farley, John. *The London Art of Cookery*. London: John Barker, 1800.

Febvre, Lucien and Martin, Henri-Jean. *The Coming of the Book: The Impact of Printing, 1450–1800*. 3rd edition. New York: Verso, 2010.

Feild, Rachel. *Irons in the Fire: A History of Cooking Equipment*. Ramsbury: The Crowood Press, 1984.

Feret, Barbara L. *Gastronomical and Culinary Literature: A Survey and Analysis of Historically-Oriented* [sic] *Collection in the U.S.A*. Metuchen, N.J.: The Scarecrow Press, Inc. 1979.

Fischer, David Hackett. *Albion's Seed: Four British Folkways in America*. Oxford, UK: Oxford University Press, 1991.

Fischer, Steven Roger. *A History of Reading*. London: Reaktion Books, 2004.

Fisher, Abby. *What Mrs. Fisher Knows About Old Southern Cooking*. Karen Hess, ed. San Francisco: Women's Co-operative Printing Office, 1881.

Fisher, M.F.K. "The Anatomy of a Recipe." In: *With Bold Knife &Fork*. New York: A Paragon Book, 1968, 13–24.

_____. *How to Cook a Wolf*. Berkeley: North Point Press, 1988.

Fitchett, Laura Simkins. *Beverages and Sauces of Colonial Virginia, 1607 -1907*. New York: The Neale Publishing Company, 1906.

Floyd, Janet and Forster, Laurel. "The Recipe in its Cultural Context." In: *The Recipe Reader: Narratives, Contexts, Traditions*. Janet Floyd and Laurel Forster, eds. Lincoln: University of Nebraska Press, 2003.

The Forme of Cury. Samuel Pegge, ed. J. Nichols: London, 1780. (From 1391 manuscript.)

Fowler, Damon Lee. *Classical Southern Cooking*. New York: Gibbs Smith, 2008.

_____, ed. *Dining at Monticello*. Charlottesville: Thomas Jefferson Foundation, 2011.

Francatelli, Charles Elmé. *A Plain Cookery Book for the Working Classes*. London: Routledge, Warne, and Routledge, 1852.

Freeman, Sarah. *Isabella and Sam: The Story of Mrs. Beeton*. London: Victor Gollancz, Ltd., 1977.

_____. *Mutton and Oysters: The Victorians and their Food*. London: Victor Gollanz LTD, 1989.

Gerard, John. *Herbal or General History of Plants*. London: Adam Islip, Joice Norton and Richard Whitakers, 1597.

Gillies, Sarah. "Seeing Through Glasse." *Petits Propos Culinaires*. 22: 32, 1986.

Gittings, Robert. *Shakespeare's Rival*. Berkeley: University of California Press, 1960.

Glasse, Hannah. *"First Catch Your Hare ...": The Art of Cookery, Made Plain and Easy*, by a Lady. Blackawton, Totnes, Devon, U.K.: Prospect Books, 2012. (Facsimile of 1747 first edition.)

Gold, Carol. *Danish Cookbooks: Domesticity and National Identity, 1616–1901*. Seattle: University of Washington Press, 2007.

Goldenson, Suzanne and Simpson, Doris. *The Open-Hearth Cookbook: Recapturing the Flavor of Early America*. Revised edition. Chambersburg, Pa: Alan C. Hood, 2006.

Goldstein, David. "Woolley's Mouse: Early Modern Recipe Books and the Uses of Nature." *Ecofeminist Approaches to Early Modernity*. Jennifer Munroe and Rebecca Laroche, eds. New York: Palgrave MacMillan, 2011, 105–128.

Görlach, Manfred. "Text-Types and Language History: The Culinary Recipe." In: *History of Englishes: New Methods and Interpretations in Historical Linguistics*. Matti Rissanen et al., eds. New York: Mouton de Gruyter, 1992.

Grainger, Sally. "The Myth of Apicius." *Gastronomica*. Spring 2007, 71–77.

Gray, Patience. *Honey from a Weed: Fasting and Feasting in Tuscany, Catalonia, the Cyclades and Apulia*. New York: Harper & Row, 1987.

Green, Thomas. *Universal Herbal*. Liverpool: Nuttall, Fisher, & Dixon, [1820?]. (Reprint of 1532 edition.)

Grewe, Rudolf and Hieatt, Constance B. *Libellus de arte coquinaria: An Early Northern Cookery Book*. London: ACMRS Press, 2001.

Grossman, Anne Chotzinoff and Thomas, Lisa Grossman. *Lobscouse & Spotted Dog: Which It's a Gastronomic Companion to the Aubrey/Maturin Novels*. New York: W.W. Norton & Co., 1997.

Hagen, Ann *Anglo-Saxon Food & Drink*. n.p: Anglo-Saxon Books, 2006.

_____. *A Handbook of Anglo-Saxon Food: Processing and Consumption*. n.p: Anglo-Saxon Books, 1992.

_____. *A Second Handbook of Anglo-Saxon Food & Drink: Production & Distribution.* n.p: Anglo-Saxon Books, 1995.

Hakluyt, Richard. *A Discourse Concerning Western Planting, Written in the Year 1584.* Charles Deane, ed. Cambridge: Press of J. Wilson and son, 1877.

Hall, Margaret Hunter. *The Aristocratic Journey: Being the Outspoken Letters of Mrs. Basil Hall Written during a Fourteen Months' Sojourn in America, 1827-1828.* Una Pope-Hennessey, ed. New York: G.P. Putnam's Sons, 1931, 20–21.

Harleian Manuscript 279 c. 1430. In: *Two Fifteenth-Century Cookery Books.* Thomas Austin, ed. London: Oxford University Press, 1964.

Harris, David R. *Origins of Agriculture in Western Central Asia: An Environmental Archaeological Study.* Philadelphia: University of Pennsylvania Press, 2010.

Hartley, Dorothy. *Food in England.* London: Macdonald, 1954.

Haywood, Eliza. *A New Present for A Servant-Maid: containing Rules for her Moral Conduct, both with respect to Herself and her Superiors: The Whole Art of Cookery, Pickling, and Preserving, &c, &c. and every other Direction necessary to be known to render her a Complete, Useful and Valuable Servant.* London: G. Pearch and H. Gardner, 1771.

Hazlett, William Carew. *Old Cookery Books and Ancient Cuisine.* London: Popular Edition, 1902.

Hecht, Jean. *The Domestic Serving Class in Eighteenth-Century England.* London: Routledge, 1956.

Henssler, Maria Paleari. *Bibliografia Latino-Italiana di Gastronomia.* Milan: Chimera Editore, 2001.

Hess, Karen, ed. *Martha Washington's Booke of Cookery.* New York: Columbia University Press, 1995.

Hieatt, Constance B. "A Cook They Had With Them For the Nones." *Chaucer's Pilgrims: An Historical Guide to the Pilgrims in* The Canterbury Tales. Laura C. Lambdin, and Robert T. Lambdin, eds. Westport, Connecticut and London: Praeger, 1996, 199–209.

_____. "Further notes on *The Forme of Cury* et al.: additions and corrections." *Bulletin of the John Rylands Library.* 70 (1): 45–52, 1988.

_____, Constance B. *An Ordinance of Pottage.* Blackawton, Totnes, Devon, U.K.: Prospect Books, 1988.

Hieatt, Constance B. and Jones, Robin F. "Two Anglo-Norman Culinary Collections Edited from British Library Manuscripts Additional 32085 and Royal 12.C.xii." *Speculum.* 61 (4): 859-882, October 1986.

Hieatt, Constance B. and Butler, Sharon. *Curye on Inglysch.* Oxford: Oxford University Press, 1985.

Hill, Bridget. *Servants: English Domestics in the Eighteenth Century.* Oxford: Clarendon, 1996.

Hill, Shaun and Wilkins, John. "Mithaikos and Other Greek Cooks." In: *Cooks & Other People: Proceedings of the Oxford Symposium on Food and Cookery.* Walker, Harlan, ed. Blackawton, Totnes, Devon, U.K.: Prospect Books, 1996, 144–48.

Hobby, Elaine. "A Woman's Best Setting Out Is Silence: The Writings of Hannah Woolley." In: *Culture and Society in the Stuart Restoration.* Gerald MacLean, ed. Cambridge: Cambridge University Press, 1995, 179–200

Hope, Annette. *Londoners' Larder: English Cuisine from Chaucer to the Present.* London: Trafalgat Square, 1992.

Houston, R. A. *Literacy in Early Modern Europe.* New York: Longman, 2002.

Hughes, Kathryn. *The Short Life and Long Times of Mrs. Beeton.* New York: Knopf, 2006.

Humble, Nicola. *Culinary Pleasures: Cookbooks and the Transformation of British Food.* London: Faber and Faber, 2005.

Hunter, Lynette. *Cookery and Household Affairs: Books Published in Britain, 1800–1914.* London and New York: Prospect Books, in association with Mansell Publishing, 1982.

Jackson, John K. *Notes and Queries: A Medium of Intercommunication for Literary Men General Readers, etc.* London. Fifth series, volume 12, July–December 1870.

Jaine, Tom. "Do Cookery Books Tell the Truth?" In: *Culinary History.* A. Lynn Martin and Barbara Santich, eds. Brompton, Australia: East Street Publications, 2004, 87–96.

Jones, Steve and Taylor, Ben. "Food Writing and Food Cultures: The Case of Elizabeth David and Jane Grigson." *European Journal of Cultural Studies* 4: 171–188, 2001.

Kellet, Susanna, Elizabeth Kellet and Mary Kellet. *A Complete Collection of Cookery Receipts.* Newcastle-upon-Tyne: T. Saint, 1780.

Kenney-Herbert, Colonel Arthur (Wyvern). *Culinary Jottings for Madras.* Madras: Higginbotham, 1878.

Kernan, Sarah Peters. " 'For al them that delight in Cookery': The Production and Use of Cookery Books in England, 1300–1600." Ph.D. diss., The Ohio State University, 2016.

Kettilby, Mary. *Collection of Above Three Hundred Receipts in Cookery, Physick, and Surgery.* London: W. Parker, 1714.

Keynes, Sir Geoffery. *John Evelyn, A Study in Bibliophily with a Bibliography of His Writings.* Oxford: Clarendon Press, 1968.

Kidder, Edward. *The Receipts of Pastry and Cookery.* London: n.p., 1720.

Kitchiner, William. *The Cook's Oracle: Containing receipts for plain cookery on the most economical plan for private families, etc.* London: J. Hatchard, 1818.

Kowalchuk, Kristine, ed. *Preserving on Paper: Seventeenth-Century Englishwomen's Receipt Books.* Toronto: University of Toronto Press, 2017.

Kunjappu, Joy. "Ink Chemistry." *Chemistry World.* London: Royal Society of Chemistry, March 2003. https://www.chemistryworld.com/news/ink-chemistry/3002158.article

Lamb, Patrick. *Royal Cookery or, the complete court cook.* London: Abel Roper, 1710.

Langseth-Christensen, Lillian. *The Mystic Seaport Cookbook.* New York: Galahad Books, 1970.

Laudan, Rachel. *Cuisine and Empire: Cooking in World History.* Berkeley: University of California Press, 2013.

Lawson, Russell. *Servants and Servitude in Colonial America.* Westport, Conn.: Praeger, 2018.

Lawson, William. *The Country Housewife's Garden.* London: A. Griffin for J. Harrison, 1637.

Lehmann, Gilly. *The British Housewife: Cookery Books, Cooking and Society in Eighteenth-Century Britain.* Blackawton, Totnes, Devon, U.K.: Prospect Books, 2003.

_____. "Politics in the Kitchen." *Eighteenth-Century Life* 23 (2): 71–83, 1999.

Leslie, Eliza. *The Lady's Receipt Book: A Useful Companion for Large or Small Families.* Philadelphia: Carey and Hart, 1847.

Lethbridge, Lucy. *Servants: A Downstairs History of Britain from the Nineteenth Century to Modern Times.* New York: W.W. Norton, 2013.

Levenstein, Harvey. *Revolution at the Table: The Transformation of the American Diet.* Berkeley, CA: University of California Press, 2003.

Lewis, Edna. *The Taste of Country Cooking.* New York: Knopf, 1976.

_____. "What is Southern?" *Gourmet,* January 2008.

Light, Alison. *Mrs. Woolf and the Servants: An Intimate History of Domestic Life in Bloomsbury.* London: Bloomsbury Press, 2010.

Lowenstein, Eleanor. *American Cookery Books, 1742–1860.* Worcester, NY: American Antiquarian Society, 1972.

Lucius Iunius Moderatus Columella. *De Re Rustica. XII 57.* London: Andrew Millar, 1745.

Maclean, Virginia. *A Short-Title Catalogue of Household and Cookery Books Published in the English Tongue, 1701–1800.* Blackawton, Totnes, Devon, U.K.: Prospect Books, 1983.

MacWilliam, Erin Louise Frances. "British Cookbooks and the Transformation of Taste, 1660–1760." Ph.D. dissertation. Vancouver: University of British Columbia, 2014.

Madgwick, R. and Mulville, R. "Feasting on fore-limbs: conspicuous consumption and identity in later prehistoric Britain." *Antiquity* 39: 629–44, 2015.

Mallmann, Francis. *Mallmann on Fire.* New York: Artisan, 2014.

Marcoux, Paula. *Cooking with Fire.* North Adams, Mass.: Story Publishing, 2014.

Markham, Gervase. *The English Housewife, Containing the inward and outward virtues which ought to be in a complete woman* …. Edited by Michael Best. Montreal: McGill-Queen's University Press, 1986. (Transcription of 1615 edition.)

_____. *The Countrie Farmer.* London: Printed by Adam Islip for John Bill, 1616.

Marshall, Agnes B. *Book of Ices.* London: Ward, Lock & Co., 1885.

May, Robert. *The Accomplisht Cook, or, The Art and Mystery of Cookery.* London: Nath. Brooke, 1660.

McCleod, Stephen A. *Dining with the Washingtons.* Raleigh: University of North Carolina Press, 2011.

Mennell, Stephen. "Gutenberg and the Cook." In: *All Manners of Food: Eating and Taste in England and France from the Middles Ages to the Present.* New York: Basil Blackwell, 1985, 64–69.

_____. "Plagiarism and Originality⊠Diffusionism in the Study of the History of Cookery." *Petits Propos Culinaires* 68: 29–38, 2001.

Menon. *La cuisinère bourgeoise.* Paris: Chez Guillyn, 1776.

Meredith, Peter. "The Language of Medieval Cookery." In: *The English Cookery Book: Historical Essays.* Eileen White, ed. Blackawton, Totnes, Devon, U.K.: Prospect Books, 2004, 28–54.

Meyer, Leland Richard. "Fireplace Cookery." In: *The American Fireplace: Chimneys, Mantelpieces, Fireplaces and Accessories.* Henry J. Kauffman, ed. Nashville: Thomas Nelson, 1972, 325–342.

Miller, Adrian. *Soul Food: The Surprising Story of an American Cuisine One Plate at a Time.* Chapel Hill: University of North Carolina Press, 2013.

Mintz, Sidney W. "The Conquest of Honey by Sucrose: A Psychotechnical Achievement." In: *Tasting Food, Tasting Freedom: Excursions into Eating, Power, and the Past.* Boston: Beacon Press, 1996, 50–66.

Moss, Kate and Kathryn Hoffman. *The Backcountry Housewife: A Study of Eighteenth-Century Foods.* Gastonia, N.C.: Schiele Museum of Natural History, 1985 (reprinted 1994, 2001).

Moxon, Elizabeth. *English Housewifery.* Leeds: James Lister, 1741.

Mundy, Peter. *The Travels of Peter Mundy in Europe and Asia, 1608-1667.* London: Hakluyt Society, 2010.

Murrell, John. *A new book of Cookerie, 1615.* New York: Da Capo Press, 1972. (Reprinted.)

Napier, Robina, ed. *A Noble Boke off Cookry ffor a Prynce Houssolde or eny other Estately Houssolde.* London: Elliot Stock, 1882. (Reprinted Verbatim from a Rare MS. in the Holkham Collection.)

Notaker, Henry. "Comments on the Interpretation of Plagiarism." *Petits Propos Culinaires,* July 2002, 58–66.

_____. *Printed Cookbooks in Europe, 1470–1700.* New Castle, DE: Oak Knoll Press, 2010.

_____. *History of Cookbooks: From Kitchen to Page Over Seven Centuries.* Berkeley: University of California Press, 2017.

Nott, John. *The Cook's and Confectioner's Dictionary.* London: Charles Rivington, 1723.

Oberlé, Gérard. *Les fastes de Bacchus et de Comus: ou histoire du boire et du manger en Europe, de l'antiquité à nos jours, à travers les livres.* Paris: Belfond, 1989.

O'Donohue, John. *Eternal Echoes: Celtic Reflections on Our Yearning to Belong.* New York: HarperCollins, 1999.

Ong, Walter J. *Orality and Literacy.* London: Routledge, 2002.

Oxford, Arnold Whitaker. *English Cookery Books to the Year 1850.* London: Holland Press, 1977.

Panich, Paula. "The Countess of Kent." *Gastronomica* 1 (3): 60–66, 2001.

Partridge, John. *The Treasurie of Commodious Conceits, & Hidden Secrets and May be Called, the Huswives Closet, of Healthfull Provision. Mete and necessarie for the profitable use of all estates both men and women.* London: By Richard Iones, 1573.

_____. *The Widdowes Treasure, plentifully furnished with sundry precious and approved Secrets in phisicke and chirurgery, for the health and pleasure of mankinde. …* London: Printed by Edward Alde, for Edward White, 1588.

Patten, Marguerite. *Victory Cookbook: Celebratory Foods on Rations!* London: Hamlyn, 2004.

_____. *We'll Eat Again: A Collection of Recipes from the War Years.* London: Hamlyn, 1985.

Peachey, Stuart. *Cooking Techniques and Equipment, 1580–1660.* Volume 2. Bristol, UK: Stuart Press, 1994.

_____. *Early 17th Century Imported Foods.* Bristol, UK: Stuart Press, 1993.

Pennell, Elizabeth Robins. *My Cookery Books.* New York: Houghton & Mifflin, 1903.

Pennell, Sara. *The Birth of the English Kitchen, 1600–1850.* London: Bloomsbury, 2016.

Pepys, Samuel. *Diaries*. Edited by Henry B. Wheatley. London: George Bell & Sons, 1895. (Abridged editions over the years of 1667 version.)

_____. *The Joys of Excess*. London: Penguin, 2011.

Phipps, Frances. *Colonial Kitchens: Their Furnishings and Their Gardens*. Stroud, U.K.: Hawthorn Press, 1972.

Plat, Sir Hugh. *Delightes for ladies, to adorne their Persons, Tables, closets and distillatoroies*. London: P. Shore, 1602.

Powell, Margaret. *The Downstairs Cookbook*. New York: Macmillan, 2012.

Price, Rebecca. *The Compleat Cook or the secrets of a Seventeenth-Century Housewife*. Compiled and introduced by Madeleine Masson. London: Kegan Paul, 1974.

A Proper Newe Booke of Cokerye. London: Richard Lant and Richard Bankes, 1545.

Raffald, Elizabeth. *The Experienced English Housekeeper*. London: R. Baldwin, 1771.

Randolph, Mary. *The Virginia Housewife*. Washington DC: Davis & Force, 1824.

Remmert, Volker R. "'Docet parva pictura, quod multae scripturae non dicunt': Frontispieces: Functions and Audiences." In: *Transmitting Knowledge: Words, Images, and Instruments in Early Modern Europe*. Sachiko Kusukawa and Ian Maclean, eds. New York: Oxford University Press, 2006, 239–270.

Richardson, R. C. *Household Servants in Early Modern England*. Manchester: Manchester University Press, 2010.

Roberts, Emma. *Scenes and Characteristics of Hindostan with Sketches of Anglo-Indian Society*. London: W.H. Allen and Company, 1825.

Rogers, Ben. *Beef and Liberty: Roast Beef, John Bull and the English Nation*. London: Chatto & Windus, 2003.

Rombauer, Irma S. et al. *Joy of Cooking*. New York: Scribner, 2019.

Ross, Alice. "Frontispieces of Old Cookbooks." *The Journal of Antiques and Collectibles*. Servants and Apprentices Bibliography, Early Modern Hub. March 2001.

Rousseau, Signe. *Food Media: Celebrity Chefs and the Politics of Everyday Interference*. London: Bloomsbury Publishing, 2012.

Rubel, William. *The Magic of Fire*. Berkeley: Ten Speed Press, 2004.

Rundell, Mrs. Maria. *A New System of Domestic Cookery*. London: John Murray, 1806.

Russell, John. *Boke of Nurture*. London: Kegan Paul, 1868. (Reprint of 1460 edition.)

Schmidt, Stephen. "What Manuscript Cooks Can Tell Us that Printed Cookbooks Do Not." *Manuscript Cookbooks Survey blog*, May 2015.

_____. "Southern Cooking: When Did Southern Begin?" *Manuscript Cookbooks Survey blog*, November 2015.

Scott, Elizabeth. " 'A Little Gravy in the Dish and Onions in a Tea Cup': What Cookbooks Reveal about Material Culture." *International Journal of Historical Archaeology* 1 (2): 131–155, 1997.

Schulick, Doug. *Ginger: Common Spice and Wonder Drug.* Chino Valley, Ariz.: Kalindi Press, 2001.

Sedgwick, Romney. "The Duke of Newcastle's Cook." *History Today* 5: 308–316, 1955.

Serjeantson, M. S. "The Vocabulary of Cookery in the Fifteenth Century." *Essays and Studies by Members of The English Association* 23: 25–37. 1938.

Shafer, Daniel L. *William Bartram and the Ghost Plantations of British East Florida.* Gainesville: University Press of Florida, 2010.

Sherman, Sandra. *Invention of the Modern Cookbook.* Santa Barbara, California: Greenwood Press, 2010.

———. "The Whole Art and Mystery of Cooking: What Cookbooks Taught Readers in the Eighteenth Century." *Eighteenth-Century Life* 28 (1): 115–135, 2004.

Shipperbottom, Roy. "Elizabeth Raffald (1733–1781)." In: *Cooks & Other People.* Harlan Walker, ed. Blackawton, Totnes, Devon, U.K.: Prospect Books, 1996, 233–236.

Simon, André L. *Biblioteca gastronomia: A Catalogue of Books and Documents on Gastronomy.* London: Wine and Food Society, 1953.

Smith, E. *The Compleat Housewife: or, Accomplish'd Gentlewoman's Companion.* London: J. Pemberton, 1727.

Smith, John. *A Sea Grammar: With Plaine Exposition of Smiths Accidence for Young Sea-Men.* London: John Haviland, 1627.

Smith, Robert. *Court Cookery: or, the Complete English Cook.* London: T. Wotton, 1723.

Snodgrass, Mary. "Charles Elmé Francatelli." In: *Culinary Biographies.* Alice Arndt, ed. Houston, Texas: Yes Press, Inc., 2006, 169–170.

Sorbiere, M. *A Journey to London in the Year 1698.* Translated by William King. London: A. Baldwin, 1698.

Spain, Nancy. *Mrs. Beeton and her Husband.* London: Collins, 1948.

Spencer, Colin. *British Food: An Extraordinary Thousand Years of History.* New York: Columbia University Press, 2003.

Spencer, Maryellen. "Food in Seventeenth-Century Tidewater Virginia: A Method for Studying Historical Cuisines." Ph.D. dissertation. Department of Human Nutrition and Foods. Virginia Polytechnic Institute and State University, Blacksburg, Virginia, 1982.

Spiller, Elizabeth A., ed. *Seventeenth-Century Recipe Books: Cooking, Physic and Chirurgery in the Works of Elizabeth Talbot Grey and Aletheia Talbot Howard.* London: Routledge, 2016.

Spours, Judy. *Cakes and Ale: The Golden Age of British Feasting.* Kew, Richmond: The National Archives, 2006.

Spurling, Hilary, ed. *Elinor Fettiplace's Receipt Book.* New York: Viking Salamander, 1986.

Stavely, Keith W. F. and Fitzgerald, Kathleen. *Northern Hospitality: Cooking by the Book in New England.* Amherst: University of Massachusetts Press, 2011.

Stead, Jennifer. "Quizzing Glasse: Or Hannah Scrutinized, Part I." *Petits Propos Culinaires* 13: 9–24, 1983.

_____. "Quizzing Glasse: Or Hannah Scrutinized, Part II." *Petits Propos Culinaires* 14: 17–30, 1983.

Suen, Wong Hong. *Wartime Kitchen: Cooking and Eating in Singapore, 1942-1950.* Singapore: National Museum of Singapore, 2009.

Swift, Jonathan. *Directions to Servants.* London: Penguin Books, 1995. (Reprint of 1731 edition.)

Swinburne, Dr. Layinka, M.D. "Dancing with the Mermaids: Ship's Biscuit and Portable Soup." In: *Food on the Move.* Harlan Walker, ed. Blackawton, Totnes, Devon, U.K.: Prospect Books, 1996, p. 314.

Takats, Sean. *The Expert Cook in Enlightenment France.* Baltimore: Johns Hopkins University Press, 2011.

Tinniswood, Adrian. *The Long Weekend: Life in the English Country House, 1918-1939.* New York: Basic Books, 2016.

_____. *Noble Ambitions: The Fall and Rise of the English Country House After World War II.* New York: Basic Books, 2021.

Tomlinson, Graham. "Thought for Food: A Study of Written Instructions." *Symbolic Interactions* 9: 201–216, 1986.

Troubridge, Lady Laura. *Etiquette and Entertaining.* London: Amalgamated Press, 1939.

Tryon, Thomas. *The Good House-wife Made a Doctor.* London: Printed for H.N. and T.S., 1692.

_____. *A treatise of cleanness in meats and drinks of the preparation of food ...* London: Printed for the Author and sold by L. Curtis .., 1682.

Turner, Katherine Leonard. *How the Other Half Ate: A History of Working-Class Meals at the Turn of the Century.* Berkeley, CA: University of California Press, 2014.

Twain, Mark. *A Tramp Abroad.* Hartford, Conn.: American Publishing Company, 1880.

_____. *Wisdom's Dictates*. London: Printed for Tho. Salisbury, 1691.

Tusser, Thomas. *A hundreth good pointes of husbandrie*. London: Trübner & Co., 1878. (Reprint of 1557 edition.)

Van Winter, Johanna Maria. *Spices and Comfits: Collected Papers on Medieval Food*. Blackawton, Totnes, Devon, U.K.: Prospect Books, 2007.

Vehling, Joseph Dommers. *Apicius*. New York: Dover, 1977.

Verrall, William. *Recipes from the White Hart Inn*. London: Penguin Classics, 2011. (Originally published 1759.)

Vicaire, Georges. *Bibliographie gastronomique*. London: Holland Press, 1954. (Reprint of 1890 edition.)

Vickery, Amanda. *Behind Closed Doors: At Home in Georgian England*. New Haven: Yale University Press, 2009.

Vogler, Pen. *Scoff: A History of Food and Class in Britain*. London: Atlantic Books, 2020.

Wall, Wendy. *Recipes for Thought: Knowledge and Taste in the Early Modern English Kitchen*. Philadelphia: University of Pennsylvania Press, 2016.

Walsh, Martin W. "Medieval English Martinmesse: The Archaeology of a Forgotten Festival." *Folklore* 111 (2): 231–254, 2000.

Walter, Eugene. *American Cooking: Southern Style*. New York: Time-Life Books, 1971.

Warnes, Andrew. *Savage BBQ: Race, Culture, and the Invention of America's First Food*. Athens, GA: University of Georgia Press, 2008.

Warner, Richard. *Antiquates Culinariae; or curious tracts relating to the culinary affairs of the old English*. Blackawton, Totnes, Devon, U.K.: Prospect Books, 1981. (Reprint of 1791 edition.)

Waterhouse, Edward. *A Declaration of the State of the Colony and Affaires in Virginia*. London: n.p., 1622.

Wecker, Johann Jacob. *Eighteen Books of the Secrets of Art and Nature*. London: Simon Miller, 1660.

Wertsman, Vladimir F. *What's Cooking in Multicultural America: An Annotated Bibliographic Guide to over Four Hundred Ethnic Cuisines*. Lanham, Md.: The Scarecrow Press, Inc., 1996.

Wheaton, Barbara K. *Savoring the Past: The French Kitchen and Table from 1300 to 1789*. Philadelphia: University of Pennsylvania Press, 1983.

White, Florence. *Good Things in England*. London: Jonathan Cape, 1932.

Willan, Anne and Cherniavsky, Mark. *The Cookbook Library: Four Centuries of the Cooks, Writers, and Recipes That Made the Modern Cookbook*. Berkeley: University of California Press, 2012.

_____. "Literacy in the Kitchen." In: *The Cookbook Library*. Berkeley: University of California Press, 2012, 52–53.

_____. "The Writing of a Recipe," In: *The Cookbook Library*. Berkeley: University of California Press, 2012, 6–11.

Wilson, C. Anne, ed. *"Banqueting Stuffe": The fare and social background of the Tudor and Stuart banquet*. Edinburgh: Edinburgh University Press, 1991.

_____. *Luncheon, Nuncheon and Other Meals: Eating with the Victorians*. Dover, N.H.: Alan Sutton Publishing Limited, 1994.

Winchcombe, Rachel. *Encountering Early America*. Manchester: University of Manchester Press, 2021.

W. M., *The Queens Closet Opened*. London: N. Brook, 1658.

Woolgar, C.M. *The Culture of Food in England, 1200–1500*. New Haven: Yale University Press, 2016.

Woolgar, C.M., Serjeantson, D., and Waldron, T., eds. *Food in Medieval England: Diet and Nutrition*. Oxford: Oxford University Press, 2006.

Woolley/Wolley, Hannah. *The Gentlewomans Companion or, A Guide to the Female Sex*. London: Dorman Newman, 1673.

_____. *Ladies Directory in Choice Experiments & Curiosities*. London: T.M. for Peter Dring, 1662.

_____. . *The Queen-Like Closet*. London: Richard Lowndes, 1672.

Wrangham, Richard. *Catching Fire: How Cooking Made Us Human*. London: Profile Books, 2009.

Wright, Clarissa Dickson. *A History of English Food*. London: Random House, 2011.

Wright, E. et al. "Age and season of pig slaughter at late Neolithic Durrington Walls (Wiltshire, UK) as detected through a new system for recording tooth wear." *Journal of Archaeological Science* 52: 497–514, 2014.

Wynkyn de Worde, *The Boke of Kervynge*. London: W. de Worde, 1508.

Zlotnick, Susan. "On the Publication of Isabella Beeton's *Book of Household Management*, 1861." BRANCH: Britain, Representation and Nineteenth-Century History. Ed. Dino Franco Felluga. Extension of Romanticism and Victorianism on the Net. Web. [Accessed March 13, 2022].

Zweiniger-Bargielowska, Ina. *Austerity in Britain: Rationing, Controls, and Consumption, 1939-1955*. Oxford: Oxford University Press, 2000.

Figure 50. Vintage Kitchenware

ACKNOWLEDGMENTS

First of all, I want to thank those people who read my books. It means a lot, especially the kind, encouraging words. (I can't say the same about the discouraging ones.)

Many, many people from the past contributed greatly to my work in this volume—chroniclers, diarists, scribes, wealthy benefactors, artists, cooks, chefs, and churchmen. Without them, none of us would know much about culinary practices. Of course, I must also thank archaeologists who dirty their hands so that the words of writers may take concrete form.

I mustn't omit a mention of librarians, particularly those who work with digitization. Their efforts make it possible for impecunious researchers like me to travel via their fingertips to parts and place and times otherwise impossible to penetrate. With digitization, the playing field levels more every day, as research no longer requires pots of gold, scarce sponsorships, sparse fellowships, or good-old-boy networking.

Speaking of artists, I would be floundering amidst stick figures like a child learning to hold a crayon if it weren't for Cathy Gibbons Reedy, my friend and marvelously creative book designer and cover wizard.

And then there are the living, breathing people offering their cheers and pats on the back. My friends, some of whom I've never met face-to-face and others from years and years of knowing, deserve thanks for the many sincere comments and support. You know who you are.

Of course, many thanks to Leo Racicot, Janet Perlman, Regula Ysewijn, Sam Bilton, Damon Lee Fowler, and Nicola Miller, who read Advanced Reading Copies and/or wrote blurbs. I really appreciate your input and support. Thanks also to Stephen Schmidt for permission to quote from his work.

The extended Bertelsen clan claims a special place in my heart for all the "huzzahs!" and "atta girls." Thanks, Kay, Alice, Ron, Jan, Dave, Maureen, and Marion for all of it. My son Erik and daughter-in-law Amanda keep me going with "Awesome" and "Cool." And as for my husband Mike, ah, what can I say? Just that I couldn't do any of it without you.

Figure 51. Alice in Wonderland

LIST OF ILLUSTRATIONS

Cover photos: Sonsedskaya

Frontispiece: John Parkinson's *Paradisi in Sole. Paradisus Terrestris* (1629)

Figure 1. The Roast Beef of Old England. A Cantata, By Theodosius Forrest, publisher Robert Sayer, circa 1749

Figure 2. Frontispiece, Hannah Woolley's *The Queene-Like-Closet* (Library of Congress)

Figure 3. Antique Cutlery (Wikiwand)

Figure 4. British Lion (Adobe Stock)

Figure 5. *Apicius*, 1541 (Wikiwand)

Figure 6. Geoffrey Chaucer (Adobe Stock 32212931)

Figure 7. Page from *The Forme of Cury* (Wikipedia)

Figure 8. Sir Toby Belch Coming to the Assistance of Sir Andrew Aguecheek (by Arthur Boyd Houghton 1836–1875)

Figure 9. Portrait of John Evelyn (Wikipedia)

Figure 10. Portrait of Gervase Markham (Wikipedia)

Figure 11. Title page, William Verrall's *Complete System of Cookery* (Wikicommons)

Figure 12. Illustration, Martha Bradley's *The British Housewife* (Wikipedia)

Figure 13. Illustration, Richard Bradley's *The Country Housewife and Lady's Director* (Library of Congress)

Figure 14. Rhubarb and Spice Seller (Henry Mayhew, *Labour and the London Poor*, 1851-1862)

Figure 15. Title page, Alexis Soyer's *A Culinary Campaign* (Gutenberg.org)

Figure 16. Queen Victoria (Adobe Stock 298550288)

Figure 17. Londoners Fetching Christmas Dinner (John Leech, artist. *The Illustrated London News* (23 December 1848), No. 350, Vol. 13: 408.

Figure 18. Isabella Beeton (Wikipedia)

Figure 19. Desserts, *Book of Household Management* (iStock 866139078)

Figure 20. Illustration, *Punch's Almanack* 1869 (iStock 1336381082)

Figure 21. William Shakespeare (Adobe Stock 42292346)

Figure 22. Portrait of Elizabeth Raffald (Wikicommons)

Figure 23. Game, *Book of Household Management* (Archive.org)

Figure 24. Soldier and His Wife (Wikipedia)

Figure 25. Oyster Stall (Gutenberg.org)

Figure 26. Lady Curzon, Vicereine of India (Alamy R528XK)

Figure 27. Vintage Engraving, Mushrooms (Adobe Stock 121583930)

Figure 28. Fish Pies, Robert May's *The Accomplisht Cook* (Wikipedia)

Figure 29. Mutton, *Book of Household Management* (iStock 66147018)

Figure 30. Berkshire Pig 1897 (Adobe Stock 255348229)

Figure 31. World War II Rationing (Wikipedia)

Figure 32. Trussing Birds, *Book of Household Management*

Figure 33. Bee (Adobe Stock 420079589)

Figure 34. Vintage Tableware (Adobe Stock 106073222)

Figure 35. Frontispiece, John Nott's *The Cooks and Confectioners Dictionary* (Wikipedia)

Figure 36. Fourteenth-century Sailing Ship (Adobe Stock 42322641)

Figure 37. Vintage Illustration, Strawberries (Adobe Stock 127565809)

Figure 38. Victorian Men Drinking Wine (iStock 1076399072)

Figure 39. Chillingham Cattle (Adobe Stock 352808819)

Figure 40. Vintage Illustration (Adobe Stock 106073222)

Figure 41. Early Printers, by Caxton (Adobe Stock 60849627)

Figure 42. Vintage Illustration, Mustard Greens (Adobe Stock 297481086)

Figure 43. Frontispiece, Hannah Glasse's *The Art of Cookery, Made Plain and Easy* (Wikipedia)

Figure 44. Vintage Serving Ware (Adobe Stock 35995602)

Figure 45. View of Early American Household (Adobe Stock)

INDEX

Figure 52. Teatime

ABOUT THE AUTHOR

After years of living overseas and working with humanitarian aid projects, Cynthia D. Bertelsen now resides in Gainesville, Florida. There she writes and cooks and enjoys ice-free winters. Summers are another story. She is the author of *Mushroom: A Global History*; *"A Hastiness of Cooks": A Handbook for Deciphering Historic Recipes and Cookbooks*; *In the Shadow of Ravens: A Novel*; *Wisdom Soaked in Palm Oil: Journeying Through the Food and Flavors of Africa*; *Meatballs & Lefse: Memories and Recipes from a Scandinavian-American Farming Life*; and *Stoves & Suitcases: Searching for Home in the World's Kitchens*. *"A Hastiness of Cooks"* won the Gourmand World Cookbook Awards in 2020 for the Best in Culinary History category for both the U.S. and the world. *Meatballs & Lefse: Memories and Recipes from a Scandinavian-American Farming Life* placed as a Finalist in the 2021 Next Generation Indie Book Awards. *Stoves & Suitcases: Searching for Home in the World's Kitchens* won Best of the USA for Food Writing from Gourmand World Cookbook Awards 2022. She contributed numerous articles to various food encyclopedias, as well as dozens of book reviews for *The Roanoke Times*, *The New York Journal of Books*, *Library Journal*, and *The Digest of Middle Eastern Studies* (DOMES). Her columns for the *Cedar Key Beacon* in Cedar Key, Florida covered culinary history when few writers and academics paid attention to the subject. She holds a B.A. degree in Latin American Studies, an M.A in History, an M.S. in Human Nutrition and Foods, and an M.L.I.S in Library Science. Read more of her writing on her blog, "Cynthia D. Bertelsen: Gherkins & Tomatoes ... Since 2008," at cynthiadbertelsen.com.

... if I had known, beforehand, that this book would have cost me the labour which it has, I should never have been courageous enough to commence it.

~ Isabella Beeton

Made in the USA
Middletown, DE
28 May 2023

31617461R00176